"When asked to recommend books for new advisers, we often suggest *Getting Started as a Financial Planner.*"

—*INVESTMENT ADVISOR* MAGAZINE

There has never been more opportunity for financial planners—or more reasons for financial professionals to consider switching the direction of their careers into this lucrative field. Today's planners will cash in on the huge surge of baby boomers preparing for retirement in the decades ahead. And as the number and complexity of investments rise, more individuals will look to financial advisers to help manage their money.

In this updated guide, Jeffrey H. Rattiner, a practicing financial planner and educator, provides a complete, systematic, turnkey framework for the aspiring planner to follow. Starting from the key question, "Why do you want to be a financial planner?" the author guides you through the development of an effective infrastructure and client management system for your practice. The many essential concepts are clearly illustrated with examples from practicing professionals. Throughout this handbook, Rattiner provides personal insights on how and why you must develop a solid understanding of client needs before you can build a comprehensive financial plan.

Getting Started as a Financial Planner has everything you need to know—from how to set up a practice and communicate with clients to how to manage investments and market your services— in order to launch your career in financial planning and to guide you to success in this high-growth profession.

PRAISE FOR THE NEW EDITION OF
Getting Started as a Financial Planner
by Jeffrey H. Rattiner

"Jeff Rattiner has been intimately involved with the development of the financial planning profession for nearly twenty years as a planner, teacher, author, and educational innovator. For anyone who is serious about entering financial planning as a first or new career, *Getting Started as a Financial Planner* provides great **insight from someone who can really say he's been there and done that. It's a must-read.**"

MARVIN W. TUTTLE, JR., CAE
Executive Director/CEO
Financial Planning Association

"*Getting Started as a Financial Planner* is a must-read for any professional interested in a career in financial planning. As one of the industry's most respected teachers and practitioners, Jeff's book is **packed with useful insights that every newcomer needs to be successful.**"

JOHN WHELAN
Vice President, Group Publisher
WICKS Business Information

"When asked to recommend books for new advisers, **we often suggest *Getting Started as a Financial Planner*.**"

Investment Advisor

"**A must-read for emerging financial planners.**"

Advisor Today

"For anyone entering the profession or transitioning to financial planning from a related field, *Getting Started as a Financial Planner* is **well worth reading**. Experienced planners who never seem to find the time to do practice planning should also benefit."

HORSESMOUTH.COM

"Right now, many people want to get into the field of financial planning but may not know how. **Jeff's easy-to-read, comprehensive primer is an excellent tool for those looking to get started in the profession and highlights the client-centered approach that is crucial to the success of any financial planning practice.**"

ROBERT P. GOSS, J.D., PH.D., CFP
Former President and CEO
Certified Financial Planner Board of Standards

"Thinking of becoming a financial planner or adding the planning discipline to your current professional practice? **Jeff Rattiner has written the perfect cookbook for those who want to enter the financial planning profession. His book is chockful of winning recipes that will undoubtedly help newcomers create truly successful financial planning practices.**"

DEENA KATZ, CFP
President, Evensky & Katz
Author of *Deena Katz's Complete Guide to Practice Management*

"If you truly want to serve your clients successfully, then you owe it to yourself and your clients to read this book. **It's a step-by-step guide that will help your clients achieve their financial dreams.**"

JOHN BOWEN
Founder and CEO
CEG Worldwide

"I wish this book had been available when I started in financial planning. The book manages to integrate how to be a financial planner with the academics of financial planning. The step-by-step, programmed approach can serve as a daily guide. **Mr. Rattiner's extensive experience as a teacher, resource person, and planner gives a perspective lacking in today's curriculum.**"

STEVEN I. LEVEY, CPA/PFS
Managing Director
GHP Horwath, P.C.

"Jeff Rattiner has done outstanding work with this new book. **Practitioners, both new and veteran, can now have a terrific road map to use to chart their success in the financial planning business.**"

JIM CANNON
Former President
AIG Financial Advisors

"I'm impressed. Jeff has done it! This book gives **hands-on advice in a logical fashion on creating, marketing, and managing a financial planning firm**."

PHYLLIS BERNSTEIN, CPA/PFS
Former Director, Personal Financial Planning Division, AICPA
Author of *Financial Planning for CPAs*

GETTING STARTED

AS A

FINANCIAL PLANNER

JEFFREY H. RATTINER

GETTING STARTED

AS A

FINANCIAL PLANNER

REVISED AND UPDATED EDITION

BLOOMBERG PRESS

NEW YORK

BLOOMBERG, BLOOMBERG ANYWHERE, BLOOMBERG.COM, BLOOMBERG MARKET ESSENTIALS, *Bloomberg Markets*, BLOOMBERG NEWS, BLOOMBERG PRESS, BLOOMBERG PROFESSIONAL, BLOOMBERG RADIO, BLOOMBERG TELEVISION, and BLOOMBERG TRADEBOOK are trademarks and service marks of Bloomberg Finance L.P. ("BFLP"), a Delaware limited partnership, or its subsidiaries. The BLOOMBERG PROFESSIONAL service (the "BPS") is owned and distributed locally by BFLP and its subsidiaries in all jurisdictions other than Argentina, Bermuda, China, India, Japan, and Korea (the "BLP Countries"). BFLP is a wholly-owned subsidiary of Bloomberg L.P. ("BLP"). BLP provides BFLP with all global marketing and operational support and service for these products and distributes the BPS either directly or through a non-BFLP subsidiary in the BLP Countries. All rights reserved.

This publication contains the author's opinions and is designed to provide accurate and authoritative information. It is sold with the understanding that the author, publisher, and Bloomberg L.P. are not engaged in rendering legal, accounting, investment-planning, or other professional advice. The reader should seek the services of a qualified professional for such advice; the author, publisher, and Bloomberg L.P. cannot be held responsible for any loss incurred as a result of specific investments or planning decisions made by the reader.

CFP® and CERTIFIED FINANCIAL PLANNER™ are certification marks owned by Certified Financial Planner Board of Standards Inc.

Revised and Updated Edition published 2005
First edition published 2000
1 3 5 7 9 10 8 6 4 2

ISBN-13: 978-1-57660-357-4 (paperback edition)

The Library of Congress has cataloged the earlier printing as follows:

Rattiner, Jeffrey H.
    Getting started as a financial planner / Jeffrey H. Rattiner.–Rev. and updated ed.
        p.   cm.
    Summary: "A guide for financial planners, includes: business plan development, client management, certification, legal compliance, client communication, and marketing strategies"–Provided by publisher.
        Includes index.
        ISBN 1-57660-185-4 (alk. paper)
    1. Financial planners—United States. 2. Investment advisors—United States. I. Title.

HG181.R278 2005
332.6'2–dc22

2005007057

To all the inspiring financial planners who crave to be the best they can be, and to those students in my Financial Planning Fast Track classes who've incorporated these principles into their daily practices and are now running them the way they have always envisioned.

To my family, who have provided me with my greatest inspiration.

CONTENTS

PREFACE

SINCE THE FIRST EDITION of *Getting Started as a Financial Planner* was published, much has changed in our profession: Fee-based financial planning is on the rise. Commissions are being commoditized. And there is now a profusion of financial planning courses and training programs. The profession continues to grow rapidly. In fact, the U.S. Department of Labor expects the number of individuals employed as personal financial planners "to grow faster than the average for all occupations through the year 2012." This is because "as the number and complexity of investments rises, more individuals will look to financial advisers to help manage their money."

Advising the public on financial planning issues continues to be one of the most profitable areas of personal consulting. Financial planners need to keep their clients focused so they will continue accumulating sufficient assets to accomplish their personal goals. Americans desire to get ahead and will need effective strategies to pass the approximately $6 trillion of intergenerational wealth to succeeding generations. These growth opportunities in the marketplace and continued federal deregulation of the financial services industry gave me reasons to update this book.

My experiences have shown that individuals aspiring to be professional financial planners want what is best for their clients. These forward-looking planners have migrated to a comprehensive needs approach to help their clients achieve financial objectives, rather than continuing to employ a purely transactional approach, which has long been the dominant theme of traditional financial planners. Historically, the main goal of this latter group has been selling "product" rather than establishing a long-term relationship. I became determined to help new financial planners evolve their view of the planning process by providing a logical, easy-to-digest, and automatic system that can help them provide comprehensive financial planning services. The result was the development of a turnkey approach to personal financial planning, which is the essence of this book.

I decided to blend my own experiences with those of very successful and well-known financial planners, including prominent members of the Financial Planning Association, the California CPA Education Foundation, the American Institute of Certified Public Accountants, members of the governing board of the Certified Financial Planner Board of Standards, and various university colleagues. I asked my associates if they were to start all over again, would they approach financial planning the same way? What would they do differently? What have they learned to become successful financial planners? Where do they see their practice and the profession headed? What does the competition look like? Most of all, what advice can they give financial planners first entering the profession? All the responses pointed primarily to one fundamental need—that entry-level financial planners have a business plan to guide them on starting a business. This action plan, they advised new financial planners, must include all the important infrastructure decisions that need to be in place before taking on the first client (as opposed to the trial-and-error approach many planners tried when they entered the profession). Much of this invaluable information was incorporated into this book in order to provide the reader with a clear, detailed, and practical approach to practicing personal financial planning across the spectrum from entry to mastering the profession.

Getting Started as a Financial Planner is written for stockbrokers, insurance agents, CPAs, attorneys, bankers, credit union reps, trust officers, wealth managers, and others who want to graduate from the transactional selling approach to the client management approach, which requires true understanding of clients' needs, capabilities, and resources. The book provides financial service professionals and non–financially trained individuals first entering the field with a method to graduate from a transaction-oriented business model to one involving a step-by-step process. This book helps explain that by using a comprehensive "client first" approach, planners can uncover more of what their clients are looking for, thus putting themselves in a better position to prepare a competent plan. This change in direction ends up providing clients with an understanding of previously unrecognized concerns and therefore with better service, ultimately making more money for both the client and the planner. This introductory book provides the basics that the narrow-based financial planner can use to create the infrastructure of a broad-based financial planning service. I decided to write this book to help make this transition successful for evolving planning advisers.

Getting Started as a Financial Planner is organized in a logical business-cycle approach. It tackles critical issues every new financial planner needs to address, from how to set up a practice through writing the business plan, marketing it, and managing clients.

The book begins by providing an overview of the profession. Chapter 1 describes who is attracted to the field, identifies the trends in the industry that will create business opportunities in the next decade, and takes the reader through the origins of financial planning to what it has become today. Chapter 2 provides the reader with the "Ten Must-Do's" for establishing the successful business infrastructure, from selecting the right business legal entity to finding a mentor and picking a specialty.

Once the business is formatted, the planner needs a proven process that will facilitate a comprehensive financial planning program. Chapter 3 describes such a process, called PIPRIM, a client management system that will help planners approach client consulting in a complete manner and create client loyalty to the process of long-term investing to accomplish financial objectives. Chapter 4 provides the reader with an overview of the many disciplines in financial planning and elaborates the concerns clients will have in each area and strategies the planner can use to satisfy these concerns. The chapter identifies the dilemmas clients will most likely encounter, explains how the planner should interpret client issues, and provides strategies for overcoming client blind spots. Chapter 5 tells the planner how to comply with the many stringent laws affecting financial services.

Chapter 6 takes the reader through all the appropriate steps for developing a business plan and offers a thorough sample business plan. It also discusses how to develop the needed business infrastructure, including establishing a compensation model that represents the planner's practice philosophy. Chapter 7 turns to marketing a financial planning practice and provides many useful strategies to help the entrepreneur become recognized and well known. Chapter 8 provides techniques and insights for maximizing dealings with clients through effective planner-client communication strategies. Understanding clients' wants and needs enables the planner to design a strategy to make clients feel comfortable and involved during this process, and enables the consultant to provide the best type of service. Chapter 10 provides additional resources that can be instrumental in establishing a practice and gaining the expertise needed in a variety of subject areas. And a new chapter in this second edition, Chapter 9, integrates the principles discussed throughout the book by presenting three common client scenarios and applying the best methods to address each of their specific concerns.

Implementing the tools and techniques discussed in the book will guide the planner through all the stages of becoming a better financial planner. Planners can assess where they are now and where they need to be in order to satisfy their financial objectives.

Please let me know how *Getting Started as a Financial Planner* helps you start, fine-tune, or expand your financial planning practice. I invite you to contact me at jeff@jrfinancialgroup.com or visit my website at www.financialplanningfasttrack.com.

ACKNOWLEDGMENTS

This book would not have been possible without the contributions of many generous people. The practitioners whom I have come to know well throughout my travels have provided me with the realities of the twenty-first-century financial planner. I want to thank at Bloomberg Press editor Tracy Tait; also Jacqueline Murphy, who initiated this project; Kathleen Peterson; Maris Williams; and Ingrid Meyer. These dedicated people provided me with the opportunity to help serious financial planners succeed in this wonderful business. A special thanks to Sheryl Garrett, of Garrett Financial Planning in Overland Park, Kansas, who acted as a sounding board and provided valuable insight into the premise for the book and who generously provided me with forms and checklists that planners can readily use in their practices, and to Ed Morrow and the staff at Text Library Support of Middletown, Ohio, and Bill Porter at Lumen Systems, Inc., of San Jose, California, who provided me with materials for inclusion in the book.

JEFFREY H. RATTINER, CPA, CFP, M.B.A.

GETTING STARTED
AS A
FINANCIAL PLANNER

CHAPTER I

THE WORLD OF FINANCIAL PLANNING

Evolution of the Profession

FINANCIAL PLANNING is a relatively new profession.

It represents the first broad-scope service profession to

emerge in recent years. Its development can be traced

back to late 1969, when a small group of financial ser-

vices professionals met at a hotel near Chicago's O'Hare

Airport to discuss the inadequacy they saw in the state of

financial services at that time. They voiced their frustrations and searched for ways to introduce a new degree of client orientation and professionalism into a field that was neither well known nor well defined.

As a result of this meeting, a trade association was formed in 1970 to give voice to the concerns of the new group. This association, initially called the International Association of Financial Planners, later changed its name to the International Association for Financial Planning (IAFP). The early mission of this organization was to provide an open forum, bringing together people representing a variety of specialized areas within financial services. The integration of these approaches eventually led to the emergence of financial planning as a profession in its own right.

To help educate this growing constituency, the IAFP created the College for Financial Planning in 1971, which gave rise to the Certified Financial Planner (CFP) designation. The first graduating class in 1973 consisted of forty-two CFP licensees. A close-knit bunch, the graduates displayed the professionalism indicated by the new certification, and thirty-six members of this group decided to form a new association specifically for holders of the CFP designation, which they named the Institute of Certified Financial Planners (ICFP). In 1985, the administration of the CFP designation was transferred from the College to an independent body that eventually changed its name to the Certified Financial Planner Board of Standards (CFP Board).

The planning pioneers who founded this profession led a movement to provide clients with better and more targeted service. They looked forward to the time when comprehensive financial planning would become an accepted and integrated means for providing service and product delivery to consumers. In doing so, they revolutionized their business, creating a new way for individuals to manage their personal finances. The pioneers' approach was to focus on the clients' needs and objectives by putting their clients' interests first and foremost, above personal gain.

The efforts toward targeted client service led to the development of two principal types of financial plans, segmented and comprehensive. Segmented plans enable practitioners to review one aspect of a client's life, such as insurance, investments, or retirement. Comprehensive plans provide a more detailed and complete approach by factoring in all of the financial concerns affecting the client's life, such as cash flow, education, insurance, investments, income tax, retirement, and estate issues. (Detailed coverage of these topics appears in Chapter 4.) These revolutionary changes in approach paved the way for a new profession: financial planning.

The next step for these innovators was to educate the public about their new service profession. They wanted to show the public how they differed from their predecessors and why it would be worthwhile to use their services.

Sellers of insurance and investment products at this time were viewed by many consumers as aggressive, pushy salesmen only concerned about maximizing their personal wealth. Skepticism and mistrust were creating a wedge between these individuals and their clients. Stockbrokers, insurance agents, and limited-partnership salespeople were seen in an unfavorable light within the financial services industry to a large extent because of the financial products they were pushing. Limited-partnership opportunities in real estate, oil, and cable entered the investment scene, some of which became a fiasco for participating holders when the tax laws relating to these structures were overhauled in 1986. Because many clients were losing money and the public was getting angry, Washington began to focus on increased regulation of professional investment activity.

To counteract negative perceptions, a number of financial service professionals began pursuing a different way of helping their clients. They strove expressly to adopt a logical and consistent format in providing good financial advice not just in one specialized area but in every aspect of clients' financial lives. Furthermore, they wanted their clients to know that they were trained specialists in their areas of practice.

The Trend toward Specialization

VIEWED AS A WHOLE, financial planning still has a close connection with stock brokerage and insurance. Close to 70 percent of all CFP licensees also hold securities and/or insurance licenses.

Today's planners are primarily midcareer people looking for a change. They receive their training from any of the three-hundred-plus registered educational program providers that offer the CFP or similar financial planning programs. However, an increasing number of college students now major or minor in personal financial planning.

To pursue their business model of fee-based financial planning, planners increasingly have begun gaining the knowledge necessary to operate in a specialty. Accordingly, growing numbers of planners are obtaining certification as a Certified Financial Planner, Personal Financial Specialist, or Chartered Financial Consultant. These designations have increased in popularity and have gained national prominence especially since the mid-1990s.

The goal of individuals practicing under these designations is to adhere to the high standards that have been created in order to protect the public. Of course, there are many other financial planners as well who, although not holding such titles, still maintain extremely high standards. However, financial planning certification holders generally have found it easier to attract clients because of their technical knowledge and the perception of many clients that certified experts are probably more knowledgeable and more professional than other practitioners. While obtaining a specialty designation may not be viewed universally as a prerequisite for success, anything a planner can do to gain the competitive edge is likely to be worthwhile. Competition is growing quickly—whereas only 42 CFPs were licensed in 1973, by the year 2004 that number had grown to 44,888.

WHO ARE TODAY'S FINANCIAL PLANNERS?

Financial planners have come from a variety of fields and hold many licenses and designations. As noted previously, many today are midcareer professionals who have retired from their first field, have grown bored with it, or wanted to branch out into something new that involves helping others. For example, many are CPAs with twenty or more years of experience who have found that their clients specifically ask for such services; if they fail to provide financial planning, they run the risk of losing clients to other CPAs who do.

Similarly, many representatives, brokers, and related employees at major brokerage firms and insurance companies find it difficult to compete solely by selling products; financial planning offers a more flexible and comprehensive approach to satisfying their clients' needs. Likewise, bankers more and more are finding that they cannot effectively compete in the service marketplace without taking an overall view of financial planning for their clientele. The banks have finally recognized that financial planning in its own right can be a very profitable revenue center.

So what does all this mean? For many financial service professionals, the days of pushing a product-centered transaction with little or no concern for client needs and objectives are gone. That approach is being replaced by the services offered by more sophisticated and better-trained financial planners who want to *understand* their clients in order to make the most appropriate choices for them.

The table on the demographics of CFP practitioners on the following page provides a breakdown of the industries in which CFP licensees originally practiced and the other licenses and/or designations they currently hold.

HOW WELL DO FINANCIAL PLANNERS GET PAID?

Firsthand knowledge and appreciation of the profession are the best platform from which to accurately assess the financial incentives of financial planning. Financial planners can tailor their practice and income to lifestyle goals. In essence, because this is a profession in which the practitioner designs a "product line," earnings potential is truly unlimited. Financial planners are fast-moving entrepreneurs. Practice growth and earnings are limited only by personal initiative, salesmanship, ability, and tenacity.

What Sources Generate Income for Financial Planners?

IN THE PAST, planners were primarily paid by commission on clients' portfolio growth. They believed that compensation should reflect the economic value of the products they sold, which yielded

Composition of Certified Financial Planner Licensees: Practitioner Demographics, 2004

TYPE OF BUSINESS OF PRESENT CFP LICENSEES	TOTAL PERCENT
Personal financial planning	31%
Securities	11%
Accounting	5%
Tax preparation	3%
Insurance	5%
Banking	3%
Education	1%
Law	1%
All other	3%
Not specified	38%

OTHER LICENSES HELD	TOTAL PERCENT
Securities	68%
Insurance	69%
CPA	16%
Investment advisor reps (IAR)	34%
Real estate	4%
Attorney	3%
No other licenses held	11%

AGE	TOTAL PERCENT
20–29	3%
30–39	19%
40–49	34%
50–59	31%
60–69	11%
70–79	2%
80+	0%

GENDER	TOTAL PERCENT
Male	76%
Female	24%

HIGHEST DEGREES EARNED	TOTAL PERCENT
Associate	3%
Bachelor's	56%
Bachelor's, and J.D.	2%
Master's	29%
Master's, and J.D.	1%
Ph.D.	2%
None	7%

expanding value to their clients over time. However, in recent years a shift has occurred in the relationship between planner and client. Gradually and quietly a revolution began, shifting the basis of compensation from higher-risk commissions to flat fees. This trend grew from the belief that planners should and could become more independent and objective if planning services were associated with financial strategy rather than recommendations for specific financial products or companies.

Planners, striving to increase their professionalism, wanted to demonstrate that client needs were paramount over agent sales. Planners could still expect substantial income opportunity, but now it was in a manner that would no longer link personal gain to commercial products. The emerging professional planner sought the neutral position held by other service professionals such as CPAs and attorneys.

Many financial planners completed this about-face on compensation in a relatively short time, giving up the appearance of possible conflict of interest. More and more, planners have abandoned fixed commissions for hourly fees or project contracts.

This change in thinking has had multiple benefits. First, trained planners feel less pressure to sell products or "ends" and can turn their attention to "means." Clients clearly have responded more favorably to the purchase of a financial planning process than to a recommendation to buy. The latter function was in fact already available from the client's stockbroker. Financial planners thus have differentiated themselves from securities traders. Planners have begun to thrive on their enhanced image as the adviser, not the salesperson.

This change came as something of a shock for some practitioners and as an easy transition for others. Some planners could not make the complete transition and went to so-called fee-based financial planning, which combines commissions and fees. The remainder went cold turkey and became fee-only financial planners. (See Chapter 6 for additional discussion of revenue generation.)

As financial planning continues to gain prominence as a profession, the future lies in fee-for-service compensation. Planners are proving to be very much worth the investment, and conse-

CFP Practitioners' Compensation

Primary Compensation (Total percent*)

Fee and commission	54%
Commission	11%
Fee only	29%
Salary	4%
Other	1%

*Does not equal 100% due to rounding

Average Fees Charged

Hourly	$162
Single-Focus Plan	$894
Comprehensive Plan	$2,316

Planner Earnings

Gross earnings in year preceding earning CFP Certification	$54,000
Gross earnings in year after earning CFP Certification	$72,000
Current average annual gross earnings	$219,000
Current average annual net earnings	$142,000

SOURCE: COLLEGE FOR FINANCIAL PLANNING'S 2004 SURVEY OF TRENDS IN THE FINANCIAL PLANNING INDUSTRY

quently more and more clients are willing to assume the risk of fees for service as they do when they consult a doctor, attorney, or CPA.

Financial planner compensation is subject to the same market pressures as the pricing of other professional services. The more unique (in range and quality) the service offered, the greater the differentiation and the greater the compensation. Careful competitive analysis, product development, and documentation of client performance directly affect earning power and sustainability. As in any business, value-added service affects pricing in financial planning. Astute financial planners lessen their risk of swings in competitive pressures and other factors such as stock market volatility by blending compensation schemes.

The tables at left show how CFP licensees structure compensation. As noted previously, the predominant model is now a combination of fees and commissions: the former ensures steady income flow, and the latter rewards planners for exceptional performance on the client's behalf. For additional information, see Appendix B: Trends in Staffing and Compensation.

Emerging Market Opportunities in Financial Planning

THE ROAD AHEAD in financial planning is leading to many new opportunities previously unavailable to financial planners. Practitioners focused on expanding their product portfolio and customer base need to be aware of these opportunities and react quickly to beat the competition.

The significant trends include the following:
- Increasing attractiveness of financial planning as a career
- Shifting demographics and corresponding wealth
- Increasing parity in two-income families
- A volatile American economy
- Online access to financial information
- Consumer need for financial planning services
- Increasing competition from full-service financial institutions

FINANCIAL PLANNING AS A NEW GROWTH INDUSTRY

According to various surveys, CFP licensees ranked the following reasons for high career satisfaction:
- Positive impact on client quality of life
- Opportunity for entrepreneurship
- High interpersonal job content
- Application of technical tools to solve client problems
- Competitive nature of the business
- Unlimited income growth
- Challenge of new business development
- Low business risk

It is interesting to note that business risk (professional liability) was the last concern of financial planners. Interviews with planners conducted by the author on why they chose to enter the financial planning field overwhelmingly revealed a motivation to help people. Planners want to see clients become financially informed and prepared for the future. This humanitarian drive in many ways rationalizes the financial return planners themselves enjoy.

The essence of a career in financial planning is a challenge—a challenge to solve quality-of-life problems in an environment limited only by the practitioner's will and creativity.

SHIFTING DEMOGRAPHICS AND CORRESPONDING WEALTH

Financial planning is headed into a major transition, propelled by changing demographics. The retirement of 40 million baby boomers is imminent. This population has new views about retirement. It is something to look forward to; it is a time to continue intellectual challenge and growth; it is a time to enjoy.

A significant opportunity exists for this baby boom generation, which stands to inherit some $6 trillion over the next decade. Furthermore, from mid-1982 through the year 2000 the stock market created record highs on a fairly consistent basis (excluding occasional market downturns). Then the market tumbled from 2001 through 2003. It is now more imperative than ever to be responsive to client demands, because it's not a sure thing that the market increases each year. More consumers than ever need good, solid financial advice.

The definition of retirement continues to change. No longer do people retire *from* something, such as a job. Now they are retiring *to* something, actively pursuing the dreams and goals they planned for during their working years. The next generation of retirees will face the inevitable decline of government assistance and shrinking retirement plans in the workplace. People will find themselves forced to take on more responsibility for financial security. Luckily, emerging service industry segments—in particular, information technology—will offer enormous opportunity for many people but greater financial risk for those who miss the information revolution. In the center is an enormous population of middle-income Americans, who today are discovering economical investing online and through discount brokers.

Financial Planning magazine states that 250,000 people are self-proclaimed financial planners. Yet only about 60,000, or about 25 percent, have qualified for certification or formal recognition as a financial planner. Clearly, this supply is not enough to deal with the demand from baby boomers and young Americans striving to save early for educational financing and retirement. This situation of demand exceeding supply for financial services will lead to much specialization in retirement planning.

INCREASING PARITY IN TWO-INCOME FAMILIES

Another important market opportunity is earnings parity in two-income families. Women are not only entering the workforce at a higher rate, but their income growth is closing the gap with men's salaries, and in particular that of their husbands. Higher joint incomes will lead to greater disposable income, higher tax liabilities with a demand for reducing taxes, and more latitude to save. On the other hand, many two-income families will give in to the desire to spend, leaving little for the future. Both scenarios create candidates for the financial planner. As time continues to be the most scarce and valuable resource to dual-income families and to the busy single person of the twenty-first century, professional help with financial planning will become increasingly necessary. Time saved by shifting the task of financial planning to a professional is time available for personal interests, family, and community.

THE VOLATILE AMERICAN ECONOMY

There are more millionaires per capita today than ever before. Conversely, more people are declaring bankruptcy than ever before. Why the conflicting signs? We are in the midst of a fast-paced and volatile economy. Many "paper" millionaires have money to burn. Other Americans, tempted by easy credit, are more in debt than ever before. More discretionary cash is finding its way into the equity markets with no sign of hesitation, since annual returns in recent years have been significant and steady.

Interest rates have been near historic lows. Inflation is practically nonexistent. Money invested through 401(k) plans is at an all-time high. However, with more baby boomers approaching retirement, it is becoming more evident that these individuals who have worked so hard may not have the retirement funds they thought they would. Because of this, baby boomers are insecure about their retirement dollars and may have to postpone their retirement date. These people are going to need more help in planning for their available discretionary funds. On the other hand, more people are going to need help managing their cash flow and preventing debt overflow. Planners will have unique opportunities catering to the needs of both populations.

INFORMATION TECHNOLOGY

Easy access to useful information has also created significant opportunities in financial planning. Myriad channels to financial information via the Internet have reached the average investor heretofore dependent on *The Wall Street Journal,* tips from daily financial columnists, or stockbroker recommendations. These consumers may well bypass financial planners in the same way they are dispensing with old-time brokers. More and more of these independent, take-charge people simply do not have the time to wait for a broker or news flash. Moreover, the Internet is there when the investor needs it. Financial planners will need to learn how to compete by joining the Internet revolution. Rather than viewing it as a threat, astute financial planners will use the Internet as *their* source of information and as *their* vehicle to reach new customers. Also, a wealth of new software can greatly assist planners in evaluating risk and return. Planners have a tremendous opportunity to show their skills to a more sophisticated audience.

CONSUMER NEED FOR FINANCIAL CONTROL

Years ago people depended on their local banker to watch the family nest egg. Today people want to control their health, their politics, their privacy, and their money. At the same time, two of the hardest things for people to do are to ration funds to accomplish certain objectives and to set plans to work toward others.

Declining dependence on government institutions and traditional financial institutions, such as the community bank, has created a great opportunity for the financial planner to fill the void.

Potential consumers of financial planning services have a broad range of worries, prioritized below:

◆ Retirement funding
◆ Income tax exposure
◆ Investment and asset growth during the earning years
◆ Managing cash
◆ Anticipating future health care costs
◆ Outliving assets
◆ Estate planning
◆ Funding education
◆ Amount of personal debt
◆ Downsizing and job loss

These worries are not temporary or linear. They occur simultaneously and stretch across social and economic distinctions. For example, funding for education *and* retirement requires special planning to increase assets with minimal risk.

INCREASING COMPETITION FROM FULL-SERVICE INSTITUTIONS

Consumer choices for financial planning are changing, too. Growing competition may result in an increase *or* decrease in independent financial planners. As stated previously, technology has influenced practices by creating opportunity that did not even exist just a few years ago. Consider accountants recently forced to redefine their profession. With the advent of tax software available for as little as $40 or bookkeeping software at $100, technology has decreased the need for accountants keeping general ledgers and doing taxes. The ongoing expense associated with bringing in a bookkeeper, accountant, or CPA on a monthly basis has been eliminated by programs performing complex calculations with a few keystrokes. Complicating the business horizon for CPAs are companies such as Vanguard that offer tax preparation software on the Internet for free. This further diminishes the long-term need for accountants. As a result, independent CPAs and larger accounting firms have expanded into a broad range of high-margin consulting areas to make up for erosion in traditional areas.

For their part, stockbrokers have been concerned about the quick development of Internet trading. For as little as $7, a client can conduct a stock trade over the Internet for which a full-service brokerage may have charged $150 in the old days. Why would a customer pay a broker several hundred dollars to execute a trade when the same service is available from an online trading company for $20 or less per trade? Many full-service brokers, such as Merrill Lynch, have radically altered the way they do business by entering the online trading market. Clients may choose to pay an annual retainer to access a brokerage firm's information products. But why would investors pay that much more money to do what they can do themselves with the same quality research? Few are willing, and many are self-educated. Technology has completely revolutionized the business. What will become of full-service brokers who do not refine their business model for consumers in this century? Seen any dinosaurs lately?

Not everyone will turn to the Internet or other new technologies to avoid traditional channels of financial services. There will always be many high-net-worth individuals and people without time or inclination who want personalized brokerage services. But again, as the changing demographics illustrated above, older individuals and younger people are not afraid to use the computer to find quality financial planning guidance. Financial planners need to find ways to link themselves to online financial information.

Insurance brokers have seen their world turn flat as life insurance sales stagnated over the past decade. Life insurance companies are turning to other products, including mutual funds, variable annuities, and financial planning as a way to make up for the insurance revenue drain. With the repeal of the Glass-Steagall Act, which prohibited insurance companies, investment companies, and banks from owning one another, many of these firms have begun to offer full-service financial products to create one-stop financial shopping. However, the small boutique financial planning firms and solo practitioners who establish their market niches and are technically good at what they do will always find a home catering to the needs of their niche markets.

Financial planners will also come from professions outside the world of finance. Engineers, architects, contractors, salespeople, and other professionals are finding a new career enticing. Some have achieved financial independence and are now motivated to build the skills to help others with what they have accomplished for themselves.

Issues Consumers Consider
When Selecting Financial Planners

GIVEN THAT market opportunities argue the need for professional financial planning services, the next logical consideration is "How should consumers select a financial planner?" The consumer will want to consider the following issues:

◆ **Do I need a specialist?** This is the same question a patient addresses in selecting a general practitioner or a medical specialist. The general financial planner provides a broad spectrum of services. The specialist provides deep expertise in a specific area. Consumers need to determine where their needs lie, now and in the future.

◆ **Is the planner affiliated with any financial product companies?** Affiliation with a financial firm can bias a planner's answers and/ or recommendations to clients. On the other hand, affiliated planners may be better informed on specific financial product options offered to consumers.

◆ **Does the planner earn significant commissions?** A high ratio of commission to total service revenue can be a warning that the financial planner is biased. Consumer confidence is likely to be higher with the more balanced fee-based (i.e., fee plus commission) service provider.

◆ **Will the planner provide professional references?** Consumers want and expect to hear success stories, especially when they are recent and relevant. Consumers will ask for references, and the astute professional financial planner will view this as an opportunity to shine, not as an inconvenience.

◆ **Can the planner answer technical questions?** Consumers of
financial services want confidence. Confidence is built when a
financial planner has earned or can demonstrate technical depth
with language targeted to the consumer. Consumers are wary of
too much jargon or too little technical depth.

◆ **What does the planner charge?** Potential clients are looking for
specific statements of charges for services linked to performance
outcomes. A fee structure based on the financial planner's delivering specified products eases the consumer's mind and makes a
commission arrangement more acceptable.

◆ **What is the planner's education and experience?** In today's
market consumers expect an adviser to have formal training and
accreditation or certification. The greater the financial risk taken
on by the consumer and planner, the more important the credentials become. Successful planners may create consumer literature
to help prospective clients make the right choices, illustrating
their expertise and displaying their credentials at the same time.

IN THE PAST, most consumers have failed to recognize the need
for professional financial counseling. Many people who recognize
the need have failed to act or have made regrettable decisions
about financial guidance. When economic times are good, many
people have greater discretionary income, and few worry about
tomorrow. This exaggerated confidence in the future leads to
procrastination. Financial planners need to recognize that people
often spend more time planning their vacations than they do
planning for financial security. Today's financial planner needs to
be a master at motivating people to take the right actions for the
right reasons right now.

CHAPTER 2

FOUNDATIONS OF A FINANCIAL PLANNING CAREER

IN ANY NEW VENTURE there is a strong impulse just to get started. While energy and urgency are fundamental to success in all competitive services industries, goal setting and practice planning are the first considerations for an aspiring financial planner. As with any new business, one must have a clear vision of what one wants to accomplish: what is the goal? The goal must be so fundamental and clear that it can be described in one to three sentences. This high-level concept is the "big picture" or mission that every business needs, whether new or well established.

The goal is not day-by-day results but rather how a professional financial planning practice will look five, ten, or even twenty years in the future. The ultimate description of the practice will address range of services, number of clients, type of clients, range of client outcomes, geographical coverage, revenue, profitability, organization size, and exit strategy. These issues and others that naturally come to mind in the process of forward thinking will help in formulating the goal.

This initial step—setting down your vision of what you want to accomplish—is by far the most important and possibly most difficult task you will encounter on the road to a career in financial planning. If the goal is wrong, all subsequent effort will be wrong. Write the goal, and share it with friends and family. Let it sit and incubate for a week. If it is still thinkable, achievable, and exciting, then it is ready for work.

A good idea for a service business becomes a great idea if a step-by-step implementation plan is crafted. What are the steps necessary to create a new business that will still be on the right track ten or twenty years down the road? Unfortunately, many financial planners have good ideas but fail in their execution. They either never really know what business they want to focus on or they do not fully consider how to differentiate their practice. When a planner's *personal* needs are synchronized with *client* needs in a well-thought-out practice start-up plan, success is much more likely.

The popular saying "If you build it, they will come" holds true for financial planning. The challenge is how to build it so that it will thrive and endure. This process has two dimensions: (1) the specific issues the planner needs to consider in planning a financial planning practice; and (2) the sequence of issues—deciding what is addressed first.

The planner must carefully design an infrastructure that will support a growing venture. Financial planning is a *service* business. A service, by definition, consists of intangibles—informal advice, good client relations, and word-of-mouth marketing—and tangibles—formal products, ancillary service alliances with complementary professionals, and value-added financial information tools. Perhaps most important, a service is making clients feel confident that they are being cared for. When these services are performed well at a fair price, clients will stay happy—and enthusiastically recommend their planner to others. This chapter introduces the beginning financial planner to the issues and steps needed to build a service infrastructure.

"Ten Must-Do's" for Developing a Financial Planning Practice

TEN KEY STEPS or "must-do" practice planning activities are necessary to get the new business launched. Each practice planning must-do is briefly described below in the sequence in which it should be considered. This chapter addresses several of the practice start-up issues in some detail, and subsequent chapters elaborate on the remaining topics.

1 Select a practice structure. Financial planning practices can be structured as sole proprietorships, general partnerships, S corporations, C corporations, or limited liability companies. Each structural option has a unique character, set of benefits, and legal limitations. This chapter reviews the differences among structural options and shows how to assess the merits of each, relative to a planner's goals and needs.

2 Prepare a business plan. All new *and* established businesses need some sort of written business plan. A good business plan starts with the business environment, that is, the market, competition, opportunities, and challenges. The plan describes the objectives, strategies, and specific actions the person or company will follow over time to master the business environment. A good business plan carefully estimates the resources and contingencies necessary to achieve objectives. Where is the business today, where is it heading, and how will it succeed are questions answered in a polished business plan. For a more detailed discussion, see Chapter 6, "Building the Practice Infrastructure."

3 Find a mentor. There is absolutely no substitute for experience. The speed with which new financial planners establish their product portfolio and client following is inversely proportional to the number of mistakes they make along the way. The best proven method to keep practice start-up snafus to a minimum is to find a mentor. To expedite your entry into the marketplace, you should team up with somebody who has been in the business for a while. Get under a mentor's wing, and you can learn from his or her experience and profit from firm guidance in the right direction. You can find mentor candidates speaking at financial planning society meetings, running seminars at local educational institutions, or through professional forums on the Web. Professional society gatherings and publications normally feature programs that place entry-level practitioners with mentors. Mentorships are often an integral part of the financial planning curriculum offered by graduate learning institutions. Check the business curricula offered by colleges in your area.

4 Get the credentials. Financial planning is technical. There is a large body of information a financial planner needs to master in the process of getting started *and* even more for staying current. Practitioners need to understand macroeconomic principles, financial markets, basic and advanced asset valuation methods, and today, the Internet. Chapter 4 describes the technical subject areas of financial planning.

5 Create an advisory board. No successful planner has the time to prospect for new clients, maintain a client base, develop new products, and remain current with the enormous volume of fast-changing information affecting the business. You will need an advisory board of directors to bring expertise, information, advice, and credibility to your practice. The more impressive your advisory board, the more certain you should feel about the quality and professionalism of your practice. Ideally, these people will provide big-picture guidance: pinpointing potential pitfalls in your business and marketing plans, providing solutions to the ongoing practice problems you will inevitably encounter, and making themselves available for the casual reality checks every business leader needs to fine-tune new ideas.

Chapter 7 explains how to build and sustain an effective advisory board.

6 Build a back-office team. As part of your business infrastructure, you will need to hire personnel to carry out many of the tasks described in your business and marketing plans. A part-time generalist with prior experience in service enterprises is a valuable, cost-effective investment. You will not want to spend your time administering the business. Your job will be sales, product development, and implementation. Many new financial planners have tried to run multiple aspects of a new practice. Invariably, the new financial planner gets diverted in accounting software, business cards, cold-calling, and other activities better suited to a strong administrative assistant. Early on, establish a system that enables your staff to do whatever needs to be done to free you to address client issues. Build the right culture in your practice from the first employee forward. See Chapter 6 for more discussion of staffing.

7 Use information technology. In an age in which technology is a threat and an opportunity for the service provider, it makes sense to purchase the best technology and train your staff to use it. This includes business software—for contact management, graphics, and database creation, for example—and business hardware—videoconferencing equipment, scanners, and high-speed/high-resolution printers, for example. Chapter 10 presents an extensive list and discussion of financial planning software.

8 Develop a marketing plan. A marketing plan is the road map you follow before and while you inform the public about your practice. Marketing, like advertising among consumer product competitors, can be addictive. Many planners do not know when to start a marketing program, or worse, when to stop. Marketing a professional financial planning practice does not need to be expensive, but it needs to be focused and monitored. An important element is an analysis of pricing. Product managers, whether selling a service or cornflakes, have to decide how to price. Is the goal to optimize price per unit or total units sold? Manufacturing organizations traditionally strive for high volume with low price points. Service organizations, on the other hand, tend to strive for high revenue per unit, as in the case of a consulting firm.

The financial planner has to make a similar trade-off: many less-comprehensive planning assignments at lower revenue per unit, or fewer more-comprehensive planning projects at high revenue per unit. Chapter 7 will guide you through the development of a marketing plan.

9 Comply with all regulations. Financial planning is a recognized professional service and is regulated accordingly. With the immense power to affect client quality of life and financial well-being comes the obligation to protect the public. Attorneys, physicians, educators, certified public accountants, and other service providers are governed first by personal ethics but also by professional licensing bodies and governmental agencies. The financial planning industry has more regulatory and compliance issues to address than many other service professions. Chapter 5 leads the reader through ethical, professional governance, and regulatory issues facing financial planners in the United States.

10 Develop and implement standardized procedures in your practice. Establishing an organized and logical set of procedures is essential to client-centered financial planning. PIPRIM is an acronym for a systematic approach to assessing and achieving client financial goals. It spans from the very beginning, when you first meet a prospective client, through the point of providing solutions, to measurement of performance. The six-step process is so comprehensive that it applies to all clients in all phases of a service relationship. PIPRIM stands for:

Preliminary meeting with a client
Integrated goal setting and data gathering
Putting it all together
Recommending solutions
Implementing the plan
Monitoring the plan

A complete discussion of the PIPRIM process appears in Chapter 3.

Selecting a Legal Business Structure

THE SELECTION of an appropriate legal business structure is extremely important. This decision will directly affect many aspects of your business. The way you can conduct business, the liability you are willing to assume, your ability to shift income among family members, the way you receive distributions from the business, the type of fringe benefits you will want to offer your employees, and the income tax code applicable to your practice are affected by the type of business structure you choose.

The selection of a business entity has been broadened through two trends:

1 The emergence of limited liability partnerships (LLPs).
2 The passage of legislation at the state level allowing for limited liability companies (LLCs).

These two options, added to traditional solo and professional group entities, have made the business structure decision more complex but more flexible to personal needs. Fee structure (described in Chapter 6) should not be affected by your choice of legal business structure. This means your preferred compensation method should apply in any of the above scenarios. One caution is to make certain that the state(s) in which you wish to do business permit the type of legal business structure you intend to choose in your specific practice (e.g., financial planning, insurance, investments, or whatever specialty practice you may choose). Also consider whether you can be licensed as a nonindividual in your state and still receive commissions under that classification. You will need to check with state regulatory agencies or legal counsel to answer these questions.

SOLE PROPRIETORSHIPS

A sole proprietorship is the most common form of business ownership due to its relative administrative simplicity. By definition, it is an unincorporated trade or business owned by a single individual. A sole proprietorship is not a legal entity separate and apart from its owner. The owner's personal assets are exposed without limitation to any and all liabilities related to the business. This unlimited liability exposure is the most significant difference between sole proprietorships and other business structures. However, if you are the business's sole owner, the only options other than a sole proprietorship are C and S corporations, and single-member limited-liability companies (LLCs) in the states that allow them.

Sole proprietorships are easy to establish and require no special state or federal registration. Sole proprietors simply file a schedule C in addition to personal tax forms. A sole proprietor can use this business structure to employ family members, thus dispersing income and tax liability. Because of the sole proprietor's unlimited liability, the business must have errors-and-omissions (liability) insurance to protect the proprietor's personal assets. In addition, under a sole proprietorship, there is no flexible ownership, continuity of life, or capital structure since the business cannot be transferred, although its assets may be sold.

Generally, start-ups begin as a sole proprietorship, but as the practice grows, other more flexible financial structures are usually considered.

When to use a sole proprietorship
—If there is only a single owner and single member, LLCs are not permitted by state law.
—If adequate liability insurance is available at an acceptable cost.
—If the business is in its early stage and more complex structures are premature and too costly.
—If the owner is not concerned about transferring interest in the business in the near term.

When not to use a sole proprietorship
—If the practice begins generating significant income and wealth for the owner exposed under an unlimited liability structure.
—If the owner is concerned about having significant personal assets at risk under an unlimited liability structure.

—If the practitioner intends to deliver financial services with inherent exposure to errors-and-omissions claims by clients.

—If there are one or more employees and the owner is concerned about how their independent actions may affect either the business or clients.

GENERAL PARTNERSHIPS

A general partnership consists of two or more owners doing business with the intention of dividing the income, expenses, and profit. The legal aspects of general partnerships are governed by state partnership statutes, most of which are in conformity with the federal Uniform Partnership Act and the Revised Uniform Limited Partnership Act. Under law, partners are jointly *and* individually liable (without limitation) for all the debts and obligations of the partnership. General partners can also be legally (and thus financially) responsible for actions taken by each other when giving the appearance of acting on behalf of the partnership. Because partners are liable to exposing personal assets through each other's acts, general partnerships are extremely risky. Each general partner has the power to act as an agent of the partnership and to enter into contracts that are legally binding on the partnership and, ultimately, on the other partners. A partner may seek legal recourse for reimbursement from the partnership *in excess* of his or her share of liabilities, depending on the ability of the other partners to yield such reimbursement from partnership funds. Partners must have a high level of trust in each other, although that trust is sometimes misplaced. Many have discovered that they really did not know their partners at all until after a disillusioning disaster.

Unlike corporations, partnerships offer no continuity of business life, management controls, or ownership transfer. A general partnership is beneficial in the following situations: (1) when a planner is seeking pass-through taxation; (2) if some or all of the potential owners are prohibited from being S corporation shareholders; or (3) if the S corporation single-class-of-stock rule prevents the principals from holding the ownership interests they want. Other than legal restrictions, the level of uncertainty built into the business plan of a financial planning practice should determine whether the advantages of a partnership outweigh the risks.

When to use general partnerships

—If the new business generates significant start-up losses that can be passed through to the partners, making it more advantageous than the various restrictions of S corporations. The partnership is not the tax-paying entity, the owners are. Thus, revenue, profit, losses, deductions, and credit are passed through the partnership to the principals, who then report these figures on their personal tax returns.

—If practice pass-through taxation benefits (using a certain percentage of business profit to pay owners' taxes) can be combined with specially tailored ownership interests that reflect each member's contributions to the business.

—If cash distributions from the partnership reduce the owners' basis for taxation. Only distributions in excess of an owner's basis can trigger taxable gain.

When not to use general partnerships

—If multiple owners will not assume common responsibility for one another's actions.

—If owners are concerned about having all personal assets at risk to liability claims.

—If the business intends to deliver financial services with the inherent risk of errors-and-omissions claims.

CORPORATIONS

Corporate structure provides the greatest business and personal asset protection of any entity. Corporations are of two types, S and C corporations. These entities are more complex than the previously discussed options for the financial planner. Corporations provide significant tax deferral and reduction opportunities but also limit the owners' entrepreneurial flexibility.

◆ **S corporation.** An S corporation is a small business that qualifies for and has elected to be treated as a pass-through entity under federal income tax laws. S corporation shareholders can choose to receive business profits as dividends. Those dividends are taxed once as income to the partners—but not twice, as happens with C corporations, where the partnership *and* owners pay taxes on the same income.

S corporations offer a range of significant advantages as well as shortcomings. On the positive side are limited liability, tax-free transfer of ownership interests (as long as there are no more than seventy-five owners), and centralized management and continuity of business life through stock ownership. The disadvantages include the filing of the sometimes complex federal tax Form 2553, less than desirable tax treatment of fringe benefits, limited flexibility in selecting a tax year, and limited methods to recognize expenses and to protect income from taxation. In addition, S corporations are subject to strict eligibility requirements. These requirements state that the S corporation must have only one class of stock and must be a domestic corporation having fewer than one hundred shareholders who are either U.S. citizens or resident aliens, estates, or certain types of trusts. Financial planning practices other than S corporations, specifically partnerships and sole ownerships, are at risk for double taxation. Limited liability *and* the legal provision for single taxation of dividends make S corporations very popular.

When to use S corporations
—If limiting owner liability is a key issue.
—If pass-through taxation is desired.
—If the strict eligibility rules can be met by current and potential owners.
—If there will be only one owner, LLCs usually are not available. S corporations are strongly preferred over sole proprietorships.

When not to use S corporations
—If one-person LLCs are available. This entity offers significant tax advantages over S corporations.
—If the owners expect to draw high fringe benefits (and thus expense) and high income. Net income could be reduced by limited deductibility of fringe benefits and other owner perks.

◆ **C corporation.** The C corporation is the most traditional corporate entity. It provides significant benefits comparable to those of the S corporation. The pluses include limited liability, flexible ownership and capital structure, continuity of business life, centralized management, and free transferability of ownership interests (unless limited by a buy-sell agreement). C corporation tax rates are slightly lower than personal rates: 15 percent on the first $50,000 earned and 25 percent on the next $25,000. As a result, the C corporation can maximize a business's retained earnings. When a business intends to retain all its earnings for an indefinite period in order to finance its growth, the difference in tax rates makes C corporations a better choice than dividend pass-through structures. A dividend pass-through business might have to distribute up to 39.6 percent of business income just so the owners can pay their personal taxes. Finally, C corporations offer better tax treatment for employer-paid fringe benefits, the ability to select a tax year, and the ability to take loans from qualified retirement plans.

The limitation of a C corporation is the double tax on profits— once at the corporate level and again for individuals receiving income distribution. However, the double taxation burden is lessened by the relatively low corporate tax rate and by the favorable offset of shareholder-employees' salaries and benefit expenses against income. In addition, C corporations can often solve the double taxation problem by "zeroing out" corporate income with deductible payments to or for the benefit of shareholders and employees. Such payments can be for salary, fringe benefits, interest on shareholder loans, and rent for property owned by shareholders. Unlike an S corporation or a sole proprietorship, C corporations do not provide for shareholders to shift income among family members. Thus, the C corporation structure should be reserved for financial planners who intend larger-scale, multiple-specialty, nonfamily businesses.

When to use C corporations

—If protection of the owners' personal assets from business liability is a significant concern.

—If the business plan assumes one owner *and* single-member LLCs are not permitted by state law.

—If the benefits of pass-through taxation are not important to the owners.

—If the owners foresee the possible need to borrow against their qualified retirement plan accounts.

—If the owners want to maximize retained earnings to finance business expansion and capital projects.

When not to use C corporations

—If the owners foresee the trade-off between double taxation and business expense deductions to be unfavorable. Double taxation can result from dividend distributions, sale of stock, or liquidation or appreciation of assets, such as real estate. If real estate assets can be owned by a pass-through entity that, in turn, is owned by C corporation shareholders, the real estate can then be leased back to the C corporation. With this arrangement, the C corporation can reduce its taxable income by making deductible rental payments that benefit its shareholders. Any gains upon the eventual sale of the appreciated assets owned by the pass-through entity will not be subject to double taxation.

—If the business owners distribute most of the income to themselves. Such a business should operate instead as a pass-through entity.

LIMITED LIABILITY COMPANIES

Limited liability companies (LLCs) are becoming more popular because they combine the best legal and tax characteristics of corporations and partnerships while avoiding many of the disadvantages. An LLC offers limited liability protection to all of its owners (called members) but still is treated as a partnership under federal income tax rules. Therefore, LLCs are unincorporated legal entities governed by state law and are not subject to restrictions on corporations or partnerships.

An LLC is a slightly tricky legal entity. It is a separate being from its members, and it owns assets and is liable for debts.

Summary Comparison of Entity Attributes

ISSUE	GENERAL PARTNERSHIP	SOLE PROPRIETORSHIP	C CORPORATION
Legal formalities of formation	None	None	File Articles of Incorporation with Secretary of State
Liability of owners	All partners are jointly and severally liable	Liability is unlimited	Shareholders liable only to extent of contributions
Ability to shift entity income among family members	Yes, within limits of family partnership rules	Yes, by employing family members	No
Number of owners and types of permissible owners	At least 2, but no maximum	1 owner. No limits	No limits
Administrative complexity	Moderate	Low	High
Double taxation and tax on contributions	Generally none	Generally none	Generally none if control test satisfied

S CORPORATION	LLC	LLP
File Articles of Incorporation with Secretary of State	File Articles of Organization with Secretary of State	File application with Secretary of State
Shareholders liable only to extent of contributions	Members liable only to extent of contributions	Not liable for professional errors and omissions of other partners or employees unless under direct supervision of partner in question. Same as general partnership for other liabilities in some states
To a degree, by manipulating wages of employee owners	No	Yes, within limits of family partnership rules
No more than 100 owners and 1 class of stock. Only individuals, estates, certain trusts, and certain tax-exempt entities may be shareholders	At least 2, but no maximum (some states permit single-member LLCs). No limits	At least 2, but no maximum. No limits
High	Moderate	Moderate
Generally none if control test satisfied, unless former C corporation and built-in gains and certain other taxes apply	Generally none	Generally none

(continued on the following page)

Summary Comparison of Entity Attributes *(continued)*

ISSUE	GENERAL PARTNERSHIP	SOLE PROPRIETORSHIP	C CORPORATION
Basis	Carryover basis from property contributed plus basis from share of liabilities	No basis	Carryover basis from property contributed. No basis from debt of entity
Tax on income	Taxed directly to partners	Taxed directly to owner on Form 1040, Schedule C	Entity-level tax. No tax to owners unless income distributed
Tax on distributions	None to extent of basis	All	Distributions taxable to shareholders. No deduction to corporation. Appreciation on any in-kind distributions taxable to corporation
Management	Each partner has general agency authority	Owner makes all the decisions	Shareholders elect board of directors. Board of directors elects officers. Officers hold authority to act on behalf of corporation. Formalities on taking corporate action
Ability to transfer all ownership rights	Transferee cannot become partner without approval of other partners	There is nothing to transfer. Owner would sell assets of business	Transferee takes all rights of transferor, including rights to participate in management

S CORPORATION	LLC	LLP
Carryover basis from property contributed. Basis from loans to corporation. No basis from other debt of entity	Carryover basis from property contributed plus basis from share of liabilities	Carryover basis from property contributed plus basis from share of liabilities
Taxed directly to shareholders. Some entity taxes on passive income or gains under certain circumstances	Taxed directly to members	Taxed directly to partners
Generally can make distributions to extent of shareholder's basis without tax. Appreciation on any in-kind distributions is taxable at the corporate level	None to extent of basis	None to extent of basis
Shareholders elect board of directors. Board of directors elects officers. Officers hold authority to act on behalf of corporation. Formalities on taking corporate action	If member-managed, each member has general agency authority. If manager-managed, only managers have general agency authority	Each partner has general agency authority
Transferee takes all rights of transferor, including rights to participate in management	Transferee cannot become member without approval of other members	Transferee cannot become partner without approval of other partners

(continued on the following page)

Summary Comparison of Entity Attributes *(continued)*

ISSUE	GENERAL PARTNERSHIP	SOLE PROPRIETORSHIP	C CORPORATION
Continuity of life	Legal dissolution on death, disability, etc., of a general partner	Legal dissolution on death, disability, etc., of owner	Perpetual existence permitted
Loans against qualified plan accounts	No, if more than 10% of profits or capital interests	Not permitted	Yes
Unreasonable owner compensation issues	None	None	Normally none. Unusually low can be challenged
Tax-advantaged fringe benefits for owners	Generally not available to partners	Generally not available to partners	Wider range of fringe benefits available to shareholder-employees

Therefore, the personal assets of an LLC member are generally beyond the reach of LLC creditors or other members. LLCs also have liberal ownership rules. Some states require a minimum of two members, others require only one. LLC covenants do not permit tax-free transferability of ownership interests. Fringe benefits and selection of tax year are unfavorably treated by LLC tax rules. Because LLCs are a relatively new type of business structure, there is a paucity of legal precedents available to guide tax courts and regulatory agencies in governing LLC business practices. Some states may not recognize one-person LLCs or permit certain lines of business to use the LLC structure. Because all members may participate fully in LLC management without losing limited liability protection, LLCs are ideal for closely held financial planning practices.

S CORPORATION	LLC	LLP
Perpetual existence permitted	Legal dissolution on death, disability, etc., of a member	Legal dissolution on death, disability, etc., of a partner
No, if own more than 5% of stock	Not permitted	Substantial flexibility in permitted allocations
Yes	None	None
Generally not available to shareholder-employees	Generally not available to members	Generally not available to partners

When to use LLCs

—If the financial planner practices under state laws permitting LLCs.

—If members desire to pass on ownership to heirs while retaining some level of management control.

—If the owners desire both pass-through taxation and limited liability.

—If the start-up company expects to have losses in the initial years that are passed through to investors.

—If the business plan includes real estate investment. Partnership taxation rules allow the investors to obtain basis from entity level debt, and special tax allocations can be made to benefit investors.

—If the business plan includes venture capital investments and state partnership laws permit pass-through taxation.

Limited Liability Partnership Attributes

ISSUE	RULE
Legal formalities of formation	File an application with the Secretary of State
Liability of owners	An LLP partner generally is not personally liable for debts and obligations of the LLP arising from professional errors, omissions, or negligence of the LLP's other partners and employees, with few exceptions
Ability to shift entity income among family members	Yes, within limits of family partnership rules
Number of owners and types of permissible owners	At least 2, but no maximum. No limits
Administrative complexity	Moderate
Double taxation and tax on contributions	Generally none

When not to use LLCs

—If state law does not permit LLCs in service industries, including banking and insurance.

—If shares of stock will continuously be issued to represent ownership interests.

—If the owners or advisers are unsure of income tax and regulatory changes, since LLCs are relatively new.

LIMITED LIABILITY PARTNERSHIPS

Because of the facility of malpractice litigation against law and accounting professionals, state LLP laws were enacted. Unlike

ISSUE	RULE
Basis	Carryover basis from property contributed plus basis from share of liabilities
Tax on income	Taxed directly to partners
Tax on distributions	None to extent of basis
Management	Each partner has general agency authority
Ability to transfer all ownership rights	Generally limited by state law and partnership agreement
Continuity of life	Legal dissolution on death, disability, etc., of general partner unless remaining partners vote to continue in existence
Loans against qualified plan accounts	No, if more than 10% of profits or capital interests
Unreasonable owner compensation issues	None

those in general partnerships, LLP partners are not liable for one another's acts. The saga of Laventhal and Horwath, before its demise one of the nation's top accounting firms, is a well-known example of the potentially ruinous consequences of joint partner liability; in that case, the firm collapsed under the weight of devastating, entangled litigation.

LLPs are a new type of entity that applies well to financial planning and asset management practices. LLPs, originally developed to control partners' personal liability, are formed and operate according to state LLP statutes. LLP partners may be personally liable for their own tort-related acts and their own professional errors, omissions, and negligence. An LLP partner may also be personally liable for the professional errors, omissions, and negligence of others who are under the partner's direct supervision or who should have been. However, LLP partners generally are not liable for the professional errors, omissions, and negligence of the other LLP partners and firm employees.

When to use LLPs

—If owners want pass-through taxation and cannot operate as a limited partnership due to active management by all the firm's partners.

—If state law prohibits use of an LLC, such as a state board of accountancy prohibiting LLC entities.

—If it is easier to convert an existing general partnership into an LLP rather than an LLC.

—If the owners want to avoid being subject to the double taxation risk of C corporations.

—If the owners want to avoid being subject to strict S corporation qualifications.

—If LLCs are subject to certain types of state taxation codes, as in Texas, where LLCs are taxed on an entity level but LLPs are not.

—If the LLP owners want to make tax-free distributions of appreciated property and create different types of partnership interests with varying rights to cash flow, liquidation proceeds, and tax allocations prohibited to S corporations.

When not to use LLPs

—When state law does not offer LLC-like liability protection to LLP partners.

—If state law does not permit this structure.

—When qualifying as an S corporation is more convenient and you want the transferability of ownership through stock.

—If the partner can "zero out" the double taxation of C corporations with deductible payments to or for the benefit of the owners.

BEFORE EMBARKING on the first of the "Ten Must-Do's," consult an experienced attorney to explain structural entity options in the state or states where you plan to practice. Remember to consider the growth phases your practice will experience in the short and long term. Your attorney will help you make structural decisions for today that will allow transition to more complex entities in the future. Plan ahead.

Finding a Mentor

SUCCESSFUL PRACTITIONERS in most fields of professional accomplishment, from music to medicine, look forward to the time when they can act as a mentor and take others under their wing. Ensuring smooth passage of a trade to a qualified next generation plus the personal satisfaction derived from helping others succeed are fundamental to the mentor's motivation. Mentors are teachers who provide specific guidance to novices. They teach techniques that have made them successful, and they are often looking to give back to their profession or community. This concept fits the financial planner profession as well.

The mentor relationship is an extremely important one for many reasons. First, most students and planners first entering this field have little or no practical experience in dealing with clients or the technical aspects of the business. Many of these students come from fields unrelated to finance. In addition, the interpersonal dynamics of the provider/client relationship are not replicated in other fields. The mentor's role is to prescribe a series of do's and don'ts to guide new planners along the path to professionalism, competency, and success. Mentors will help prioritize what needs to be done and will coach the student through the planning process described in Chapter 3.

Second, students of financial planning lack technical experience. Planners must be well educated in multiple disciplines of financial planning, including insurance, investments, education funding, retirement, income tax, and estate planning, among others. The future planner must know how to explain a financial objective to a client in very easy to understand terms, including the cost, the expected return, and the financial plan needed to accomplish the desired results. Because the knowledge base is so vast, few planners can be expert in all areas; today planners should specialize in a financial planning subfield, since it is important to differentiate themselves. Mentors are frequently specialists who train students to become experts in their field and expand the total knowledge base for the next generation.

Where can you find mentors? Try your local Financial Planning Association (FPA) society. Many have organized programs that give new members the opportunity to work with mentors and to form discussion groups focusing on specifics they find in practice. Often students are allowed to join at reduced prices.

Internships are another alternative. There are many practitioners willing to hire interns, generally on an unpaid or nominal-pay basis, in exchange for the experience that will assist them greatly in their first jobs. These internships can be found through finance and accounting departments of colleges and universities as well as through local organizations, such as the FPA.

Because of the complexities of financial planning work, working with a mentor in this type of arrangement is an excellent opportunity for newcomers to the profession, especially for those at midcareer transition. Many midcareer entrants to the field have sufficient funds to hold them over temporarily so they can get the needed experience to come out of the gate running. The other advantage to guidance from a mentor is that it is better to learn on someone else's nickel! In other words, you are better off making mistakes with someone who can then show you a better way to handle issues and minimize your learning curve. When you feel confident about handling difficult client issues, then you will be on your way to becoming an independent financial planner.

Getting the Credentials

WHAT KIND of background does one need to be a successful financial planner? How can you differentiate yourself from the other 250,000 self-described financial planners? Is it beneficial to earn a specialty designation? These are questions you need to consider when entering this profession. The fact is that more and more planners are earning professional designations and certifications. The drive to demonstrate professional expertise in specialty fields is definitely on the rise.

The personal financial planning certification process protects the public by ensuring a minimum level of competence among service providers through the successful completion of a certifying examination. Certification improves the personal financial planning skills of practitioners, resulting in increased professional competence across the industry. It enhances the profession's image as one that requires rigorous training. Furthermore, it helps keep the practitioner up-to-date with new developments in the profession. Once certified with any professional designation, practitioners need to take continuing education classes.

Following is a discussion of the most widely held designations financial planners pursue. Certification requirements are from the administering organization's official guidebook. For more information, contact the appropriate organizations listed here.

CERTIFIED FINANCIAL PLANNER (CFP) CERTIFICATION REQUIREMENTS

The CFP designation is offered by the CFP Board of Standards and has four initial requirement categories: education, examination, experience, and ethics.

1 Education. Before taking the certification examination, you must first complete the academic financial planning curriculum. The CFP Board does not specify or publish an official study manual; however, completion of the curriculum is available through three educational paths—registered program, challenge status, or transcript review.

The registered program encompasses many college or university classes affiliated with the CFP Board. Each CFP Board Registered Program provides coverage of all topics determined by the CFP Board to constitute the core curriculum for personal financial planning practitioners. Registered institutions presenting these programs often do so under different course names, yet they must cover the required content. More than three hundred programs are now registered with the CFP Board, and a new type of boot-camp format—Financial Planning Fast Track—

provides a revolutionary way of obtaining the necessary education. For more information, visit www.financialplanningfasttrack .com. These programs are neither approved nor disapproved by the CFP Board. Rather, they are registered as having met the CFP Board's requirements to ensure that the appropriate curriculum will be covered so that students can be prepared for the examination.

There is no time limit between completion of a CFP Board Registered Program and sitting for the Certification Examination. The educational program is designed to cover all of the tested topics; however, in reality it may not be adequate preparation for the examination. You should check with the registered institution to determine what the pass rate has been for students completing its program. The list of registered programs is available in the CFP Board's General Information Book on its website, www.CFP-Board.org.

Aspirants who already hold certain degrees and professional credentials are allowed to sit for the Certification Examination without having to verify their educational preparation. The following degrees and credentials have been approved by the CFP Board as fulfilling the education requirement: Certified Public Accountant (CPA), licensed and/or inactive attorney, Chartered Financial Consultant (ChFC), Chartered Life Underwriter (CLU), Chartered Financial Analyst (CFA), Ph.D. in economics or business, and Doctor of Business Administration.

The transcript review process is applicable to aspirants who have already completed the necessary coursework to sit for the Certification Examination. The CFP Board may waive some or all of the education component required for certification if the applicant can demonstrate successful completion of upper-division-level college or university coursework and the applicant is a holder in good standing of a CFP Board–recognized credential that can be transferred to meet the education requirement. Examine the checklist on the transcript review application to determine if you have completed some or all of the mandated courses.

The CFP Board also recommends courses in finance, accounting, economics, computer programming, and communications, especially for those who are new to the area of financial services.

2 Examination. When you have successfully completed the coursework or have satisfied the examination challenge requirement, you are eligible to apply for the ten-hour certification examination. It is administered three times a year, generally on the third Friday and Saturday in March, July, and November. The test is divided into one four-hour session (Friday afternoon) and two three-hour sessions (Saturday).

The test is designed to assess your ability to apply your financial planning education to financial planning situations and your understanding of the requirements of a successful CFP licensee. These requirements, which are updated approximately every five years, are derived from an extensive job analysis that specifies what CFP licensees do in practice. These requirements cover the areas of investment planning, estate planning, individual income tax planning, retirement planning, risk management, insurance, and finance.

3 Experience. To become certified you will also need work experience in personal financial planning to show that you have acquired the counseling skills that are part of the job. The usual requirement is three years, performed before or after successfully completing the certification examination, but exceptions apply in certain situations, such as five years' full-time experience without an undergraduate degree. Six months' experience must be gained within twelve months of submitting the résumé form, and internship programs may qualify for partial credit.

4 Ethics. Once you have completed the education and experience requirements, you will receive a declaration packet that includes an ethics statement form and your license application with a bill for your initial licensee fee. Before certification, you must disclose past or pending litigation or agency proceedings and acknowledge the right of the CFP Board to enforce its *Code of Ethics and Professional Responsibility* through the due process described in its *Disciplinary Rules and Procedures*. If you have any questions about the effect of any past or pending action on your certification, you may contact the CFP Board counsel directly.

Becoming a CFP licensee is a good idea if you are concerned about designation recognition. With more than 73,000 CFP licensees in the marketplace, it is far and away the most popular designation, which should prove valuable in establishing credibility with consumers. Also, the name itself—Certified Financial Planner—resembles other licenses and designations that incorporate the term *certified* and as such is readily recognizable to the consumer/client. For more information, contact the CFP Board at 888-CFP-MARK (888-237-6275) or visit its website at www.CFP-Board.org.

PERSONAL FINANCIAL SPECIALIST (PFS) INITIAL ACCREDITATION REQUIREMENTS

To qualify for the PFS designation, which is offered by the American Institute of Certified Public Accountants (AICPA), you must:

◆ Be a member in good standing of the AICPA. This means being a licensed CPA and not having any professional or ethical violations against you.

◆ Hold a valid and unrevoked CPA certificate issued by a legally constituted state authority.

◆ Have at least 250 hours of experience per year in personal financial planning activities for the three years immediately preceding the application. These activities must include the following:

—Personal financial planning
—Personal income tax planning
—Risk management planning
—Investment planning
—Retirement planning
—Estate planning

◆ Agree to comply with all the requirements for reaccreditation after you earn the right to use the PFS mark. These include earning continuing education credits and submitting three client references every time you apply for renewal.

◆ Pass the PFS examination. This examination is a six-hour practice-oriented exam. There are no formal education requirements or specific course topics as with the CFP Certification Examination. Rather, the test is based on one's practical knowledge as a CPA specializing in financial planning.

Professional Financial Planning Designations

DESIGNATION	ISSUED BY	TELEPHONE/WEBSITE
CFP licensee Certified Financial Planner	CFP Board of Standards	888-237-6275 www.CFP-Board.org
PFS Personal Financial Specialist	American Institute of Certified Public Accountants	888-777-7077 www.aicpa.org/pfs
CFA Chartered Financial Analyst	CFA Institute	800-247-8132 www.cfainstitute.org
ChFC Chartered Financial Consultant	The American College	888-263-2765 www.amercoll.edu

◆ Satisfy a point system, whereby successful attainment of professional designations, examinations, authoring of books or articles will go toward these requirements.

◆ Submit six written references that discuss your working experience in personal financial planning.

This designation is especially meaningful when you have an active CPA practice and want to branch out and become a specialist in financial planning. Since it is limited to practicing CPAs only, it has never attracted the number of designates that the CFP mark has. To date, very few CPAs have earned this designation. To receive additional information, contact the AICPA at 888-777-7077 or online at www.aicpa.org.

CHARTERED FINANCIAL ANALYST (CFA) REQUIREMENTS

The Chartered Financial Analyst Institute (CFA Institute) offers a CFA charter. To receive one, you must:

◆ Pass the Level I, Level II, and Level III examinations, which test three levels of investment analysis; the exams are offered once a year.

◆ Have at least four years of acceptable professional experience working in an investment decision-making capacity. Acceptable work experience means performing, teaching, or supervising the collection, evaluation, or application of financial, economic, or statistical data as part of the investment decision-making process. Eligibility of a candidate's experience for meeting the CFA requirements is reviewed only after the candidate passes the first examination.

◆ Apply concurrently for membership in the CFA Institute and in a local member society (these local organizations are affiliates of the CFA Institute).

◆ Sign and submit a professional conduct statement.

◆ Sign and submit a form agreeing to comply with CFA Institute rules and ethical standards.

◆ Exhibit a high degree of ethical and professional conduct.

This designation focuses on investment calculations. It is very specific to investment and does not emphasize a comprehensive approach toward financial planning. If you want to become an investment specialist, then earning a CFA is highly worthwhile. For more information, contact the CFA Institute at 800-247-8132 or online at www.cfainstitute.org.

CHARTERED FINANCIAL CONSULTANT (ChFC) REQUIREMENTS

Through self-study courses offered by the American College of Bryn Mawr, Pennsylvania, students are eligible to become candidates for a Huebner School Chartered Financial Consultant (ChFC) designation. The program to obtain this designation requires coursework, three years of business experience, and thirty hours of continuing professional education every two years, along with maintenance of ethical standards. An undergraduate or graduate degree from an accredited institution qualifies as one year of business experience. Examinations are administered after each course. Ten courses are needed to obtain the ChFC designation.

For more information, contact the American College at 888-263-7265 or online at www.amercoll.edu.

Licensing Requirements for Insurance and Investment Advisory Practitioners

FINANCIAL PLANNERS who want to become fee-based investment advisers need to pass the so-called Series 65 or Series 66 securities examinations. These tests generally are a prerequisite to becoming a Registered Investment Advisor (RIA) in most states. However, if you plan to go for your CFP, PFS, or ChFC designation, obtain that first, because many states now waive the Series 65 or 66 exams if the applicant possesses any one of those designations. Note, however, that some states may require you to pass the Series 6 or Series 7 exam in addition to either passing the Series 65 or 66 exam or obtaining the financial planning designation waiver. Check with your state licensing board first.

If you are interested in becoming a commission-based investment salesperson, generally it is better to take the Series 7 exam rather than the Series 6. Passing the Series 7 provides you with the opportunity to sell more products, such as stocks, bonds, options, mutual funds, variable life, and variable annuities, whereas the Series 6 enables you to sell only mutual funds and variable insurance products. If you want to sell life, health, and disability insurance products, you need to obtain a life and health insurance license. If you wish to sell automobile, home owners, and umbrella insurance, you will need a property and casualty license.

The easiest way to obtain your licenses for insurance or investment advising is to affiliate with a financial services organization that will sponsor you, such as a brokerage or insurance company. Such firms usually will pay your licensing fees and provide you with the training necessary to pass the examinations. This approach will enable you to get your licenses quickly and easily while learning about the industry firsthand.

DESIGNATION CONSIDERATIONS

Many of the designations discussed above originated in related industries. The ChFC designation, for example, is an offshoot of the Chartered Life Underwriter (CLU) designation, which has existed in the life insurance industry for many years. Planners holding the ChFC designation often approach planning issues more from an insurance perspective, given that the primary training associated with this designation reflects that orientation while also incorporating other elements of the financial planning process. For a planner with a strong interest in insurance concerns who wishes to become a specialist in this area, the ChFC or CLU title may be the most appropriate. However, it is worth noting that this designation is not well known or understood by the general public; in fact consumers may tend to view ChFCs as strictly sellers of insurance products due to an association of the mark with that industry.

CPAs wishing to emphasize their financial planning skills can obtain the PFS certification, which, as noted previously, is open only to CPAs and denotes the CPA as a financial planning specialist. The drawback of this mark, however, is that it has not been heavily promoted to the public as a mainstream designation, so that most consumers are unfamiliar with it. This in part reflects the fact that the AICPA has not rallied around this specific designation since many within the organization want to promote the CPA holder as the financial planner of choice. In fact, one faction holds that the CPA degree itself confers the appropriate skills necessary to be a competent financial planner.

However, CPA training in and of itself does not provide exposure to the spectrum of skills needed by the planner. The full range of these disciplines, discussed in Chapter 4, is usually not found in the standard college and university accounting curricula. On the other hand, some AICPA members believe that an accounting specialty for financial planners is warranted. They see CPAs who practice as Certified Financial Planner specialists as analogous to physicians and lawyers who practice in specialties. These conflicting views among its constituency have made it difficult for the AICPA to lend major support to a single designation.

The must-have certification for practitioners wanting to denote their financial planning specialization is the Certified Financial Planner (CFP) designation. Held by more than 73,000 planners, this is the best-known mark that the public associates with the financial planning profession. The press often includes the CFP designation along with a planner's name after a quote in a newspaper or magazine. Since the mark is the predominant one among financial planners who hold designations, industry representatives who are CFP licensees tend to have more clout with regulators. Also, consolidation has occurred within the financial planning industry, notably the International Association for Financial Planning (IAFP) and Institute of Certified Financial Planners' (ICFP's) historic January 1, 2000, merger into a single professional organization, the Financial Planning Association (FPA). The American College, sponsor of the once rival ChFC mark, now also offers training leading to the CFP designation and has become the largest enrollment base for those hoping to become licensed as Certified Financial Planners. All these factors suggest that the CFP program is likely to continue to predominate as the industry standard in the profession in the years to come.

For planners seeking a formalized training program, the CFP designation provides the most comprehensive and generic industry training. Since one of the requirements for obtaining the mark is to go through an education program covering a mandated range of topics, would-be planners have an opportunity to receive adequate training in the full spectrum of planning disciplines, which is especially valuable both for novices and for planners entering from other industries.

Other designations, namely the CFA and RIA, do not provide for a comprehensive approach to the entire range of financial planning services. They are for planners wishing to highlight an industry specialty in investment planning and advising, but these designations do not suggest a practice with broad financial planning.

CHAPTER 3

DEVELOPING A CLIENT MANAGEMENT SYSTEM

CREATING THE CLIENT management procedures, methods, and tools to get started as a financial planner is fundamental to success. Like an attorney or CPA, a financial planner needs to master the content of the profession, then develop good client management skills to put the theory into practice. The preliminary steps to establishing your financial planning practice, such as deciding what type of business structure to adopt and the other crucial initial tasks, are outlined in Chapter 2. The final step among the "must-do's" is to design and perfect a client management system for your practice—the steps and procedures you will use over and over again to take your clients' needs to results. Your client management system will become turnkey in that each new client relationship will follow the same planning process: one key opens one door to all clients for your services.

Your client management approach must become so automatic and fail-safe that any planning associate on your staff can perform client services in the same way. Repetition and fine-tuning of "best practices" leads to a superior client management system, competitive advantage, and better client results. Your methodology must be efficient, manageable, and perhaps most important, easy to execute. In essence, a well-developed turnkey client management system takes the planner's practice to the next level of professionalism, quality, and productivity.

The client management approach introduced in Chapter 2 is described by the acronym PIPRIM, outlining the six straightforward but crucial activities involved in financial planning. This chapter takes you through each step in detail and provides a complete methodology for managing clients.

The PIPRIM Client Management System— Six Steps to Successful Client Management

IN ORDER to translate a client's personal financial needs into goals and objectives and ultimately into a plan, planners can use a client-centered financial planning process, PIPRIM.

Preliminary meeting with a client
Integrated goal setting and data gathering
Putting it all together
Recommending solutions
Implementing the plan
Monitoring the plan

BEFORE YOU MEET THE CLIENT, UNDERSTAND YOUR ROLE

Financial planning is a process that concludes as a highly personalized service. It is not a product, bought and consumed by the client. Rather, financial planning is a cycle that constantly renews as client needs change over time. Your clients must understand and accept the fundamental nature of the financial planning process if they are to value your services. Your job is not to make clients rich, as a stockbroker might. Rather, your role is to probe and study your clients' needs, lead them through the PIPRIM system, and prepare a financial plan for now and for the future.

Unlike stocks that are bought and sold, a financial plan is long-range. You and your clients are investing in a relationship that must weather short-term gains and setbacks. Your ability to maintain client confidence is dependent not on the dollar gain from the financial plan but rather on the integrity of your relationship and the financial planning system you employ. In the end, clients will be financially independent if the process you follow has been tested, challenged, and improved with each engagement. Your clients will expect nothing less.

A NOTE ABOUT ETHICS

Your role is to help clients achieve financial well-being. This requires that you accept and occupy a position of trust. Financial planners, like other service professionals, are by definition held to a high standard of ethics, since clients entrust them with their financial future. Planners must put client interests above their own and ensure that objectivity and independence are never compromised.

The Certified Financial Planner Board has prepared a *Code of Ethics and Professional Responsibility*. This invaluable guide for the financial planner ensures that the practitioner is employing the "right environment for the clients." The CFP Board has initiated the challenge of elevating the status of the profession, for CFP licensees and non–CFP licensees alike, through the creation and promulgation of this professional practice standard. All financial planners should understand and apply this code consistently in every client assignment. Through self-directed standards, the financial planning professional will continue to invest in his or her own future. Section I of the *Code of Ethics and Professional Responsibility* appears in Appendix A.

A PROSPECT CALLS

On day one of your career as a financial planner, you need to be ready for your first contact with a prospective client. It is not as simple as picking up the telephone and talking. Remember that lasting impressions are made in the first few sentences of any conversation, whether face-to-face or over the telephone.

What do you say when someone calls you on a referral from a colleague or friend? First, do not try to "sell" anything. Rather, you need to conduct yourself in a manner consistent with the credibility you have already achieved from the referral source. The reputation of the person who referred you is on the line, too. Next, remember that the prospect does not really know what to ask for—that is why you are being contacted. Resist diagnosing the prospect's situation on the first call. More important, do not offer advice. Keep the conversation light and informal, but professional. Thank the prospect for the call, then explain your background and, very briefly, how you work with clients. While you are not attempting to gain a commitment in the first conversation, you are trying to establish enough interest for the prospect to take the next step, a meeting.

In general, the flow of the first conversation with a prospect is as follows: The prospect may approach you with a specific question, express various concerns, or indicate a need for direction. Assume that the prospect calls you and wants to know what financial planning is all about. What do you say?

SCENARIO I

Prospect: I got your name from a mutual friend, Bill Williams. He said you might have some ideas. I have questions concerning some immediate financial issues that I haven't really planned for.

Planner: I appreciate the call, what are your concerns?

Prospect: My son will attend college in three years, but I would also like to seriously plan for retirement just about when he finishes school. I'm not sure how to handle both.

Planner: That's a challenge but not impossible. [Offer confirmation of the problem, but link yourself to a professional solution.] I specialize in both of those areas, and have helped many people build a financial plan to meet personal goals. My approach is to first of all meet a prospective client, understand the current financial situation, and, assuming there is a good match between your goals and my capabilities, build a financial plan. The best way to start is with an informal meeting in my office to study your situation more closely. Would you be willing? [Some planners like to offer a free thirty-minute consultation. While this approach works for some prospects, it may cheapen the service to others. Price should not be the motivating factor for a client to retain a financial planner.]

Prospect: Sure, it's certainly worth an hour of my time to learn more. When should I come in?

SCENARIO 2

Prospect: I have heard that you work with people in need of financial advice—that's me.

Planner: I do have several new clients whose financial goals range from very general to specific. What advice are you looking for? [Do not attempt to stretch your client base, expertise, or specialization beyond reality. It is more credible to state your credentials *and* limitations up front, particularly if you are new.]

Prospect: I don't have a great deal of money to worry about, but I'm concerned about what I do have. I need advice so I don't make decisions now that I'll regret in the future. Can I even afford professional advice with a bank account my size?

Planner: It's not the size of the bank account now that is important, it's the size you'll need to meet your goals. [It is very important to get people thinking about goals from the beginning. Without goals, the prospect cannot value the financial future you will chart through a plan.] I think the best way to proceed would be a no-obligation meeting in my office. We can talk more about your current situation and start setting some goals. [In this scenario, a "no-obligation" meeting does make sense because the prospect has already established limited resources.] Would you be interested?

Prospect: Since it's no obligation, I can afford that. When should I come in?

SCENARIO 3

Prospect: My attorney, Lester Jones, referred me to you. He speaks very highly of the way you have started your financial services practice.

Planner: Yes, Lester and I have known each other for a long time. He is very good; we have worked together with common clients. [Since the prospect respects Mr. Jones, mention situations when you have worked together. This gives you fast and unquestioned credibility.] What are your particular financial issues?

Prospect: I have a significant and growing income every year, yet I worry that almost all of it goes to taxes or just evaporates. I hate to say it, but there is social pressure to drive the right car and go to the right vacation spots in my circle of friends. They seem to afford it all, but I can't anymore. I need a financial plan before I spend my family into ruin. I need advice, and quick.

Planner: Let me first say, you're not alone. Very few people have the discipline and fewer have a financial plan to manage money. I recently worked with a family in a similar situation. The process leading to financial security was difficult for this couple, but we worked together and continue to work together. I was able to help them set financial goals, prioritize their current needs, and feel comfortable with financial decisions in spite of the urge to spend. I would be happy to show you the format of the plan I created for this family. It might take an hour of your time, but you'll see the benefit. When could we meet? [In this example, the prospect is expressing self-doubt and is looking for confirmation that there is a solution. Without promising results, the financial planner offered a true case study. This told the prospect two things: (1) there are other people with the same problem, and (2) there are solutions. The planner was fairly assertive in asking for a meeting. This prospect cannot afford to turn down the offer. There was no need to bring up "no obligation."]

THESE ARE scenarios that financial planners run into constantly. They all begin with a specific or vague problem, concern, or need. However, you approach every situation the same way. Communicate understanding, give examples of similar situations you have addressed, and never diagnose or promise anything over the phone. Never provide free advice. Always invite the prospect to come into the office for a thirty- to sixty-minute initial consultation. Mention "no obligation" only if asked or if you think the issue of payment could be a demotivator. This meeting allows you *and* the prospective client to find out whether a legitimate need exists, whether your client management system can help, and whether there is adequate symbiosis to sustain a relationship.

Once you have set a date and time for your initial consultation, keep the interest level warm by sending the prospect a follow-up packet of information introducing yourself and your firm. This shows the prospect that you are serious about helping, and it gives factual information to increase confidence in your ability and to confirm that talking with you was the right decision. Every interaction with a prospect is important. You want to control the image you portray and sustain interest at the same time.

EXHIBITS 3.1 AND 3.2 (see pages 75–77) show a sample packet adapted from one used by Garrett Financial Planning in Overland Park, Kansas. The letter should be short, professional, goal focused, nonintimidating, and motivating. Give the prospect good reasons to want to do business with you. The information packet must not be overwhelming; it must establish your background, credentials, and track record; and it must include preparation work sheets (homework) to discuss at the first meeting. The information packet is not a sales pitch. The more you say, the greater the potential for overkill.

Step 1:
Preliminary Meeting with the Client

YOU AND the prospect have taken the first step. You have agreed on the practical value of investing one hour of time in each other. You have set up an appointment and have provided the prospect background information and homework. The meeting time has arrived, and the prospect is waiting in your reception area. A strong, friendly, and confident greeting is important to first impressions. By all means, greet the prospect yourself. Do not send an assistant or ask the prospect to find his or her way to your office.

> Welcome to Financial Planning Associates, John. Did you have any trouble finding us or parking? Downtown is a disaster these days with the new one-way traffic rules. Did you have a chance to read the information packet I sent you and to fill out the personal financial profile? Great. We will start with an overview of your current situation, talk about your goals, and see if I can't find a way to help you.

During the preliminary meeting in your office, which typically lasts thirty to sixty minutes, you and the prospect will explore, and ultimately conclude, whether your abilities match the prospect's needs. Prospective clients will give you either too much or too little information about themselves and their financial aspirations. You will need to constantly stop the conversation, repeat your understanding of what the prospect has said, and move the conversation forward step-by-step. You will, of course, ask yourself if you can work closely and successfully together. Be sure you talk about the following issues:

◆ Why is the prospect here?
◆ What is the prospect's current financial situation?
◆ What are the prospect's immediate and long-term needs?
◆ Is the prospect capable of helping design and implement a financial plan, taking charge of his or her success?

◆ Is there confluence between your financial and investment philosophies?

◆ What services can you apply to the prospect's needs?

◆ Do you have a strong initial sense that you can help?

◆ How would the prospect benefit from your service portfolio?

◆ What is the estimated time frame to complete the plan and accomplish goals?

◆ What compensation models apply to this prospect's situation?

◆ Is your role likely to be adviser, motivator, teacher, or director? Are you ready to take on any or all of these roles with this individual?

The most important part of the initial meeting is to get the prospect to summarize the discussion in his or her own words. Do not be afraid to ask the prospect, "What do you think?" If the prospect can more clearly see how his or her financial situation can be improved through a co-administered financial plan, the message has succeeded. The prospect's own verbalization is requisite to commitment.

If you and the prospect have reached a clear understanding of needs and capabilities and reasonable confidence in the potential for results, you should suggest the next step. Schedule a follow-up meeting within the next two weeks. Meet as soon as possible to maintain momentum and commitment. A plan to reconvene within two weeks will help the prospect stay focused and thinking about the tasks to be accomplished before your next appointment. Do give the prospect an assignment: for example, to rank his financial goals by importance, time frame, and degree of monetary risk he is willing to accept.

No more than two days after the initial meeting, summarize your understanding in an engagement letter. By now the prospect knows that the free meetings are over. You have started to deliver value, professional knowledge, and commitment of your time. It is totally reasonable for you to now draft an engagement letter governing the transition from prospect to client relationship. **EXHIBIT 3.3** (see pages 78–80) shows a sample engagement letter. This particular example is designed for performing comprehensive financial planning services.

Ask the client to read the agreement carefully and call you with any questions. Many prospective clients will have little experience with legal agreements or contracts. Your attorney should review the language in the letter of engagement before you send it. Do not be surprised if the letter gets to the prospect's attorney, who will undoubtedly find ways to amend the letter to his client's advantage. Try to avoid the cost and delay of two attorneys working out the details of phraseology. Once all parties are satisfied, have the prospect sign and return the letter to you before your next meeting. If the engagement letter is not signed before your second meeting, hold off on working with the prospect until the letter is signed. This document describes in legal terms the obligations of the client and planner in a contractual relationship.

The second meeting, usually lasting sixty minutes or more, is to start designing a working relationship. This session is in essence a test of what the next ten to fifteen hours of planning would be like with this client. If the client passes your *team test,* and if you pass your client's *credibility test,* then you are in a position to proceed to the next step—the integrated goal-orientation and data-gathering session.

Step 2:
Integrated Goal Setting and Data Gathering

IN THE THIRD session with your client, you will start researching and collecting information that will help you design and implement a successful financial plan. The meeting should last for as much time as you need; some planners spend as much as two hours with a client in this meeting.

FORMULATION OF GOALS

Begin by asking clients to describe their goals as explicitly as possible. Point out to the client that as more information is provided, the plan becomes more concrete. You cannot gather too much; all information is useful either now or later. At this stage, your job is to take in everything clients can tell you about themselves and their financial aspirations. Do not attempt to go through the details of all the information the client provides at this time. Rather, skim through it to ensure that you have everything significant. During the actual formation of the plan, you will review this information again in detail.

It is important that the third session be interactive. You must probe clients with open-ended questions designed to elicit nonfinancial as well as financial information, since both significantly affect the development of the plan. Your questions must be direct, targeting the goals that have been discussed or written down previously. As noted above, you will go through the information in detail later, as you formulate a financial plan.

If you are working with clients who are life partners, be sure to meet with them together. Spouses and partners often give contradictory information to the same questions. Meet as a triad to ensure that you have a common and focused set of goals.

Your questions can be divided into two sections: those that address specifics of the client's *financial situation* and those that address the client's *goals*. The first area to elucidate is the client's vision of the ideal future life, which will become the basis for financial goals. Both should be stated as explicitly as possible. Clients must clearly articulate their picture of the future, and you must restate this vision in goals that the client can reasonably achieve. Unrealistic goals are damaging to the client, to his or her family, and to your relationship and reputation.

FORMULATION OF OBJECTIVES

Goals are by definition long-term descriptions of a future condition. Objectives are the short-term steps to a goal. Setting objectives is the heart of planning, because they define what the client expects to achieve through the financial planning process.

Pay careful attention to both the broad, relatively open-ended forecasts of what the client wants to achieve (goals) and how those goals translate into specific objectives. Clients sometimes tell planners that they want to be rich. What does that really mean? How does the client define rich? Specific objectives, on the other hand, are quantifiable and provide you with a road map to meeting a client's needs. For a particular client, rich might mean retiring in a certain number of years with a specific lifestyle. Perhaps a couple wishes to retire at age fifty with $1 million in the bank, or at age sixty with an income of $100,000 a year, or with enough residual wealth to pay for the educational needs of an unknown number of grandchildren. These are specific, meaningful goals, and you can design strategies to achieve them. Objectives, therefore, are both definite (specific time frame) and measurable (dollar amount).

Once the client has stated clear, quantifiable outcomes for financial planning, the next step is to rank those objectives in order of importance. Most clients will not be able to achieve all their objectives fully. None but the truly wealthy clients will have sufficient resources to accomplish more than a few of their objectives. You need to tell the client this up front before the plan is prepared. You must force your clients to be realists. Oddly enough, if they were realists from the beginning, they probably would not need your services. Explain that based on their current financial condition and future outlook, they can totally achieve one or two objectives, but at the expense of others. A client's objectives may be at cross-purposes, one competing with another. Not bringing this conflict to the client's attention and reaching consensus is an ethical breach of confidence.

The most common reason that a client seeks legal restitution from a financial planner is a promise of more service or financial gain than is either perceived or actually delivered. Often the client fails to understand or accept the risk involved in preparing a financial plan, blaming the planner for weak results. Other times the financial planner fails to remind the client verbally *and* in writing of the inherent risk in financial planning. In either case, client expectations have not been properly set or managed. (See Chapter 8 for more detail on managing client expectations.)

Consider a hypothetical client who has interview appointments with two planners. The client's goals are sufficient net assets for retirement and long-term earnings on assets equal to or greater than average interest rates. The client is willing to take on low to moderate investment risk. Planner 1 meets with the client and, after analyzing his portfolio, tells the client that he can get him a 40 percent annual rate of return with moderate risk. The client then sees planner 2 and poses the same goals. After careful deliberation, planner 2 tells the client that he can probably achieve an 8 percent rate of return with moderate risk. Not knowing whom to trust, the client invests half his portfolio with each planner. A year goes by during which both planners deliver a 20 percent return. The client is pleased with planner 2, who did 12 percent better than he had predicted, but is angry with planner 1, whose strategy underperformed by 20 percent. Both planners offered their best prediction of future asset performance and risk. Still, planner 1 in a sense "guaranteed" a 40 percent return. Not only was this imprudent, but it could be interpreted as willful. This could be the basis of a malpractice lawsuit, which, win or lose, is devastating to a planner's reputation. It is crucial to be realistic with your clients and protect yourself from any remote misinterpretation.

SPECIFIC CLIENT OBJECTIVES AND STRATEGIES

◆ **A client is concerned about his family's financial well-being in the event of his or her death.** A life insurance plan can be purchased to neutralize this worry. Life insurance protects against the following:

—Loss of the client's future earning power in the event of death

—Expenses associated with the transfer of estate to survivors

—Money for replacing the services (such as homemaking) the client provided to his or her family

—Income taxes the surviving spouse may pay when filing as a single head of household

—Loss of the client's private business valuation

Other insurable financial objectives include perpetual income in the case of disability, coverage for catastrophic illness, and protection against property loss and liability. While no one can predict the future, many clients have lifestyle profiles that are characterized by high personal or business risk. For more detailed information on insurance planning, see Chapter 4.

◆ **A client wants to protect capital accumulation.** An investment plan must be structured to enable clients to meet financial goals, given their tolerance for risk and discretionary spending.

A client's need for cash, market liquidity, and diversification also affects portfolio construction. In addition to a medium- to long-term investment strategy, clients should set aside cash for three to six months' household expenses as a hedge against unforeseen financial events. Emergency funds serve as a cushion against job loss or sudden catastrophic expenses. This strategy helps protect clients from the need to spend down investment principal. See Chapter 4 for more detail on investment planning.

◆ **A client wants to minimize tax exposure.** Reducing a client's tax burden can be accomplished through income and estate tax planning. During a long-term relationship with a client, you can build a financial plan to:

—Avoid or reduce taxes

—Shift the tax burden to family members in a lower tax bracket

—Allow wealth to accumulate while postponing taxation

—Take returns as capital gains by making lifetime gifts

In connection with a client's expected life span (based upon actuarial tables), you may be able to improve the tax situation for the client's family by providing for a will and through the transfer of property by contract, operation of law, or disclaimer.

In summary, the planner assists the client in articulating short- and long-term life goals and in establishing realistic and quantifiable objectives. Since objectives are the central focus of the financial planning process, it bears repeating that financial objectives should be quantified in dollar amounts, time frames, and risk assumptions instead of remaining general and open-ended. A series of specific objectives are further defined by investment *strategies*. Strategies are detailed optional programs for achieving specific objectives. Strategies should compete for attention, meaning that the best strategy to reach an objective will most closely match the client's predisposition to investment vehicles and risk.

THE FACT-FINDING SESSION: GATHERING DATA TO HELP SOLVE CLIENT PROBLEMS

There are two types of data to gather from the client: quantitative and qualitative. Quantitative information provides basic but specific identifying information concerning a family along with numerical details concerning the family's financial status. It also provides the basis for the many financial analyses you will perform.

Qualitative information provides general information concerning a family's goals, lifestyle, health status, risk tolerance level, employment status, hobbies, attitudes, and fears. Qualitative data give a financial plan life. Knowing a client's specific goals, such as planning to move when retiring at age fifty-five, funding a child's college education and expenses, starting an expensive hobby just before retirement, or traveling extensively during retirement, is important to the success of any financial planning.

◆ **Examples of quantitative data include the following:**
—General family profile
—Names, addresses, and phone numbers of family members
—Assets and liabilities
—Cash inflows and outflows
—Insurance policy information
—Employee benefit and pension plan information
—Tax returns for the last three years
—Details on current investments
—Retirement benefits available
—Client-owned business information
—Copies of wills and trusts
—Lifetime gifting programs

◆ **Examples of qualitative data include the following:**
—Goals and objectives
—Health status of client and family members
—Interests and hobbies
—Expectations about employment
—Risk tolerance level
—Anticipated changes in current/future lifestyle
—Other planning assumptions

After the interview concludes, set up the next appointment for approximately four weeks after the data-gathering session. Before you do any work, send the client a synopsis of the meeting, stating your recollection of the issues and objectives you discussed and the conclusions to which you came. Ask the client to sign the synopsis and return it to you. The synopsis should follow this outline:

> Dear Mr. and Mrs. Client:
> On November 3 you and I discussed... You had the following concerns and objectives:... I provided you with an outline of how I would approach your issues... If these responses meet your recollection of the issues, please initial, date, and return a copy of this letter to me by... Sincerely, Joseph Smith, CPA, CFP

This initiative ensures that you and the client are expecting the same things from the work that is about to begin. It also limits your liability.

EXHIBIT 3.4 (see pages 81–91) represents a sample form that can be used to gather client data.

Step 3:
Putting It All Together

INTERPRET FINANCIAL INFORMATION

The information you have gathered by talking to a client and reviewing his or her economic condition will lead you to reaching conclusions about the client's financial strengths and weaknesses. Interpretation of financial information is where the science ends and the art takes over. Here is where your experience with other similar clients is applied. Your practice history kept in a case study format will help you learn the do's and don'ts of interpreting financial information for financial planning. Take, for example, a client's insurance information:

◆ **Life insurance**

—Approximate need is roughly seven times gross earnings. Of course, you will need to perform a needs analysis to determine a more exact amount. You can do this by adding up all the expenses that the client will be responsible for and arriving at a total need.

—Primary beneficiary named. In the event of death of the insured, this is the person who receives the insurance proceeds.

—Contingent beneficiary named. In the event of death of the insured and primary beneficiary, this is the person who receives the insurance proceeds.

—Disability waiver of premium included. In the event the insured becomes disabled, this provision continues payment of the insurance premium.

—Strength of issuing company. You undertake research to determine the strength of the insurance company that is underwriting the policy.

◆ Disability insurance

—Approximate need is roughly 60 percent to 70 percent of gross monthly earnings. Because of the extreme moral hazard in providing an insured 100 percent benefits for not working, insurance companies provide usually about two-thirds of the earned income amount. Determine what the client's earned income is and use 60 to 70 percent of that amount as the disability benefit.

—Own occupation definition. If the insured becomes disabled performing the duties of his or her specific occupation, the insured may be able to receive benefits from his or her specific job and still work in a field outside the insured's primary occupation.

—Noncancelable and guaranteed renewable. As long as the insured continues to pay the premium, the insurance company cannot cancel the policy nor raise the premium on the insured. However, the insurance company can raise the premium on an entire classification of insureds.

—Partial and residual disability. If the insured is not totally disabled, does he or she receive benefits while going back to work part-time?

—Cost of living adjustment (COLA) rider. Do annual benefits increase according to the increase in the consumer price index?

—Strength of issuing company. You undertake research to determine the strength of the insurance company that is underwriting the policy.

◆ **Health insurance**

—$1 million or higher lifetime catastrophic coverage. In the event of serious illness, the insured needs plenty of coverage in order to avoid catastrophes.

—Strength of issuing company. You undertake research to determine the strength of the insurance company that is underwriting the policy.

◆ **Home owners insurance**

—HO3 and HO15 coverage. Replacement cost coverage on the client's dwelling (HO3) and the contents (HO15) is necessary.

—Riders on items not fully covered by policy. If your client has a valuable item worth more than the underlying coverage found inside the policy, the client needs to purchase a rider to increase the limits. Items of this magnitude would include fur coats, jewelry, and collectibles.

—Minimum $300,000 liability coverage. Having too little liability coverage can prove extremely risky. In the event that someone tries to sue the client, you want to ensure that your client's personal assets are not at risk.

—Strength of issuing company. You undertake research to determine the strength of the insurance company that is underwriting the policy.

◆ **Automobile insurance**

—Minimum $300,000 liability coverage. Having too little or not having any liability coverage can prove extremely risky. In the event that someone tries to sue your client, you want to ensure that your client's personal assets are not at risk.

—Uninsured/underinsured coverage. This coverage enables your client to increase liability coverage to the $300,000 amount in the event someone gets into an accident with him or her and has too little or no coverage.

—Physical damage coverage. This coverage protects your client in the event his or her automobile gets into an accident with another car or object and allows the client to restore the automobile to its condition prior to the accident.

—Strength of issuing company. You undertake research to determine the strength of the insurance company that is underwriting the policy.

REVIEW IMPORTANT DOCUMENTS

As personal financial planner to your client, you have every reason to ask for full disclosure of pertinent information. You also have the responsibility to ask the client if there are financial issues you need to know in confidence. Among the legal documents that may need your review are wills, trusts, buy-sell agreements, deeds, divorce settlements, and any other legal claims on your client's assets. Other standard documents to be studied are investment and retirement plans, the last three federal and state income tax returns (since you can amend an income tax return up to three years out), private notes payable and notes due, criminal records, and court settlements. You need to know everything to help your client and to protect yourself.

TIE CLIENT RESOURCES TO CLIENT OBJECTIVES

Your client's assets and liabilities and other information pertaining to financial stability or jeopardy must be organized in a series of financial statements. This will enable you to determine the strengths and weaknesses in the client's financial position and evaluate the likelihood of your clients' achieving their objectives in view of available resources. It is important to stress the concept of *available resources*. A solid financial plan is based on predictions of growth in current asset base and not on the best-case scenario, which might include an estimate of future income or windfalls. For example, the prudent financial planner will discount an inheritance in a client's financial plan. Relations between family members change. Similarly, the deft financial planner will discount a client's estimate of future earning power. We all like to believe that we are worth more than we are being paid. On the reverse side, a client's liabilities should be fully accounted, since liabilities are by definition the worst-case scenario. Thus, an evaluation of the client's current economic condition adjusted for future capital accumulation *and* liability is the basis upon which to build a financial plan.

When analyzing the client's financial and personal information, do not lose sight of:

◆ **Qualitative information that may help you understand client motivation and personal traits predictive of future behavior.** Is your client a short-term thinker, spontaneous, impulsive? Is your client conservative, indecisive, even timid? The plans you create for clients must fit their personality and likely behavior in the future.

◆ **Helping clients maintain control over their financial lives.** You may need to encourage, if not demand, that your client adopt a budget and stick to it. A recalcitrant client is a failure in the making and is bad advertising.

◆ **Effect of unknown events.** The financial plan you create for a client is a fluid tool. It must be flexibly designed to accommodate changing client goals, objectives, and strategies. The plan must also anticipate the unknown: reversal of the stock market, sudden illness, business failure, divorce, and death. These topics are very unpleasant and even painful for some clients, but they must be discussed and anticipated in the financial plan.

◆ **Long-term effects of poor planning.** What if your plan fails? What is the client left with? You must talk to your client about some residual capital and assets that will remain outside of the financial plan. No planner is good enough to risk a client's entire basis of wealth in a financial plan. As a general rule, a client should reserve enough liquidity to maintain a family for one year. Certain investments—401(k) plans and deferred income plans—are untouchable and thus lie outside a self-directed financial plan.

CREATE CLIENT FINANCIAL STATEMENTS

From the information you have collected during the integrated data-gathering step of PIPRIM, you should create two standard financial statements to summarize the multiple dimensions of a client's financial condition. The first, a *Statement of Financial Position,* shows change in a client's assets, liabilities, and net worth over a three-to-five-year period. The second, a *Cash Flow Statement,* shows a client's cash inflow less outflow at a point in time, usually by quarter for the previous four quarters. Chapter 4 describes the cash flow management process in more detail.

Step 4:
Recommending Solutions

THE NEXT STEP in the client management system is to develop recommendations (or strategies) to achieve a client's financial goals. These recommendations are solutions to a client's goals and priority objectives. Before you submit your recommendations to a client in a formal proposal, do a test drive. Remember that your recommendations are the financial plan the client has been anticipating. It is the solution to a problem, the end point of a long process of probing, information collecting, interpretation, and synthesis. It has to be acceptable the first time. Often, your recommendations will be fine-tuned before the client fully buys in. This is to be encouraged.

It is advisable to test your general recommendations with the client over an informal lunch or morning coffee. Let the client give you direction among the options you have designed. This puts the client's fingerprints on the plan; it builds ownership and commitment. Once you and the client agree on recommendations, prepare a concise written proposal. The following outline is a professional but easy-to-use format for a client's financial plan:

◆ An overview of the client's short- and long-term goals

◆ The client's current financial strengths and weaknesses and implications for the financial plan

◆ The client's financial objectives anchored to current resources

◆ A detailed summation of all recommendations, showing pluses and minuses

◆ The financial plan from mutually selected recommendations

◆ A comprehensive economic overview of the client's financial plan, supported by financial statements

◆ A step-by-step implementation and monitoring plan

Step 5:
Implementing the Plan

YOU HAVE TESTED your recommendations with the client over lunch. You have agreed to a refinement of your recommendations. You have written and presented a final draft of the financial plan to the client, and the client is delighted. You have at least solved the client's problem on paper. Now the really hard work begins. It is time to turn recommendations into reality. The last section of your final plan proposal is perhaps the most important. It describes how you *and* the client will work together to implement the plan. The step-by-step blueprint must be specific. It lays out in order the tasks, decisions, and assessments to be made along the way to financial success. Talk to the client about who will initiate action on each recommendation, and with what results. **EXHIBIT 3.5** (see page 92) is an outline of action for implementing a financial plan.

If your compensation structure is fee-only, your involvement in the actual implementation of the financial plan—that is, selection of investment vehicles—will not be direct. In this scenario, you will refer the client to an internal associate, stockbroker, lawyer, or other financial product specialist. A specialist is a product salesperson or fee-based expert who works in highly defined, technical financial areas, such as commodities or futures for the risk-inclined client. Technical experts know their fields very well and can suggest products tailored to the client's objectives, resources, and risk profile. You will want to review a specialist's proposal to make sure it fits your client's needs and other parts of the financial plan. Offer several specialists in the same field to your client. This ensures your neutrality and places some of the selection task on the client. Make sure the specialists' perspective—aggressive or conservative—is compatible with your own, or it may be difficult for the client to work with you and the selected specialist.

If the client stops after step four of PIPRIM, short of implementation, then little good has been achieved. The client is no closer to financial security, and you have likely received some payment but have paid an opportunity cost. A client's financial plan is worthless on paper but potentially priceless in practice.

Step 6:
Monitoring the Plan

DEPENDING ON your compensation model (see Chapter 6)—fully paid on the delivery of the financial plan or commission on plan performance—you will take a low or high profile in monitoring the plan with the client. It is definitely to your benefit to show interest even if your fee is fully paid. First, you will want to use all clients as references. Second, financial and personal conditions change, and you may be retained to do more work. Third, if you are a specialist selling products, there is always the potential for second-generation sales. Fourth, you will want to know what strategies work and why. This is your competitive advantage. In any event, schedule periodic review sessions with each client to evaluate the course of the financial plan. Plan to meet twice a year: in April after taxes, and near the end of the year to evaluate forward strategies.

When you meet with clients to review progress, pay attention to both personal and economic changes. Is the client getting married or divorced, having children, moving to the suburbs, buying a new car, or changing jobs? How has the plan been affected by changes in federal tax laws, economic conditions, inflation, and investment rate of return? Are new investment techniques available? If you drafted a plan for a client in the late 1970s, when inflation stabilized at 12 percent per year, your strategies and results would need to be completely different in today's minimal-inflation environment. Work with the client to modify the plan as circumstances change. If necessary, return to the early stages of the PIPRIM client management system to reevaluate goals and collect new information in order to make plan adjustments that fit a client's changing needs.

A good model to use in monitoring a financial plan is to start with the assumptions. When the plan was written, what assumptions were made about the client's financial condition and personal situation and the general economy? How have these assumptions changed in the last six to nine months? Are the assumptions now more or less favorable? Do we expect the new assumptions to prevail long enough to make changes to the financial plan? If new assumptions can be expected to persist with a good degree of probability (80 percent or more), then adjusting the financial plan is warranted. Work with the client closely to challenge the assumptions. Do not feel responsible if the conditions you and the client predicted months ago have changed. It is the nature of life. Do feel responsible for forcing the client to face changing circumstances even if the realization of personal issues is painful. Financial plans are not built on emotion, they are built on facts.

Elements of a Personal Financial Plan

THE PIPRIM client management system is a systematic and logical process designed to help clients reach their financial destination. Beyond the six steps of PIPRIM there are three underlying values that must be communicated to the client throughout the process. First, a solid financial plan is built on *trust*. The client trusts the planner's experience, ethics, and analytical ability. The planner trusts the client's intentions and commitment to self-improvement. Second, the financial plan is built on *change*. No final plan is either permanent or perfect. The planner and client must be committed to honest evaluation of changing conditions and to continuing refinement of goals, objectives, and strategies. Both parties must accept the inevitable ambiguities of change and its impact on financial planning. Third, the financial plan is built on *results*. A great plan on paper is not a plan; it is no more than imagination. The planner and client must work together to put a plan into action and to achieve success, which is the real payoff for both of them.

EXHIBIT 3.1

Sample Information Packet Cover Letter

Financial Planning Corporation

January 10, 2005

Mr. and Mrs. Brandon Matthews
9824 Cliff Drive
River City, KS 12345-6789

Dear Mr. and Mrs. Matthews:

Enclosed you will find our firm's New Client Information Packet. It includes biographies of our principals and a confidential client questionnaire we would like to ask you to complete for our initial meeting on Friday, January 31, at 3 P.M. in my office. The questionnaire is all-encompassing and may ask for more information than you have at hand. We will talk through any open areas. The most important section relates to your personal financial goals. There is where you should spend most of your time.

I am looking forward to meeting you on January 31. I'll have my assistant, Mary Jacobsen, call you in a few days to give you directions to our offices and answer any questions you might have about the materials enclosed.

Please feel free to call me at any time.

Sincerely,

Lisa White, CFP
Financial Planning Corporation
SG:gs
enc.

EXHIBIT 3.2

New Client Questionnaire

Your Personal Financial Health Checkup

Please take a few minutes to complete this checklist. Any "no" or "not sure" answers can point to potential problems you may wish to ask me about.

MONTHLY INCOME AND EXPENSES

1 Do you use a budget? ☐ Yes ☐ No ☐ Not sure
2 Do you have any financial problems ☐ Yes ☐ No ☐ Not sure
that require immediate attention
(i.e., child going to college, loss of
job, immediate retirement, poor
investment returns, etc.)?

RETIREMENT

1 Are you saving for retirement? ☐ Yes ☐ No ☐ Not sure
2 Do you know what rate of return ☐ Yes ☐ No ☐ Not sure
you need now to maintain your
lifestyle after retirement and keep
ahead of inflation and taxes?

CHILDREN'S EDUCATION

1 Have you planned for this expense? ☐ Yes ☐ No ☐ Not sure
2 Is the ownership of your education ☐ Yes ☐ No ☐ Not sure
savings designed to reduce taxes?

YOUR INVESTMENTS

1 Are your investments well ☐ Yes ☐ No ☐ Not sure
diversified?
2 Are you satisfied with their ☐ Yes ☐ No ☐ Not sure
performance?

RISK AND INSURANCE

1 Will your insurance cover your   ☐ Yes   ☐ No   ☐ Not sure
family's needs in the event of death
or disability?

2 Do you have an umbrella liability   ☐ Yes   ☐ No   ☐ Not sure
policy?

ESTATE PLANNING

1 Are your wills current?   ☐ Yes   ☐ No   ☐ Not sure

2 Is your estate designed to minimize   ☐ Yes   ☐ No   ☐ Not sure
taxes and fees?

EXHIBIT 3.3

Sample Engagement Letter

Financial Planning Corporation

CLIENT SERVICE AGREEMENT—
COMPREHENSIVE HOURLY ENGAGEMENT

Please review this letter carefully as it outlines the understanding between you ("Client") and Financial Planning Corporation ("FPC") for the services FPC will provide you. If you have any questions about the content or purpose of this letter, we should discuss them before you sign this letter.

This letter covers consultations that address a specific issue or issues that concern the Client and a detailed financial analysis. This agreement confirms and clarifies the financial planning to be provided by FPC. This agreement covers those services as indicated below at a billing rate of $200 per hour per CFP licensee, $100 per hour per Financial Planner, and $75 per hour per Educational Consultant, billed in six-minute increments. FPC principals and staff are responsible for maintaining an accountability record for billing purposes. Client agrees to submit one-half of estimated fee range upon signing of this agreement, with the balance of actual fees due immediately upon presentation of recommendations to Client. Specific issues to be addressed by FPC are indicated below with the Client's initials.

_____   Cash flow analysis
_____   Retirement capital needs analysis
_____   Current portfolio review or analysis
_____   Insurance review
_____   Portfolio allocation and investment recommendations
_____   College education funding
_____   Estate plan review
_____   Income tax planning
_____   _____
_____   _____

Total estimated fee range: _____

1   FPC will analyze the financial situation of the Client and provide recommendations to guide the Client toward the achievement of his/her financial objectives. In limiting FPC's analysis to the specific areas indicated above, the Client understands that information regarding specific issues not revealed to FPC may have a direct impact on Client's overall financial picture.

2   The Client will provide FPC with the necessary information to provide the services agreed upon. FPC will regard any information provided by the Client as confidential.

3   The Client understands that the responsibility for financial decisions is his/hers and that he/she is under no obligation to follow, either wholly or partially, any recommendations or suggestions provided by FPC.

4   The Client agrees that FPC cannot guarantee the accuracy of the information or success of the advice that it may provide, that the information or advice is based upon such investigations as FPC deems reasonable, and that FPC is not liable for errors of fact or judgment as long as it acts in good faith.

5   The Client understands that a bill for fees and expenses will be submitted as services are performed and will be due and payable at that time.

6   The Client understands that FPC will not receive commissions on transactions that may result from the implementation of the Client's financial plan.

7   The Client understands that due to the limited nature of this engagement, FPC is under no obligation to contact the Client regarding changes in the financial markets or particular mutual funds or investments that FPC may have recommended.

8   This agreement may be terminated at any time upon written notice of either FPC or the Client.

9   If the Client should terminate this agreement, at the direction of the Client, FPC will assist with concluding any investment actions.

10 FPC will not initiate a transaction on accounts without prior approval of the Client.

11 By giving FPC written notice of the termination within five (5) business days of execution of this agreement, any fees that the Client has prepaid will be refunded to the Client in full. After the initial five (5) business day period, fees earned from the first day through the receipt of written notice of termination will be due and payable at FPC's regular hourly rate. FPC will not assign the agreement to any other party without the written consent of the Client.

ACCEPTED this _____ of _____ , _____

(Day)   (Month)   (Year)

Client   _____

Client   _____

_____

Signature on behalf of
Financial Planning Corporation

SOURCE: ADAPTED FROM DOCUMENT USED BY GARRETT FINANCIAL PLANNING OF OVERLAND PARK, KANSAS

EXHIBIT 3.4

Sample Client Data Collection Questionnaire

Financial Planning Corporation
Confidential Questionnaire

Please take time to fill out the following forms and mail, e-mail, or fax them (along with any related statements) to us at least 10 days prior to our upcoming service appointment.

This information will help FPC to provide you financial advice that applies to your current situation.

CLIENT(S) PERSONAL INFORMATION

Client 1 name _____

Home address _____

_____

_____

Home phone _____

E-mail _____

Social Security number _____

Driver's license _____

Expiration date _____

State _____

Birth date _____

Client 2 name _____

Home address _____

_____

_____

Home phone _____

E-mail _____

Social Security number _____

Driver's license _____

Expiration date _____

State _____

Birth date _____

Family members (Please list children and other dependents.)

Name _____

Relationship _____

Date of birth _____   Dependent □ Y □ N
          (Month / Day / Year)

Resides _____
          (City & State)

Name _____

Relationship _____

Date of birth _____   Dependent □ Y □ N
          (Month / Day / Year)

Resides _____
          (City & State)

Name _____

Relationship _____

Date of birth _____   Dependent □ Y □ N
          (Month / Day / Year)

Resides _____
          (City & State)

Name _____

Relationship _____

Date of birth _____   Dependent □ Y □ N
          (Month / Day / Year)

Resides _____
          (City & State)

Name _____

Relationship _____

Date of birth _____   Dependent □ Y □ N
          (Month / Day / Year)

Resides _____
          (City & State)

Objectives (Please list in order of their time horizon.)

OBJECTIVE	TIME HORIZON	TODAY'S COST
1. _____		
2. _____		
3. _____		
4. _____		
5. _____		
6. _____		

CLIENT(S) BUSINESS INFORMATION

Client 1 name _____

Employer _____

Address _____

_____

_____

Work e mail _____

Work phone _____

Work fax _____

Job title _____

Current salary $ _____

Annual growth (%) _____

Years employed with this employer_____

Anticipated changes _____

Client 2 name _____

Employer _____

Address _____

_____

_____

Work e-mail _____

Work phone _____

Work fax _____

Job title _____

Current salary $ _____

Annual growth (%) _____

Years employed with this employer_____

Anticipated changes _____

1 Planned retirement age
Client 1 _____ Client 2 _____

2 Do you see any significant changes in your monthly expenses upon retirement? (i.e., increased travel, major purchases, etc.) _____
_____

3 What after-tax rate of return do you expect to earn on your investments?
_____

4 What inflation rate do you feel comfortable using in these projections?
_____

5 Do you want all your debts paid after your death? _____

6 How much money, if any, do you want to leave to your heirs? _____
_____

7 Who prepares your tax return?
☐ Self
☐ Paid preparer
Name   _____
Address   _____
            _____
            _____
            _____
Phone   _____
Fax   _____

8 Do you have estate-planning documents?

9 When and in what state were the estate-planning documents drafted?

		Date	State
Will	☐ Y ☐ N	_____	_____
Living trust	☐ Y ☐ N	_____	_____
Power of attorney	☐ Y ☐ N	_____	_____
Living will	☐ Y ☐ N	_____	_____
Other documents	☐ Y ☐ N	_____	_____

10 How were your current investments selected? _____ _____

_____

_____

_____

_____

_____

_____

11 Evaluate how well the following statements reflect your attitudes or beliefs using a scale of 1 to 5 (1 being *most* true and 5 being *least* true).

_____ I would rather work longer than reduce my standard of living in retirement.

_____ I feel that I/we can reduce our current living expenses to save more for the future if needed.

_____ I am more concerned about protecting my assets than about growth.

_____ I prefer the ease of mutual funds over individual securities.

_____ I am comfortable with investments that promise slow, long-term appreciation and growth.

_____ I don't brood over bad investment decisions I've made.

_____ I feel comfortable with aggressive growth investments.

_____ I don't like surprises.

_____ I am optimistic about my financial future.

_____ My immediate concern is for income rather than growth opportunities.

_____ I am a risk taker.

_____ I make investment decisions comfortably and quickly.

_____ I like predictability and routine in my daily life.

_____ I usually pick the tried and true—the slow, safe, but sure investments.

_____ I need to focus my investment efforts on building cash reserves.

_____ I prefer predictable, steady return on my investments, even if the return is low.

12 **Rate your working relationships with each of the following advisers that apply** (1 being *most* satisfied and 5 being *least* satisfied).

ADVISER						N/A
Financial planner	1	2	3	4	5	X
Broker	1	2	3	4	5	X
Broker	1	2	3	4	5	X
Accountant	1	2	3	4	5	X
Tax preparer	1	2	3	4	5	X
Attorney	1	2	3	4	5	X
Insurance agent	1	2	3	4	5	X
Insurance agent	1	2	3	4	5	X

INSURANCE POLICIES

TYPE OF POLICY	COMPANY	PERSON INSURED	ANNUAL PREMIUM	CASH SURRENDER VALUE	OWNERSHIP	PREMIUM DUE DATE
Life						
Life						
Life						
Life						
Disability						
Disability						
Health						
Health						
Automobile						
Automobile						
Home owners						
Umbrella						
Long-term care						
Professional						
Liability						
Other						

Your Balance Sheet

If you have this information in a format of your own design, please feel free to attach that rather than filling in the charts below. **Please also attach all brokerage, financial adviser, and mutual fund investment statements, and any other necessary documentation**.

Determining Your Net Worth:
Analyzing Your Assets and Liabilities

PERSONAL ASSETS

NAME OF ASSET	CURRENT VALUE
Primary residence	$ _____
Secondary residence	$ _____
Automobile(s)	$ _____
RVs (boats, campers, etc.)	$ _____
Household belongings, etc.	$ _____
Other personal assets	$ _____

CASH RESERVES

BANK NAME	NAME OF ASSET	CURRENT VALUE	RATE OF RETURN (%)	MATURITY DATE	ANNUAL ADDITIONS	PURPOSE
	Checking accounts	$				
	Savings accounts	$				
	Credit union accounts	$				
	Money market accounts	$				
	Certificate of deposit 1	$				
	Certificate of deposit 2	$				
	Certificate of deposit 3	$				

BROKERAGE ACCOUNTS

BROKERAGE NAME	CURRENT VALUE	STOCK, BOND, MUTUAL FUND, OTHER	OWNERSHIP	CURRENT BALANCE
	$			$
	$			$
	$			$
	$			$
	$			$
	$			$

RETIREMENT INVESTMENTS

NAME OF ASSET	CURRENT VALUE	RATE OF RETURN (%)	MATURITY DATE	ANNUAL ADDITIONS	PURPOSE
Company retirement plan	$				Retirement
Company retirement plan	$				Retirement
Company retirement plan	$				Retirement
Company retirement plan	$				Retirement
IRA	$				Retirement
IRA	$				Retirement
IRA	$				Retirement
Other	$				
Other	$				

NONRETIREMENT AND BUSINESS INVESTMENTS

NAME OF ASSET	CURRENT VALUE	RATE OF RETURN (%)	MATURITY DATE	ANNUAL ADDITIONS	PURPOSE
Real estate	$				
Real estate	$				
Real estate	$				
Personally owned business	$				
Other business interests	$				
Note receivable	$				
Note receivable	$				
Note receivable	$				

NAME OF ASSET	CURRENT VALUE	RATE OF RETURN (%)	MATURITY DATE	ANNUAL ADDITIONS	PURPOSE
Life insurance cash value	$				
Life insurance cash value	$				
Life insurance cash value	$				
Other	$				
Other	$				
Other	$				
Other	$				

LIABILITIES

NAME OF LIABILITY	INITIAL BALANCE	CURRENT BALANCE	MONTHLY PAYMENT	INTEREST RATE	PAYOFF DATE
Home mortgage					
Home equity loan 1					
Home equity loan 2					
Second home mortgage					
Auto loan 1					
Auto loan 2					
Credit card					
Credit card					
Credit card					
Credit card					
Real estate loan					
Real estate loan					
Real estate loan					
Business loan					
Business loan					
Business loan					
Retirement plan loan					
Retirement plan loan					
Other loan					
Other loan					
Other loan					
Other loan					
Other loan					

Your Monthly Budget

MONTHLY EXPENDITURES	AMOUNT
Auto loan payment	$
Auto maintenance	$
Child care	$
Clothing	$
Contributions	$
Credit card payments	$
Dues	$
Entertainment	$
Food	$
Household maintenance	$
Income and Social Security taxes	$
Insurance	$
Personal care	$
Property taxes	$
Rent or mortgage payment	$
Retirement plan investments	$
Savings/investments	$
Transportation (gas, fares)	$
Utilities	$
Vacations (monthly allotment)	$
Other	$
TOTAL MONTHLY EXPENDITURES	$

MONTHLY RECEIPTS	CLIENT 1	CLIENT 2
Wages or salary	$	$
Capital gain (long-term)	$	$
Capital gain (short-term)	$	$
Dividends (mutual funds, stocks, etc.)	$	$
Interest (CDs, savings account, etc.)	$	$
Pension	$	$
Rental and/or royalty	$	$
Social Security	$	$
Other taxable	$	$
Other nontaxable	$	$
TOTAL MONTHLY RECEIPTS		$

NET CASH FLOW = TOTAL MONTHLY RECEIPTS – EXPENDITURES = $ _____

Items to Bring to Your First Meeting

☐ Your completed Confidential Questionnaire
☐ A copy of each person's most recent pay stub
☐ Tax returns for the last three years
☐ Estate planning documents including wills, powers of attorney, living wills, deeds, trust documents, or legal agreements that are relevant
☐ Investment portfolio statements from other advisory firms, banks, or investment companies (no need to bring information on any investments held through Financial Planning Corporation)
☐ Employee benefit plan statements and employee handbook
☐ Pension plan information or projections and current company retirement plan statements such as 401(k), TSA, 403(b), ESOP, Thrift Savings Plan
☐ Insurance policies, including health, life, disability, home owner, automobile, umbrella, and long-term care
☐ Business insurance policies, including buy-sell, disability over-head, key person insurance, executive bonus, etc.
☐ Annuity statements
☐ Divorce decrees, prenuptial agreements
☐ Educational funding statements
☐ Charitable gifting programs established
☐ Any information on unique financial situations that have occurred since our last conversation (i.e., major debts, company buyout offers, inheritances, etc.)
☐ Any other information you would like to discuss

EXHIBIT 3.5

Sample Summary Action Plan

Action List for Brandon and Keri Matthews
July 10, 2005

ACTION	PERSON RESPONSIBLE	DUE DATE	COMPLETED
Increase withholdings	Keri	07/10/05	x
Purchase life insurance	Brandon	07/10/05	
Purchase disability insurance	Brandon	08/15/05	
Begin dollar-cost-averaging plan with mutual funds	Keri	09/01/05	

CHAPTER 4

THE SPECTRUM OF FINANCIAL PLANNING

FINANCIAL PLANNING—or personal financial planning (PFP), as the field is also known—is more than just investment planning. In fact, investment planning is just one of the many disciplines involved in comprehensive financial planning, although clients often tend to equate the two. It is crucial to educate clients so that they understand that financial planning involves a variety of disciplines, each necessary in the process of integrating all of a client's needs and concerns into a cohesive format. Taking a comprehensive approach is the only way clients can know where they stand vis-à-vis their short- and long-term objectives.

PERSONAL FINANCIAL PLANNING DEFINED

Personal financial planning is the process of determining whether and how an individual can meet life goals through proper management of financial resources. It is the development and implementation of an integrated, coordinated plan for achieving overall financial objectives.

As noted in Chapter 3, financial planning is a process, not a product. It may lead to recommendation of a product, but financial planners are not order-takers. Instead, planners help people achieve their financial objectives by constructing a complete, comprehensive plan that addresses all client concerns.

WHY CLIENTS DO NOT PLAN

There are many reasons why clients may not undertake financial planning on their own, including the following:
◆ Thinking they have insufficient assets or income to warrant planning
◆ Assuming their financial situation is in good order
◆ Putting off what is complex and worrisome
◆ Not wanting to consider unpleasant events, such as death, disability, unemployment, or property loss
◆ Thinking financial planning is expensive

All of these assumptions are faulty. Of course, failing to plan ahead also costs money. The consequences of not planning include the following:
◆ Inadequate protection against personal catastrophes such as death, disability, serious illness, an automobile accident, prolonged unemployment, or other major negative events
◆ Too little money set aside for retirement or for the family's educational needs
◆ Higher than necessary income or gift taxation

◆ Unplanned estates, with higher taxes and settlement costs
◆ Not reaching financial goals in life

WHY YOUR CLIENT NEEDS YOUR HELP

Many people have inadequate skills in making informed, systematic decisions about their own finances. They have little exposure to good decision-making models. Planners help clients identify needs and good ways to meet them while avoiding potential obstacles. The planner's job incorporates elements of counseling, information management and processing, education planning, investment planning, income tax planning, risk management, retirement planning, and estate planning.

CORE DISCIPLINES OF PERSONAL FINANCIAL PLANNING

Financial planning consists of the following core disciplines:
◆ Cash flow management
◆ Insurance planning
◆ Investment planning
◆ Education planning
◆ Income tax planning
◆ Retirement planning
◆ Estate planning

This chapter provides a framework for deciding in which discipline or combination of disciplines you should focus your practice.

Cash Flow Management

CLIENTS SEEK cash flow management services to obtain more effective control of their financial situation. For many, that means learning to manage their monthly cash flow better. Often, clients would like to save a larger portion of their income while maintaining their lifestyle. Some have critical cash flow problems, such as excessive debt, little or no savings, or significant fluctuations in cash inflow. Others are concerned about having sufficient resources to fund retirement and seek to control their spending in order to avoid consuming assets too fast. Therefore, these clients have financial objectives that relate specifically to cash flow management.

Cash flow management has two chief purposes:

1 Management of income and expenditures, including establishing and maintaining a reserve of cash or near-cash equivalents to meet unanticipated or emergency needs, such as those caused by illness, injury, death, or sudden loss of employment; and

2 Systematic creation and maintenance of a surplus of cash for capital investment.

Planners sometimes underestimate the importance of cash flow management as a service to provide to clients. This is a mistake, because solving problems in this area can play a significant role in the client's ability to reach a wide range of financial goals.

The three primary components of cash flow management are budgeting, cash flow planning, and determination of net worth. Without the planner's help in these areas, clients will have difficulty accomplishing their goals.

YOUR ROLE IN CASH FLOW MANAGEMENT

As a planner your role is to assist the client in developing a cash flow plan. This process involves compiling financial information, identifying income sources and spending patterns, establishing reasonable objectives, developing a budget, and monitoring performance. Cash flow planning can have a significant effect on a client's lifestyle, and the planner frequently needs to educate the client about the importance of saving money. As part of this process, the planner must help the client assess which goals are realistic, given the client's current level of saving, and how much more money would be needed to reach goals that appear impossible now. Thus, a planner's key aim often is to help clients set up a cash flow system that generates an appropriate level of savings. If clients still are unable to save enough, the planner needs to help them revise their objectives to a level they can attain.

BUDGETING AND BUDGET ANALYSIS

Budgeting is a time-consuming yet essential task; it requires a comprehensive analysis of how fast clients are spending and whether and at what rate they are investing toward short- and long-range goals. To manage their money effectively, clients need to learn how to plan their budgets from the bottom up. Clients must project income, document and monitor spending and investing, and compare projected and actual figures. The task can be accomplished only if the client maintains accurate, detailed accounts of income and spending patterns. That may sound more difficult than it is, however. Budget-related data can be retrieved from income tax returns, home improvement records, bank and brokerage statements, financial statements (such as the balance sheet and income statement), insurance policies, retirement and Social Security information, pension benefits, and credit card and checkbook records.

Successful budgeting usually means controlling spending. The planner must make realistic estimates of how much clients will spend. If that number is likely to exceed income, the planner should help clients reduce or eliminate expenditures. In addition, he or she should review the budget periodically and make adjustments based on what has or has not worked in the past.

If a client is burdened with excessive debt, has marginal success in controlling spending, or presents a complicated situation that is beyond the capacity of the planner to handle, then the planner should consider referring the client to a financial counseling service.

Preparing personal budgets and performing analysis require three steps:

Step 1: Establishing reasonable goals and objectives
Step 2: Determining the client's current financial situation
Step 3: Forecasting future expenses and income

The first step is to help clients establish reasonable goals and objectives. Long-range goals might center on retirement and education needs, while a short-term goal might be to improve cash flow. When clients understand their objectives and establish that they are realistic, they are in a better position to determine whether their current spending patterns will help get them there.

The second step is to determine the client's current financial situation by analyzing expenses and income flows over the last six months to see what regular and lump sum costs the client has. Use old cash receipts, checks and check registers, and charge accounts to organize expenses by category. One technique is to have clients list expenses in a notebook divided into twelve sections, one for each month, with each section further subdivided into types of expense categories. Distinguish between fixed and variable expenses, for example. The former are defined as necessities—that is, rent, mortgage, food, clothing, automobile payments, insurance, utilities, taxes, loans, and charge account balances—over which the client has little control. Variable expenses, on the other hand, are more discretionary in nature and often can be modified or even postponed, if necessary. Note items that have tax implications, such as mortgage interest, real estate taxes, and charitable contributions. The process of recording all expenses may have the positive effect of discouraging clients from unnecessary spending.

If you are providing this service for a special purpose, such as in connection with a client's qualifying for a loan, you will need to select the appropriate budget forms. Banks and other financial institutions may require use of special forms. Clients may want to adopt such forms for their ongoing budget planning, especially if they do a lot of business with a specific bank.

The third step is to help clients realistically forecast future monthly revenue from salary, business income, interest, dividends, and personal loans as well as disposable income after taxes (including costs of medical insurance and other payroll deductions). Identify every income source a client has, and verify each source from past income tax returns. Once you have estimated income and expenses for each month, ask the client to predict expenses for the entire year.

Aim to balance income with expenses in each category. Irregular expenditures such as vacations and holiday gifts should be spread over the entire year. Mark the client's calendar with the dates that large expenditures are due. Compare actual and planned spending on a monthly basis. If significant variances exist, go to the budgeted items and rework them with flagged queries and recommendations to determine where the client might reduce costs while preserving as much as possible of the desired discretionary outlays.

Use current fixed and variable expenses as the basis for making a three-to-five-year projection of these expenditures. Remember to allow for an emergency fund to be set aside in a money market account (equaling six months' worth of gross living expenses), and take inflation, tax rates, salary changes, and other variable factors into account. Expenses will change, too, if clients care for aging parents, pay college fees, have children, buy a new car or home, or otherwise alter their circumstances. Remind clients that these changes may affect their ability to meet long-term goals. **EXHIBIT 4.1** (see page 142) presents a sample work sheet for preparing a monthly budget.

CASH FLOW PLANNING

Once you have analyzed your client's cash flow, the next step is to help the client maximize discretionary income by implementing specific strategies. To do this, you will need to help clients control spending, adjust their goals if they cannot save enough money to reach their initial objectives, and periodically revisit their projected and actual cash flows to make sure they are staying on track.

There are a variety of tools at your disposal to help clients increase their discretionary income. They include the following: debt restructuring, asset reallocation, qualified plan vehicles, employee benefit plans, and separate treatment of children's assets.

◆ **Debt restructuring.** Clients may be able to pay off all outstanding credit card balances by consolidating debt into one personal bank loan or mortgage. The planner should recommend that they then stop using their credit cards as much as is practical.

◆ **Asset reallocation.** This technique involves moving money to make it work harder. The planner may recommend moving underperforming assets into more productive investments that are still in line with the client's goals and time frames. Or the planner might suggest substituting growth investments for income-producing ones and taxable investments for tax-exempt ones.

◆ **Qualified plans and other personal retirement account (before-tax) vehicles.** Clients should use tax-deferred savings plans— including 401(k) plans, tax-deferred annuities, Keogh plans, other employer-sponsored plans, IRAs, and deferred compensation plans—as much as possible. If the client is saving for retirement outside of a qualified plan, such as in an after-tax investment account, the planner should illustrate the long-term benefits of tax-deferred savings, since taxes are not paid annually. Incidentally, qualified plans need not consist of only 401(k) plans. Self-employed clients can invest in a Keogh or a simplified employer-sponsored plan as well. Also, IRAs, deferred compensation plans, and nonqualified savings plans might be available to both employer-employed and self-employed clients.

◆ **Employee benefit plans.** The client's employee benefit plans can pay for some expenses with pretax dollars. Clients whose employers offer such plans can use a 401(k), 403(b), SEP, or flexible spending account to pay allowable child care or medical expenses, for example, thereby minimizing taxes.

◆ **Separate treatment of children's assets.** Planners can encourage clients to save for a child in a custodial account or trust. The marginal tax bracket applicable to the taxable investment earnings is likely to be lower for the child than it would be for the parent.

DETERMINING NET WORTH

In addition to determining appropriate budgets and the cash flow that can be saved and invested from future earnings, you also need to know where your clients stand today—their overall financial standing, or net worth. In simplest terms, net worth constitutes assets (items you own) less liabilities (amounts you owe). In determining net worth, the financial planner does much more than merely constructing and reviewing a net worth statement. The process, to be most beneficial, involves calculating current net worth, setting a realistic goal for the upcoming year, and developing specific strategies for meeting that goal. Planning efforts that focus on net worth help clients to do the following: (1) establish financial discipline, (2) organize financial life around a future target, (3) measure financial progress on a regular basis, and (4) feel financially secure about the future.

◆ **The basic calculation.** The planning begins with calculating a client's net worth. Net worth, the basic measure of financial health, is the total fair-market value of all assets owned, such as real estate and stocks, bonds, and other securities, minus all outstanding liabilities, such as mortgages and revolving-credit loans. Thus, net worth is the amount by which assets exceed liabilities at a specific point in time.

To calculate net worth, pull together the relevant financial records. These include the latest tax records, bank statements, canceled checks, credit card information, other itemized living expenses, brokerage accounts and mutual fund records, mortgage payments, real estate closing records, insurance policies, pension account records, and loan repayment schedules. Gathering all this information may seem daunting, but it is essential for net worth planning. The data in these documents also lay the foundation for other planning areas.

The planner should analyze the information by categorizing assets as liquid, investment, or personal. Further classify investment assets as short term or long term. Label long-term assets as equity, debt, or miscellaneous, and categorize liabilities as short term or long term. Subtracting total liabilities from total assets then provides the net worth figure for the family as of a given date.

◆ **Forming a strategy.** The net worth figure is the basis for an appropriate net worth planning strategy. If net worth is negative, which is not only possible but in some cases quite likely, it does not necessarily mean that the family is on the verge of declaring bankruptcy. It does mean, however, that the planner should develop aggressive strategies for debt reduction, higher investment return, and realistic goal-setting.

Just as a negative net worth does not necessarily point toward impending disaster, a positive net worth does not mean the financial planning process is over. Net worth should be viewed yearly, generally with a new target set for saving in the coming year. If the client meets or exceeds that goal, the planner should take steps to preserve or increase the rate of saving. If the client falls short, however, the planner should either develop new strategies for correcting the situation or help the client set a more realistic net worth goal.

To increase net worth, clients must spend less and save more. It is that simple, and the planner cannot emphasize this point too strongly. An inability to control spending is the root cause of most personal financial disasters, well ahead of inadequate income, unwise investments, and catastrophic changes in circumstances. **EXHIBIT 4.2** (see page 143) is a work sheet that can be used in calculating net worth.

INTEGRATION OF CASH FLOW MANAGEMENT WITH FINANCIAL PLANNING DISCIPLINES

Once your clients have planned to maximize income and minimize spending, they also will need your help to plan for insurance, investment, education, income tax, retirement, and their estate.

Because cash flow management is the means for funding client goals in other planning areas, generally it is the starting point of the planning process. The chart at right describes integration of cash flow management with other key planning disciplines.

Insurance Planning

PURCHASING INSURANCE is the most common way of handling various risks that can cause financial loss. In order to reduce these risks, people must seek to minimize or eliminate hazardous elements that can increase the chances of harm, injury, danger, or destruction. Insurance accomplishes this in two ways: it transfers or shifts risk from an individual to a group, and it pays for losses.

Clients buy insurance to provide themselves with the funds necessary, for example, to maintain their existing lifestyle after the death of a loved one (life insurance), to replace earned income (disability insurance), to pay medical bills (health insurance), or to replace or repair a tangible item (home owners and automobile insurance). If a client cannot write a check to cover a loss, it is time to buy insurance.

Your job is to help clients identify the risks that can keep them from attaining their personal financial goals and construct a plan of action to provide adequate insurance against those risks. The information from the client's comprehensive financial plan,

Integration of Cash Flow Management with Financial Planning Disciplines

PLANNING AREA	INTEGRATION OF CASH FLOW PLANNING
Insurance planning	To provide for insurance costs or to establish cash reserves for emergencies
Investment planning	To determine annual amount available for investing and to determine investment income to include in cash flow
Education planning	To provide periodic savings to be used to fund future education costs and to reduce annual cash flow used to pay education costs currently
Income tax planning	To provide for payment of income taxes and to increase or reduce available cash flow based on income tax plan
Retirement planning	To provide periodic savings to be used to fund retirement and to provide retirement income
Estate planning	To determine the impact of the loss of cash flow from transfer of assets for estate planning purposes and to provide cash income and liquidity for heirs after death

including lists of assets and liabilities, cash flow sources, and objectives, can be used to develop and implement an appropriate insurance program for the client.

The financial planner typically focuses on estimating how much insurance the client needs and determining what type of policy is best. Insurance contracts can be confusing, and your specialized knowledge can greatly help your clients.

Insurance can be broken into two subcategories: life and health, and property and casualty.

LIFE INSURANCE

Life insurance policies require that a policy owner, who may or may not be the person insured, invest money with an insurance company that has agreed to pay money to a beneficiary on the insured's death. The need for life insurance can come from either business or personal relationships.

The rules for life insurance are quite simple. The primary objective is to buy enough life insurance for the beneficiary to keep the same lifestyle that existed before the insured person died. Life insurance can also be used as a form of forced savings, since several types of policies accumulate cash value.

How much life insurance does the client need? The financial planner needs to determine what the economic loss would be if the insured person died. **EXHIBIT 4.3** (see pages 144–147) presents a work sheet that can be used to estimate the client's life insurance needs. Once that need is determined, the next critical step is to determine the resources the client has to expend on this necessity. Based on that response, the planner determines what types of policies are affordable. The planner discusses the merits of these policies with the client, who can then choose one.

◆ **Term insurance** is temporary insurance designed for a specified period of time, such as one year, five years, or ten years, or to a specified age, such as age sixty-five. At the end of the specified period, the contract expires. Good term policies have two key features: *guaranteed renewability,* which means that as long as the client pays the premiums, the insured does not have to furnish evidence of insurability; and *convertibility,* which means that the term policy can be converted to one with cash value, such as whole life, during the term of the contract.

Term insurance policies are appropriate for policy owners who have a short-term insurance need, generally of fourteen years or less.

◆ **Whole life insurance** policies have level premium payments and are designed to remain in force over the insured person's entire lifetime. Premium payments during the early years are deliberately higher than would be required to cover the probability of death alone. This excess charge in the early years is invested in long-term bonds and mortgages, allowing the policy to build cash value. That cash value is then used to pay the cost of insurance in the policy's later years, when the insured is older and more likely to die. The cash value and/or dividends may offset some or all of the premiums as they build.

The policy owner can also access that cash value by borrowing it from the insurer or surrendering the policy. The cash value of a surrendered policy may be taxable. Policy interest rates are generally low, and premiums are paid for the insured person's entire lifetime or until age one hundred, when the policy usually matures. The maturity date depends on state law and the insurance company's rules. At death, the death benefit is payable to a designated beneficiary or to the state if no beneficiary is identified.

Whole life policies are appropriate for clients who want to shift the investment burden over to the insurance company and who like fixed-income investing.

◆ **Universal life insurance** is a type of cash-value policy. It provides flexible premiums and flexible benefits; its interest rate is tied to those of short-term money market accounts. These policies separately disclose the operating expenses and mortality charges paid by the policy owner. As with all cash-value policies, universal life policies let policyholders access cash value through loans or by surrendering the policy.

The first year's premium is the only required premium under a universal life policy. After the first policy year, the policy owner is free to raise, lower, or even skip premium payments as desired, as long as there is enough cash in the policy to keep it in force. An upper limit on premiums in universal life policies is established by the IRS under Code Section 7702. The lower limit on premiums is the cost of the term insurance that the policy must have to keep it in force.

Universal life policies come with two death benefit options. Option 1 provides a death benefit equal to the face amount. Option 2 provides a death benefit equal to the policy's cash value plus the face amount. The premium is usually the same under each option. However, because the death benefit is increasing at a faster rate under option 2, less funds are available to keep in the cash-value account. Option 1 will therefore have more cash value than option 2 and will allow the policy to last longer. Option 1 generally works better for individuals age fifty and over because of the increased mortality charges under option 2.

Universal life policies are appropriate for clients who want the flexibility to increase or decrease premiums and who want their investments tied to short-term money market rates.

◆ **Variable life insurance** is similar to whole life insurance in that it has fixed premiums and a minimum guaranteed death benefit. The difference is that the investment risk and return are shifted to the policy owner. The policy owner directs the funds backing the policy into one or more of a group of segregated investment accounts chosen by the life insurance company. The policy owner can allocate assets among a stock fund, a bond fund, and a money market fund. Because the policy owner picks the portfolio of investments, there is no minimum cash value guarantee.

When the portfolio performs well, both the cash value and the death benefit of a variable life policy increase accordingly. When the portfolio's performance is below expectations, the death benefit may drop, but if the owner maintains premium payments, the death benefit will never drop below the amount of coverage agreed to when the policy was issued. Variable life policies are suitable for clients who want to choose how the portfolio backing the life insurance policy is invested and who are willing to assume the investment risk that goes with that responsibility.

DISABILITY INSURANCE

Disability income insurance is a form of health insurance that replaces a percentage of income lost due to a physical or mental incapacity. Clients need disability income insurance whenever ongoing living and medical expenses might exceed income from investments, a spouse's income, and existing earned-income-replacement provisions. Most clients need disability income insurance—fewer than one in six consumers typically have adequate protection.

The most important point to consider when purchasing a new disability policy can be found in the definition. The best type of policy to purchase is one that's defined as "own occupation," or "own occ" for short. With this type of policy, if the insured is unable to perform the specific duties and responsibilities of his regular job, then he can collect benefits regardless of whether or not he decides to go back to work at a different job. The alternative definition, "any occupation" (or "any occ" for short), means that if you are capable of re-entering the workforce, the insurance company—if it feels that your disability will ultimately not affect your ability to earn a living—can decide to reduce, or in some cases, even eliminate, your benefit. Then there is a middle ground called "split definition," which provides the favorable "own occ" definition of coverage for a limited period of time and the "any occ" definition thereafter.

Other terms to look for include "noncancelable," which means the insurance company cannot cancel the policy as long as you continue to pay the premiums; and "guaranteed renewable," which means the insurance company cannot raise your premiums as an individual insured, although it reserves the right to raise premiums for an entire classification of insureds, such as teachers or forty-year-old females.

PROPERTY AND CASUALTY INSURANCE

Anyone who cannot or does not want to have to write a check to replace or repair a home, automobile, or other property needs property and casualty insurance, which usually consists of home owners, automobile, and umbrella (liability) insurance.

◆ **Home owners insurance** covers a variety of risks, including physical property damage and personal property theft. It also covers compensation for loss of use if clients need to move out of their home temporarily, as well as public liability protection if an accident occurs on their premises.

For home owners, the best type of insurance is HO3 coverage, or all-risk (open peril) coverage. This type of policy provides replacement-cost coverage on the dwelling itself for any peril except for those specifically excluded by the policy. An HO15 policy provides full replacement cost (up to policy limits) on a home's contents. For renters, an HO4 policy provides replacement-cost coverage on the home's contents. For condominium and co-op owners, an HO6 policy provides replacement-cost coverage and covers the insured for damage to interior walls. Finally, for home owners with older homes, an HO8 policy covers them only at actual cash value, which is replacement cost less depreciation. Full replacement coverage on an older house (usually pre–World War II) is usually very expensive, if available at all. If you have upgraded your older house, such as redoing the electric wiring, heating, or plumbing, then you would probably qualify for the better HO3 coverage.

◆ **Automobile insurance** covers both personal injury and property damage. It has two major components. First, liability coverage provides protection against personal injury to others. That includes pain and suffering, protection of passengers against uninsured and underinsured motorists, lost wages, and medical expenses. Second, property damage or collision insurance also provides protection for any property damaged by the insured.

Most states require evidence of insurance for an individual to register an automobile. These minimum or statutory requirements for the amount of insurance necessary for bodily injury or property damage are almost always inadequate. An appropriate amount of coverage for bodily injury or property damage is $300,000.

◆ **Liability insurance.** Many times the underlying liability coverage found in a home owners or automobile policy is inadequate. People have assets well beyond those covered under these policies. To protect yourself from lawsuits that can eat away at your personal assets, liability coverage, such as an umbrella policy, is warranted. These policies are relatively inexpensive, such as $175 for $1 million worth of coverage, and kick in only after the liability limits from the home owners or automobile policy have been reached. Premium discounts exist for coverage purchased above $1 million.

Investment Planning

INVESTMENT PLANNING is critical for helping clients reach their financial goals. There is no one right way to invest—the right way is the one that works for the client. Your job is to discover what that method might be.

There are three principal steps in the investment planning process: first, defining investment parameters; second, managing client expectations; and third, selecting appropriate investment vehicles.

DEFINING INVESTMENT PARAMETERS

The financial planner must perform an assessment of six overall investment parameters for the client: risk tolerance level, time horizon, liquidity concerns, marketability concerns, income tax consequences, and diversification concerns.

1 Risk tolerance level. Clients generally are not risk averse; they are loss averse. They want to earn high rates of return without losing principal. Risk tolerance is a measure of how much risk someone is willing to take in purchasing an investment. A client's tolerance for risk determines which investments are appropriate for that client, and those investments in turn determine whether clients reach their objectives. To assess clients' risk tolerance, ask them to complete the Client Risk-Tolerance Questionnaire, which appears as **EXHIBIT 4.4** (see pages 148–152), and then you complete the accompanying Client Score Sheet.

2 Time horizon. A client's investment time horizon is the amount of time available to attain a financial objective. The time horizon affects the investment vehicles used to attain the goal. For example, if the client has a high-priority goal with an extremely short time horizon, a low-risk money market instrument (such as a U.S.

Treasury bill, money market fund, or short-term certificate of deposit) may be a suitable investment vehicle. If the time horizon is ten years or more, an illiquid investment (such as real estate) that has a higher expected rate of return may be suitable. A consideration related to time horizon is the degree of volatility that investment carries. The longer the time horizon, the less concern there is about an investment's short-term volatility.

3 Liquidity. Clients with limited investments or those saving for a particular personal or business expenditure, such as a down payment on a home, will be concerned about investment liquidity, or their ability to convert an investment into cash without losing a significant part of their principal. Liquid investments include short-term government securities, money market funds, and savings accounts.

4 Marketability. Marketability and liquidity are often confused. Marketability is the speed and ease with which a security can be bought or sold. Investments such as real estate can have high marketability but may not be liquid, especially during slow markets, because significant principal would be lost in a sale under those conditions.

5 Income tax considerations. Investment selection is influenced by a client's tax bracket, available tax credits, and amounts and types of income, deductions, and depreciation. The return on an investment is a combination of the tax benefits, the type and amount of cash flow, and the type and amount of final distributions. Certain investments make more sense for high-income clients, whereas others are more appropriate for clients with lower incomes. High-tax-bracket clients generally benefit more from tax-free, tax-sheltered, and tax-deferred income. To see which investments will provide a higher rate of return for a particular client, you must compare the after-tax returns of those investments. Never make an investment solely for the income tax benefits without also weighing the investment return.

6 Diversification. The old adage "Don't keep all your eggs in one basket" holds true for investing. To maximize returns and minimize risk, it is a good idea to spread risk among different instruments and asset classes—such as allocations among blue-chip stocks, Treasury bills, municipal bonds, small-cap stocks, and money market funds—rather than putting 100 percent of investment money in any one of these categories.

MANAGING CLIENT EXPECTATIONS

Once the financial planner understands client concerns, he or she needs to help clients feel comfortable with investing and understand what it can and cannot do for them. It is important to explain key concepts such as the types of risk investors are exposed to, rates of return, and the risk/return trade-off present in investing.

Risk comes in two forms: systematic and unsystematic.

1 Systematic risk stays with you as long as you are an investor in the marketplace, and you cannot reduce or eliminate it. In assuming this risk, you gain the potential that the market will reward you. Systematic risk can be divided into the following three types:

—*market risk*, or the risk present merely by virtue of being in the marketplace;

—*interest rate risk*, or the risk that changes in interest rates will adversely affect stock and bond prices; and

—*purchasing power risk*, or the risk that inflation will adversely affect stock and bond prices.

2 Unsystematic risk can be controlled through diversification and includes the following two types:

—*business risk*, which is based on the particular sector of the marketplace in which one is investing; and

—*financial risk*, which is based on debt levels incurred by a company in which one is invested.

Return is typically referred to in three forms: expected, minimum required, and actual.

1 Expected return is what you would normally expect to earn in the future from a particular investment. It is based on anticipated growth, earnings, or income generated by the investment. Expected return is directly correlated to the amount of risk an investment vehicle carries, which in turn is related to the particular asset class of the investment. Equity issues, for

STOCK ASSET CLASS	MARKET CAPITALIZATION RANGE
Large capitalization (large cap)	More than $5 billion
Midcapitalization (midcap)	$1 billion–$5 billion
Small capitalization (small cap)	$300 million–$1 billion
Microcapitalization (microcap)	$10 million–$300 million

example, are often classified as one of four classes, based on the value of the company assets, as shown in the table above.

According to the Chicago-based Ibbotson Associates, which tracks returns of asset classes in its annual handbook, *Stocks, Bonds, Bills, and Inflation,* from 1925 to 2003 small-cap stocks returned 12.7 percent, followed by large-cap stocks at 10.4 percent, long-term government bonds at 5.4 percent, and Treasury bills at 3.7 percent. During this period, inflation averaged 3 percent.

2 Minimum required rate of return refers to the return an investment needs to earn in order to warrant its purchase. Before you invest any money, calculate an acceptable rate of return that will allow the client to achieve the set objectives.

3 Actual return refers to the real return you earn by holding a particular investment. The return consists of interest, dividends, and the investment's price appreciation.

SELECTING APPROPRIATE INVESTMENT VEHICLES

The financial planner must help the client objectively determine investment strategies for achieving financial goals. In selecting investment vehicles, investors essentially have two options: becoming owners or lenders. Owners hold interests in equity instruments, such as stocks; in real estate; or in commodities, such as gold. Lenders invest in bonds and other fixed-income instruments.

INVESTMENT TYPES

◆ **Money market instruments** are generally the safest but provide the lowest returns. Examples include U.S. Treasury bills, commercial paper, and certificates of deposit.

◆ **Fixed-income investments** can be broken down into three categories: (1) U.S. government obligations, which consist of Series EE and HH bonds, U.S. Treasury notes (with one- to ten-year maturities), and bonds (with ten- to thirty-year maturities); (2) municipal obligations (general obligation bonds backed by the credit of the local taxing authority) and revenue bonds (backed by the earning capability of the specific project); and (3) corporate bonds (issued by corporations to raise money).

EQUITY INVESTMENTS

Key categories of equity securities include blue-chip, income, growth, cyclical, defensive, and interest-sensitive stocks.

◆ **Blue-chip stocks** are stocks of highly regarded and well-established companies. They generally pay dividends in good and bad years. Examples include IBM, Merck, and McDonald's.

◆ **Income stocks** are those such as utility stocks that pay dividends.

◆ **Growth stocks** are from corporations with increasing profits that reinvest a large percentage of their earnings to achieve continued expansion. Growth stocks are expected to increase in value faster than the market average.

◆ **Cyclical stocks** are from companies that tend to prosper in growing economies and do poorly during down cycles. Examples include industries such as airlines, automobiles, and steel.

◆ **Defensive stocks** are relatively unaffected by general fluctuations in the economy because their companies produce necessities: "eat-'em, drink-'em, and smoke-'em" products like groceries, beverages, and tobacco.

◆ **Interest-sensitive stocks** rise and fall with changes in interest rates. Examples include stocks in the housing and banking industries.

MUTUAL FUNDS

An alternative to purchasing individual securities is investing in mutual funds. A mutual fund invests in cash, bonds, stocks, or other investments. The purchasers of the fund's shares essentially own a portion of each investment owned by the fund.

For diversification purposes, mutual funds can be an appropriate investment vehicle for small to medium portfolios. If an investor cannot afford to purchase one hundred shares of fifty different stocks, he or she may be able to afford one hundred shares of a mutual fund that invests in those same fifty stocks. The investor's shares are pooled with those of other investors, enabling the pool to invest in more securities than might otherwise be feasible.

Among other advantages of mutual funds is the fact that professional managers oversee the portfolios, using their expertise to maximize returns. Mutual funds are liquid, meaning that investors can cash out at will. Investors can purchase over time in small increments, as low as $50 per month. Mutual funds may also offer dividend reinvestment plans, periodic withdrawal and investment plans, check-writing privileges, and investor services via the telephone and Internet.

INSURANCE INVESTMENTS

Cash-value life insurance policies provide an investment alternative. See the preceding discussion of this category in the Insurance Planning section of this chapter.

SELECTING A BROKER-DEALER

Financial advisers who sell investment products usually work with a broker-dealer (BD). Affiliation with a broker-dealer opens up a vast network of relationships with mutual fund companies; insurance companies; clearing firms; training firms; and experts on taxation, retirement plans, financial plans, and other relevant areas. However, be aware that advisers can be affiliated with only one broker-dealer at a time.

Advisers who are just starting out should not expect BDs to actively recruit them. They tend to look for proven producers, so few consider beginners. However, most will still welcome a serious candidate who is committed to financial planning.

Ultimately, the decision comes down to which broker-dealer the adviser feels comfortable working with for both the present and the long term. A way to start would be for the adviser to ask colleagues which broker-dealer firms they use and why. The next step would be to narrow the list down to three and visit each. The planner should insist on talking with the people with whom he or she would have the most contact, for example, the branch manager, the person who processes trades or pays commissions, or the individual responsible for record keeping.

Here is a partial list of topics to explore when inquiring about the services of a broker-dealer:

◆ Training programs for advisers
◆ Research services used by the BD
◆ Research tools available to advisers
◆ Certification requirements for advisers (e.g., RIA)
◆ Financial condition of the BD
◆ Products offered for fee-based advisers
◆ Capabilities of servicing client accounts
◆ Payout rates on investments sold
◆ Errors and omissions liability coverage
◆ Back-office operations: frequency and manner of billing, whether certain assets can be excluded from billing, costs to advisers
◆ Clearing firm used
◆ Adviser marketing support
◆ Capacity for identifying adviser on client account statements

Education Planning

WITH TUITION COSTS spiraling upward faster than inflation, it is critical that clients plan early for the cost of their children's education. Because many clients are having children later in life, planning for education can directly conflict with planning for retirement. Funds for both may be needed at the same time.

The financial planner needs to educate clients about the rising costs associated with education and the urgency to begin planning sooner rather than later. During early discussions the planner should carefully review with clients the hierarchy of options that exist for paying for college. Parents should look into grants and scholarships first, followed by financial aid, then loans, and lastly their own personal resources.

Another approach is to look to grandparents who are trying to liquidate their estates. Direct gifts covering tuition payments to schools, colleges, and universities can be made without interfering with the annual gift-tax exclusion (for more on this topic, see the Estate Planning section in this chapter).

Planners must ensure that the client funds "through" college and not just "to" college. In other words, if the student takes five years to complete college and graduates at age twenty-three, planning should be done through age twenty-three, not just through age eighteen.

Planners who provide college-education planning to their clients should use the following nine-step process, adapted from *A Professional's Guide to College Planning*, by Raymond D. Loewe, CLU, ChFC, National Underwriter Co., of Cincinnati, Ohio.

1 Learn the basics.

2 Help your clients complete a trial financial aid test.

3 Help your clients construct a college budget based on the adequacy of their retirement plan.

4 Teach your clients and their children how to select the proper colleges.

5 Plan the financial aid strategy while the student is still in high school.

6 Fill out financial aid forms correctly.

7 Compare and evaluate every financial aid award.

8 Integrate any college-borrowing plan into a retirement plan.

9 Help clients to save, save, save—the right way.

◆ **Learn the basics.** You will be asked many questions by clients pertaining to their children's education plans. You may want to develop answers to common, basic questions, such as:

—How much is college going to cost (including room, board, tuition, fees, books, travel expenses, laundry money, etc.)?

—What are the four types of financial aid?

—How does financial aid work?

—How can students find the best college within an acceptable price range?

— Is it possible to negotiate a college financial aid package?

—What can we do if our child doesn't receive enough financial aid?

◆ **Help your clients complete a trial financial aid test.** This will help you to steer clients away from common mistakes and toward selecting the college that fits best with the student's criteria. Remember, the most expensive school is not necessarily out of reach. The net cost after financial aid may make that college affordable after all.

◆ **Help your clients construct a college budget based on the adequacy of their retirement plans.** In constructing a college budget, start by evaluating the client's retirement resources. Often, an answer to the college cash flow problem is for parents to share the cost of college with their student rather than bearing the entire cost alone. It is essential to make realistic assessments of a family's financial situation and not to jeopardize one need while serving another.

◆ **Teach your clients and their children how to select the proper colleges.** Different colleges use different kinds of financial aid to attract the students they want. There are many college information books available at local bookstores and libraries that provide background on this important aspect of college selection.

◆ **Plan the financial aid strategy during high school.** The earlier one plans, the better. Clients would do well to start planning when their student is a sophomore in high school. Colleges track income and assets for financial aid purposes from the tax return for the year before the financial aid package is distributed. Help clients preserve their eligibility. Prevent clients from putting money into the student's name, since a higher percentage of student assets and income than parent assets and income is figured into the financial aid calculation. Carefully time the liquidation of investments and taking of capital gains, as well as a spouse's going back to work.

◆ **Fill out financial aid forms correctly.** In January and February of the student's senior year, parents begin the process of completing financial aid forms. The planner should ensure that clients file all required forms, make all deadlines, value the home realistically, and avoid volunteering any information not asked for.

◆ **Compare and evaluate every financial aid award.** Do not let clients assume that a financial aid award is correct or that an initial award is the best that a college will offer. Using college reference books, you can determine approximately what kind of mix (financial aid vs. self-help) a client will be granted.

◆ **Integrate any college-borrowing plan into a retirement plan.** Once the financial aid amount is determined, figure out how the clients will actually pay for college. How much of their savings and investments should they liquidate? How big an emergency fund should they keep? Should the parents tap into home equity?

◆ **Help clients to save, save, save—the right way.** Make sure the client takes into account the following principles:

—Avoid the kiddie tax.

—Control taxation of savings growth.

—Control taxation during the withdrawal phase.

—Provide flexibility to deal with future financial aid eligibility.

—Allow multiple investment options for staying ahead of college inflation rates, diversifying investment risk, and making changes at a reasonable cost both as markets change and as clients need to make changes.

—Maintain a sufficient amount of life insurance to cover the death or disability of the breadwinner.

—Consider a pay-yourself-first option that allows automatic, systematic plan deposits.

Income Tax Planning

INCOME TAX planning is using any allowable strategy to reduce, time, or shift either current or future income tax liabilities. Income tax planning is driven by overall financial objectives and is not an end in itself. For many families income taxes are their biggest expense, so the subject deserves special attention.

Your role in the income tax planning process is not necessarily to do your client's income tax return. Rather, it is to locate potential tax savings opportunities, which may result in the need to reposition your client's investment allocations. You may want the client to work with a certified public accountant (CPA) to handle the more complex issues surrounding income taxes.

Your job is to help clients minimize taxes, which is legal, not evade taxes, which is illegal. As a result, you should look at techniques for tax deferral (deferring tax until the following year) or tax acceleration (accelerating tax into the current year), if appropriate. The following checklists highlight a variety of year-end timing techniques that you can recommend to assist your clients in minimizing their taxes.

TECHNIQUES FOR ACCELERATING EXPENSES AT YEAR-END

◆ Pay certain expenses this year that might otherwise wait until the following year. Do repair work; order supplies or equipment.

◆ Charge deductible expenses on your credit card. Charitable contributions and medical expenses are deductible when you charge them, not when you pay the credit card company. This is an especially astute move to consider at the end of a tax year.

◆ Ask your employer to increase your withholding of state and local taxes.

◆ Pay fourth-quarter estimated taxes before year-end rather than by January 15 of the following year.

◆ Bunch miscellaneous deductions. Because miscellaneous itemized deductions are deductible only to the extent they exceed 2 percent of adjusted gross income (AGI), it may make sense to move deductions into the current year in order to exceed your marginal tax rate (which is the tax rate on your last dollar of income) if it is higher. Alternatively, if you do not think that will provide you an allowable deduction, defer paying certain tax-related expenses until the following year. This essentially lets you deduct two years' worth of miscellaneous expenses in one tax year. Miscellaneous expenses include unreimbursed employee business expenses, such as business meals and entertainment, transportation and lodging while away from home, subscriptions to professional journals, union or professional dues, job-related continuing education, job-hunting expenses, and uniforms. Other miscellaneous expenses include investment advisory fees, investment publications, and safe-deposit-box rental charges.

TECHNIQUES FOR DEFERRING INCOME AT YEAR-END

◆ If you are self-employed, delay client billing until the following year. As a self-employed person, you have total control over when bills are generated and sent to clients.

◆ Defer bonuses until the following year by arranging this in advance with your employer.

◆ Use the installment method to defer taxable gain on property sales. If you sell capital-gain property at a profit, you may want to elect installment-sale treatment. If you arrange a sale in which payments are made over more than one year, you automatically qualify for installment-sale treatment. Because the profit from a sale is taxable in the year of sale, choosing an installment sale means that only a portion of the gain will be recognized during the current year, postponing the rest of the gain into the following year.

◆ Delay the closing dates for asset sales into the following year.

OTHER TAX-PLANNING MOVES

◆ Realize stock losses or gains while maintaining your investment position. The lower tax on long-term gains makes sales timing important, because you are required to offset capital gains with capital losses before figuring the tax. If you have already taken long-term gains as the end of the year nears, it may pay to put off selling shares that would create a loss until the next year and use those losses to offset more highly taxed regular income. Capital gains rates keep changing (based on whomever is President). At the time of this writing, the maximum is 15 percent (but don't expect it to stay at that rate forever).

◆ Dispose of passive investments to free up previously disallowed losses.

◆ Increase your level of participation in business activity to meet the material participation standard under passive loss rules.

◆ Consume expiring loss and credit carryovers that you were unable to take in prior years because your income was too high.

◆ Exchange matured E bonds for HH bonds to avoid realizing accrued interest, since this allows you to defer the interest until a later date.

◆ Increase or decrease vacation home use in order to have it treated as either a personal residence or passive activity.

◆ Pay contested taxes during the current year. This gives you an automatic deduction while letting you continue fighting these taxes during the next year.

◆ Settle insurance or damage claims to maximize the current year's casualty loss deduction.

◆ Establish an individual retirement account (IRA) to reduce your taxable income.

◆ Defer premature IRA payouts to avoid the 10 percent early withdrawal penalty. However, IRA distributions used to pay medical expenses are penalty free.

◆ Establish a full spousal IRA deduction. You can contribute $4,000 for a taxpayer and $4,000 for a spouse into an IRA. This applies to households where only one spouse works, as long as the aggregate contributions do not exceed the couple's combined compensation for the year.

◆ Incur adoption expenses. Moderate-income taxpayers can claim a tax credit of up to $10,990 in qualified adoption expenses per child. The full credit is available for taxpayers whose AGI is $75,000 or less and is phased out over the next $40,000 of modified AGI. Qualified adoption expenses consist of reasonable and necessary adoption fees, court costs, attorney's fees, and various other related expenses.

◆ Consider moving into your vacation home after retirement in order to make it your principal residence and qualify for up to $500,000 of tax-free profit ($250,000 for singles).

◆ Under Code Section 179, a calendar-year business taxpayer may be able to elect to expense qualifying property such as office equipment (up to certain annual limits) rather than depreciate it over a period of time. This provides a larger write-off of expenses and reduced income.

◆ If a taxpayer furnishes more than half of the support for a parent, he or she can deduct the medical expenses he or she paid for this parent, subject to the taxpayer's overall 7.5 percent floor.

◆ A self-employed business owner with an individual retirement plan can make a current-year contribution up to the due date plus extensions for filing his or her current-year tax return.

Retirement Planning

A FINANCIAL PLANNER will discuss two broad aspects of retirement with clients. The first is determining the total amount of money that a client needs for retirement. This is accomplished by guiding a client through a retirement needs analysis (see **EXHIBIT 4.5** on pages 153–156). The second aspect is advising the client on retirement plan options. These two aspects of retirement planning cannot be considered until quantitative and qualitative information is prepared with the client as in Step 2 of the PIPRIM financial planning process (see Chapter 3).

DETERMINING CLIENT NEEDS

Once clients have some idea of their retirement goals, the planner's task is to help them determine the amount of money necessary to overfund the goals, thus allowing for unforeseen financial and life changes. Engage clients in discussions about what is important to them in retirement. Respond to the clients' concerns, so that realistic retirement goals can be set and a financial plan designed. It is necessary to calculate the required level of savings and investments today and in succeeding years to achieve the client's desired retirement income.

In order to invest for a retirement goal, your clients need an accurate estimate of how much money they will need the day after they stop working. Of course, the future is uncertain, a simple but often forgotten fact that clients must understand. You need to encourage each client to make a set of reasonable assumptions about future life scenarios (one home or two homes, number of vacations per year, major expenditures, number of cars) along with your assumptions about economic conditions during the client's retirement span. Together you must build the most reasonable and probable picture of the client's minimum and maximum retirement expectations. This foundation serves as the point of departure for retirement investment planning. Exhibit 4.5 will assist your client to develop a retirement needs analysis and funding plan.

Three Phases of Retirement Planning

ANOTHER WAY for the financial planner to look at retirement planning is in the context of three phases: accumulation, conservation, and distribution. Once you and your clients calculate how much money they will need during retirement, you will need to design an investment plan to get there. Clients can accumulate money in three different types of retirement plans: qualified, personal retirement, and nonqualified plans.

The conservation phase of retirement planning refers to the efforts that ensure that clients maximize principal throughout their working years. For an analysis of methods of maximizing assets, see the Investment Planning section earlier in this chapter.

Finally, for the distribution phase of retirement planning, the planner determines the best method and timing for withdrawing the money that is needed for retirement. Retirement distributions can be either lump sum or paid out as an annuity.

Qualified Retirement Plans

QUALIFIED PLANS offer a great income tax benefit for employers and employees. Employers get a current tax deduction for amounts contributed to the plan, while employees do not recognize the amount as current income in that taxable year. Employees can defer tax until the time of distribution, which may be many years down the road. The box on the following page summarizes the principal types of qualified plans.

VESTING

Vesting is a key ingredient of any qualified retirement plan. Vesting is applicable to two separate components: employee contributions and employer contributions. Employee contributions and salary deferral contributions are always 100 percent vested. Employer contributions must provide for minimum standards of vesting under one of two schedules as presented in the table on page 125: five-year cliff vesting or three-to-seven-year graded vesting.

This means that at a certain point during employment, an employee acquires a nonforfeitable, guaranteed interest in

Principal Types of Qualified Plans

QUALIFIED PLANS	PERSONAL RETIREMENT PLANS	NON-QUALIFIED PLANS
Defined benefit	SEP	Deferred comp
Pension	SIMPLE	Salary red
Cash balance	IRA	Salary continuation
Hybrid	Traditional	Rabbi trust
Defined contribution	Roth	Secular trust
Target benefit	Coverdell	SERP
Tandem		
Money purchase		
Profit sharing		
401(k)		
Savings (Thrift)		
ESOP		
Stock bonus		

benefits under either a defined contribution or defined benefit plan. A plan cannot have a vesting schedule longer than seven years. Under a SIMPLE plan (see page 132), however, vesting must be immediate and nonforfeitable for both employee and employer contributions. Special vesting rules apply to top-heavy plans.

Generally, a qualified plan must provide that participants are fully vested in (have full entitlement to) the portion of the plan attributable to employer contributions on a schedule that does not exceed one of the following two alternatives.

◆ **Five-year cliff vesting.** After five years of service, the participant is fully vested in his or her account. Employees who leave the company before working there for five years are not entitled to any portion of the plan account attributable to employer contributions other than the elective deferral contributions, since the employer is not required to offer any.

Five-Year Cliff Vesting

Nonforfeitable employer contributions

YEARS OF SERVICE	PERCENTAGE
Less than 5	0%
5 or more	100%

Three-to-Seven-Year Graded Vesting

Nonforfeitable employer contributions

YEARS OF SERVICE	PERCENTAGE
Less than 3	0%
3	20%
4	40%
5	60%
6	80%
7 or more	100%

◆ **Three-to-seven-year graded vesting.** Vesting must occur at a rate of at least 20 percent per year beginning after three years of service. The participant is fully vested after seven years of service.

Alternative vesting schedules can be used as long as they are as favorable to employees as the two schedules described above. Regardless of the vesting schedule, an employee is considered fully vested at the plan's normal retirement age.

To reiterate, the vesting schedule applies only to employer contributions; employee contributions, elective deferrals, and the interest earned from those contributions are always fully vested. Employees also become fully vested upon the termination of a plan.

CATEGORIZING QUALIFIED PLANS

Qualified plans are generally categorized as either *defined contribution* or *defined benefit* plans. Defined contribution plans are also referred to as individual account plans, since each participant has a separate account for accruing plan contributions and investment earnings. Defined benefit plans, in contrast, pool the plan funds; participants receive statements that reflect their accrued benefits, but the plan may not segregate funds into individual accounts.

Another method of categorizing qualified plans is to differentiate between pension and profit-sharing plans. Pension plans provide set benefits—either a fixed benefit or a fixed contribution level. Defined benefit pension plans provide specific retirement benefits; money-purchase pension plans and target benefit plans specify the annual employer contribution to the plan. The profit-sharing (including stock bonus) plan stands alone as the only type of qualified plan that does not specify a fixed contribution.

DEFINED CONTRIBUTION PLANS

Under a defined contribution plan, a participant's benefit is fixed but not guaranteed until the participant reaches pay status. The participant's benefit is based solely on the following three features:

1 The amount of contributions made for the participant
2 Reallocated forfeitures from terminated nonvested participants
3 Increases or decreases resulting from income gains, losses, and expenses

Since investment gains or losses over the life of the plan will ultimately affect the participants' benefits, a primary characteristic of a defined contribution plan is that the risk of investment gain or loss is borne by the participants rather than the employer. Increases or decreases in plan assets will not affect the employer's contributions or obligations under the plan. Rather, such increases or decreases will affect only the participants' ultimate benefits. A defined contribution plan may, but is not required to, allow employees to direct the investment of some or all of the money allocated to their accounts.

There are several types of defined contribution plans. These include the money-purchase plan, target benefit pension plan, traditional profit-sharing plan, age-weighted money-purchase and profit-sharing plan, stock bonus plan, employee stock-ownership plan, and section 401(k) plan.

◆ **Money-purchase plan.** A money-purchase plan is a formal type of defined contribution plan in which the company's contributions are mandatory and are usually based solely on each participant's compensation. The employer annually pays this percentage of compensation to a trust for the benefit of the participant. Generally, the account balance at retirement is used to purchase an annuity that provides annual income for the participant's retirement.

◆ **Target benefit plan.** A target benefit plan is a hybrid or cross between a defined benefit plan and a money-purchase plan. Its defined benefit feature uses a target formula to determine an annual contribution in order to pay a projected benefit amount at retirement. As in a money-purchase plan, the contributions are directed into a separate account for each participant. As in a defined contribution plan, employers do not have to make up earnings if expected results differ from actual; only the participant's earnings will be higher or lower than projected. The difference between a money-purchase plan and a target plan is that in a money-purchase plan, contributions are generally determined and allocated as a percentage of current compensation, whereas in a target benefit plan, contributions are determined as if the plan provided a fixed benefit.

◆ **Profit-sharing plan.** In a profit-sharing plan, the oldest type of defined contribution plan, the company agrees to make "substantial and recurring," though generally discretionary, contributions. Amounts contributed to the plan are invested and accumulate tax-free for eventual distribution to participants or their beneficiaries either at retirement, after a fixed number of years, or upon some event such as layoff, illness, disability, retirement, death, or severance from employment.

Unlike contributions to a pension plan, contributions to a profit-sharing plan are usually tied to profits. However, since 1985, neither current nor accumulated profits are required for a company to contribute to a profit-sharing plan. The plan must provide a predetermined formula for allocating contributions among the participants and for distributing the accumulated funds.

◆ **Age-weighted plan.** An age-weighted plan is a defined con-tribution plan that allows higher contribution levels for older plan participants. The plan is based on the participant's age and compensation level. The advantage of this type of plan is that it allows older participants to build an adequate retirement account balance in a shorter period of time. It benefits owners of small businesses and key employees who are older and have been with the company for a long time.

◆ **Stock bonus plan.** A stock bonus plan is similar to a profit-sharing plan except that benefit payments are made in shares of company stock. A stock bonus plan may distribute cash to a participant instead of stock, subject to the participant's right to demand a distribution of employer securities. If the plan per-mits cash distributions and the employer securities are not read-ily tradable on an established market, participants must be given the right to require the company to repurchase the stock it dis-tributes to them under a fair valuation formula. Because these plans require the use of the sponsor's own corporate securities, they do not exist for proprietorships, partnerships, and limited liability companies.

◆ **Employee stock-ownership plan (ESOP).** An ESOP is a special type of profit-sharing or stock-bonus defined contribution plan that can qualify for favorable tax treatment. As in a stock bonus plan, the employer can contribute company stock instead of cash. However, the plan must be primarily invested in company stock. ESOPs not only provide qualified retirement benefits for employees but also benefit the employer, by creating a market for the employer's stock, increasing the firm's cash flow, supplying financing for business growth or expansion, and providing an estate-planning tool for the owners of a closely held corporation. ESOPs can borrow money to provide the contribution. When used to borrow money, these plans are called LESOPs (leveraged employee stock-ownership plans).

◆ **Section 401(k) plan.** Also called a cash or deferred plan, a section 401(k) plan is an employer-sponsored stock bonus plan or profit-sharing plan that meets certain Internal Revenue Code requirements. Unlike other qualified plans, 401(k) plans permit employees to make before-tax contributions through a salary reduction agreement. All 401(k) plans contain a cash or deferred arrangement (CODA). Under a CODA, employees can opt to have compensation that their employers would otherwise have paid directly to them deferred to the plan instead. An employee can agree to a salary reduction or to defer a bonus that he or she has coming.

Personal Retirement Plans

THESE PLANS provide many of the same tax benefits as qualified plans but differ in two ways. First, money cannot be borrowed from a personal retirement plan. Any distributions are taxed as ordinary income. Second, in qualified plans participants born before 1936 can qualify for ten-year income averaging, but this feature is not available to employees with personal retirement plans. Personal retirement plans can include individual retirement accounts (IRAs), simplified employee pension plans (SEPs), and savings incentive match plans for employees (SIMPLE plans).

TYPES OF IRAS
◆ **Traditional IRA.** There are two types of traditional IRAs: individual retirement accounts (trusts and custodial accounts) and individual retirement annuities (contracts). Either or both can be established by an individual to save for his or her retirement.

An IRA must be established with a bank, savings and loan association, credit union, brokerage firm, or other organization that can demonstrate to the Internal Revenue Service the ability to lawfully administer the trust. An individual may contribute to an IRA if he or she satisfies the following requirements:

Age requirement. The law imposes a maximum age restriction on traditional IRA contributors. An individual must not attain age seventy by the end of the taxable year. For example, if Marty is seventy years old on May 31, 2005, he is not eligible to make an IRA contribution in 2005 because he became seventy before year-end. However, there is no minimum age requirement for making IRA contributions.

Annual IRA Contributions

YEAR	LIMIT	CATCH-UP PROVISION (50 AND OVER)	MAXIMUM ANNUAL CONTRIBUTION
2005	$4,000	$500	$4,500
2006	$4,000	$1,000	$5,000
2007	$4,000	$1,000	$5,000
2008	$5,000	$1,000	$6,000

Beyond 2008: Annual limitations are adjusted for inflation in $500 increments.

Earned income requirement. Income must be earned from personal services rendered. The personal services must be rendered in the year the income is received.

Rollover requirement. IRA rollovers must be from a qualified retirement plan.

Contribution limit. Individuals may contribute to an IRA according to the limits shown in the chart above.

If an IRA holder has more than one traditional IRA, the aggregate contributions cannot exceed the limit. Further, the eligible contribution amount is reduced by the amount contributed to a Roth IRA, as discussed below.

◆ **Coverdell Education Savings Account (formerly Education IRA).** You can make a $2,000 per year, per beneficiary, nondeductible contribution to a Coverdell ESA. The money must be allocated for education expenses. These include tuition at a qualified elementary, secondary, or post-secondary education institution, books, supplies, equipment required for attendance and enrollment, room and board, and fees.

The earnings in the account grow tax-free as long as distributions are used for eligible expenses. Coverdell ESA accounts contributions must be made in cash, be made before the designated beneficiary reaches eighteen years of age, and be less than or equal to $2,000 per year per beneficiary.

Contributions can be made to one or several Coverdell ESAs for the same beneficiary provided that the total contributions are not more than the limits for a year. And contributions can be made, without penalty, to both a Coverdell ESA and a Qualified Tuition Program (QTP) in the same year for the same beneficiary. Funds must be used by the time the beneficiary turns thirty years old or transferred to a younger relative (including cousins, step-relatives, and in-laws).

◆ **Roth IRA.** The Roth IRA generally offers the tax benefit of having all withdrawals available tax-free. The downside is that contributions to the IRA are not deductible. The basic rules and regulations of the Roth IRA are the following:

—Contributions can be made after a taxpayer reaches 70½ years of age (if the combined earned income of the taxpayer and his or her spouse equals or exceeds the Roth IRA contribution).

—Taxpayers do not have to start taking distributions when they reach 70½ years old.

—Contributions can be made even if the taxpayer participates in an employer-sponsored retirement plan.

—The phaseout for the contributions for married couples does not arise until AGI is $150,000. Once AGI reaches $160,000, the Roth IRA contribution amount is totally phased out. For singles, the AGI phaseout begins at $95,000 and ends at $110,000.

—Distributions are tax-free if qualified. Qualification is met if:

   (a) the withdrawal is not made within the five-tax-year period beginning with the year of contribution; and

   (b) the distribution is received at or after age 59½, *or* the distribution is received in the event of death or disability, *or* the distribution is for a first-time home buyer.

—The five-year-tax period in (a) above starts with the year for which the contribution is made. This means that if a Roth IRA contribution for the year 2004 were made between January 1, 2005, and April 15, 2005 (the date for filing the 2004 income tax return), the five-year waiting period would still start with 2004, not 2005.

—Nonqualified withdrawals are included in taxable income if they come from earnings on the Roth IRA account. However, the withdrawals are considered to be made from contributions to all of the taxpayer's Roth IRAs first.

—A 10 percent early withdrawal penalty applies if the taxpayer is not yet 59½ years old, unless the withdrawal is for death, disability, periodic payments (meeting certain requirements), home ownership, or higher-education expenses.

—The maximum annual contribution is the lesser of 100 percent of earned income or $4,000, less any amounts made to a regular IRA. The contribution must be made by April 15 of the following year, the deadline for filing the previous year's tax return.

—The Roth IRA must be designated as such when it is established.

◆ **SEP.** A simplified employee pension (SEP) is a pension plan established by a business on behalf of the employee in which the contributions are deposited into IRAs and are tax deductible by the employer. This simpler version of a qualified plan is especially suitable for small businesses. Any employer, including a sole proprietor with no employees, can establish a SEP for all eligible employees. The owner of the business is also eligible to receive a SEP contribution. Since an employer contributes directly to the SEP IRA, no separate pension trust is needed.

A SEP is primarily distinguishable from an IRA by its higher annual contribution limit. An employer may contribute as much as 25 percent of compensation, up to a maximum of $42,000, to an employee's SEP.

◆ **SIMPLE plan.** The savings incentive match plan for employees, or SIMPLE plan, offers a retirement-plan option for businesses with one hundred or fewer employees. Available since 1997, the plan was introduced as part of the many-faceted Small Business Job Protection Act of 1996. SIMPLE retirement plans are designed to offer greater deferral opportunities than ordinary IRAs. They also have fewer restrictions and administrative requirements than traditional pension or profit-sharing plans. SIMPLE plans can be in either an IRA format or a 401(k) format.

Under a SIMPLE IRA plan, any employee with compensation of at least $5,000 must be permitted to enter a "qualified salary reduction arrangement." Under this arrangement, employees can elect to contribute up to $10,000 of their compensation per year by deferring a portion of their salary to an IRA. This portion must be expressed as a percentage of compensation, not as a flat amount. The $10,000 maximum contribution may be increased periodically to reflect cost-of-living adjustments. In addition, if you are over age fifty, an annual catch-up provision of $2,000 (in addition to the $10,000 maximum contribution) can be made.

DEFINED BENEFIT PLANS

A defined benefit plan is an employer-sponsored plan providing a predetermined or defined benefit. Each year that a participant is in the plan, the participant earns or accrues an additional portion of that ultimate promised benefit. Participants who leave the company before normal retirement age are generally entitled to the portion of their accrued benefit that is vested.

A defined benefit plan typically provides benefits based on a combination of compensation and service or plan participation. However, it is not unusual for a collectively bargained defined benefit plan to provide benefits based on a flat dollar amount. The maximum promised benefit is calculated assuming that the participant remains in the plan until the normal retirement date.

A defined benefit plan must provide determinable benefits. If the plan realizes forfeitures from nonvested employees, those forfeitures must be used to reduce future employer contributions and cannot be used to increase the benefits of the remaining participants. These plans may not provide for in-service distributions; in other words, defined benefit plans may not allow distributions to participants who are still working unless the participant has attained the plan's normal retirement age.

◆ **Pension plan.** A pension plan is a qualified employer plan that guarantees a specified benefit level at retirement. It is used to provide older employees with the maximum amount of tax-deferred savings and to provide an adequate level of income to employees regardless of their age at plan entry. Employers are obligated to fund the plan annually and assume the risk of bad investment results. Benefit levels are guaranteed both by the employer and by the Pension Benefit Guaranty Corporation

(PBGC). The annual employer contribution is determined each year by an actuary.

◆ **Cash balance plan.** A cash balance plan is a qualified employer pension plan that provides for annual employer contributions at a specified rate to hypothetical individual accounts that are set up for each plan participant. The employer guarantees not only the contribution level but also a minimum rate of return on each participant's account.

◆ **Hybrid plan.** Where defined benefit plans have a defined contribution component that is based partly on the balance of participants' separate accounts, these plans are known as hybrid plans and are considered both defined contribution plans and defined benefit plans.

Nonqualified Plans

PLANS THAT do not meet federal Employee Retirement Income Security Act (ERISA) guidelines and Internal Revenue Code requirements are considered nonqualified and cannot avail themselves of the preferential tax attributes. The best example of a nonqualified plan is an individually designed deferred compensation arrangement set up exclusively for one or more executives.

Generally, employees recognize income in the year that their rights to plan benefits become nonforfeitable. Only then are employers allowed to deduct contributions made. Nevertheless, due to the expanded coverage rules enacted under recent tax law changes, some employers might find it less costly to establish a nonqualified plan.

Nonqualified plans represent contractual arrangements in which the company compensates key executives at a later date for current-year services. Nonqualified plans are not subject to the coverage, funding, or distribution rules that apply to qualified plans. Therefore, nonqualified plans can be designed to meet each executive's specific needs.

One type of nonqualified plan, a rabbi trust, is essentially an irrevocable trust involving retained administrative powers under which assets can be used to pay other liabilities. Therefore, it is considered to be a grantor trust, with the employer being taxed on the income. To avoid this tax, the trust assets should be invested. The assets remain subject to the employer's creditors in the event of insolvency, but no other condition need be imposed on payment of the benefits. The benefits of key employees are typically vested. Since the assets of a rabbi trust remain subject to creditors' rights, there has been no transfer of property. Consequently, no income is imputed to the intended beneficiary until benefits are actually received.

Distributions from Retirement Plans

GENERALLY, all distributions from qualified retirement plans are included in the recipient's gross income when received. Taxation of certain types of distributions may be postponed through a tax-free rollover to an IRA or another qualified retirement plan. In some cases, favorable tax treatment may be available for a lump-sum distribution. Loans taken from qualified retirement plans are not taxable if certain requirements are met. Distributions to beneficiaries generally are included in the deceased participant's estate for federal estate tax purposes.

LUMP-SUM DISTRIBUTION

A lump-sum distribution is a distribution of the balance held in a qualified retirement plan made on account of the employee's death, attainment of age 59½, separation from service (except for self-employed individuals), or disability (for self-employed individuals only).

A distribution will not qualify as a lump-sum distribution unless the employee was a plan participant for at least five years prior to the year of distribution. The IRS has ruled that plan participants who have their entire account balances transferred directly from an old plan to a new plan may include years of participation in both plans to satisfy the five-year participation requirement. This five-year participation requirement does not apply to a beneficiary receiving a distribution after the participant's death.

Lump-sum distributions may qualify for favorable income tax treatment. Further, the participant (or surviving spouse) may elect to defer payment of taxes by rolling over the distribution into an IRA or another qualified retirement plan.

◆ **Lump-sum distribution to a deceased participant's beneficiary.** If the beneficiary is the surviving spouse of the deceased participant, the same options that would have been available to the participant are available to the spouse.

◆ **Taxation of a lump-sum distribution.** An employee who has attained age 59½ and who has completed at least five years of plan participation prior to the year of distribution has several income tax options:

—The entire distribution may be reported as ordinary income and might qualify for ten-year forward averaging.

—The entire distribution may be reported as ordinary income without electing ten-year forward averaging.

—All or part of the distribution may be rolled over to an IRA or to another qualified retirement plan; no tax is paid on the amount rolled over, and the rest is taxed as ordinary income without the option of electing either five-year or ten-year forward averaging.

If more than one lump-sum distribution is received in a single tax year, all of the distributions must be aggregated, and the election to use forward averaging will apply to the aggregate amount.

◆ **Early distribution of benefits.** A 10 percent penalty is charged on benefits distributed from a qualified retirement plan, and the distribution is included in the employee's income, unless the distribution is:

(1) made on or after the date the employee attained age 59½;

(2) made to a beneficiary (or to the estate of the employee) after the death of the employee;

(3) attributable to the employee's disability;

(4) part of a series of substantially equal periodic payments (not less frequently than annually) made for the life (or life expectancy) of the employee, or the joint lives (or joint life expectancy) of the employee and the employee's beneficiary, that begin after the employee separates from service;

(5) made to an employee after separation from service after attainment of age 55;

(6) a dividend paid on stock held by an employee stock-ownership plan (ESOP);

(7) a payment to an alternate payee pursuant to a qualified domestic relations order (QDRO); or

(8) an amount equal to or less than the total medical expenses deductible for the year by the employee.

Exceptions 5, 7, and 8 above are not applicable to a distribution from an individual retirement plan; and for exception 4 to apply to an individual retirement plan, separation from service is not required. The penalty tax applies only to distributions from qualified retirement plans, individual retirement plans, and tax-sheltered annuities.

The 10 percent penalty tax applies only to the portion of the distribution subject to income tax and is in addition to the income tax. Thus, the 10 percent penalty tax does not apply to the portion of the distribution that is income-tax-free. The penalty tax applies to a participant who made an irrevocable election to defer receipt of the distribution prior to both the effective date and the date of enactment of the penalty tax and then received the distribution thereafter. The 10 percent penalty tax can be avoided if the early distribution qualifies for rollover treatment and it is rolled over into another qualified plan or an IRA.

◆ **Loans.** If the plan permits, a participant may borrow from any type of qualified retirement plan, including a pension plan. In fact, loans that meet the requirements of relevant tax laws are not treated as distributions. As a result, they are not taxable at the time they are made. However, if a loan fails to meet the tax law requirements, or if it goes into default or is foreclosed, the participant may be taxed on the principal of the loan.

Estate Planning

THE PURPOSE of estate planning is to pass property to named beneficiaries either during life or at death. Estate planning is crucial as a means of providing for one's family over the long term. Failing to plan for the legal and financial aftermath of death will not spare loved ones from the consequences. They will simply have less control over their finances than they otherwise would have.

Planners need to provide information about the various estate planning tools and techniques that are available to the client. Most planners are not attorneys and therefore will not be able to draft estate planning documents for clients—those who do are practicing law without a license. The biggest responsibility of planners in estate planning is to ensure that appropriate tools and techniques are used to successfully achieve client objectives as reflected in the client's estate plan.

The pitfalls of inadequate estate planning are illustrated in the example of two brothers who owned a $4 million manufacturing business. Both brothers were in their forties, and each had a son who planned to step into the family business. At family functions it was always joked that the sons would inherit the business from their fathers and double its size. Unfortunately, one of the brothers died of an unexpected heart attack. The executor of the deceased brother's estate read the will, which stated that his half of the business would go to his son. After the funeral, the son of the deceased brother went to the office to work with his uncle. The uncle asked what the nephew was doing there. The nephew responded that he was going to help the uncle create an $8 million business, because he was taking over for his father. The uncle excused himself and came back with a piece of paper describing the ownership of the business. The piece of paper established joint tenancy with right of survivorship (JTWROS). This type of property ownership supersedes a will and caused the portion of the deceased father's will related to the business to be invalid.

The lesson to be learned from this example is to make sure client goals are documented and clear. Make sure they are consistent with other business and estate documents. If they are not, changes need to be made immediately. Beyond that, refer clients to an attorney who specializes in estate planning.

TRANSFERRING PROPERTY DURING LIFE

◆ **Gifts.** The best transfer technique for reducing the size of a probate estate is gift giving. Probate is a procedure established by law for the orderly distribution of estates. It is designed to ensure that all of a decedent's property is collected and protected, that all debts are paid, and that the beneficiaries promptly receive designated assets.

The law allows every person to give anyone each year up to $11,000 for an individual recipient or $22,000 for a married couple. The law does not limit the number of recipients, although gifts exceeding $11,000 for a single person or $22,000 for a married couple are considered taxable gifts, with the tax paid by the giver in most cases. At the time of death, the IRS totals the taxable gifts made during a lifetime and subtracts this total from the estate exemption (unified credit) limit.

The amount that a beneficiary is entitled to receive without incurring estate taxes was $1.5 million in 2005.

TRANSFERRING PROPERTY AT DEATH

Property can be transferred at death by will, intestate, contract, trust, or operation of law.

◆ **Will.** A will is a legal document that specifies how a person (the testator) wants to dispose of the real and personal property owned at the time of death.

◆ **Intestate.** When a decedent dies intestate, or without a will, the state decides where the property will go. Each state has different rules on how property passes. These laws are usually based on a lineal or collateral family relationship to the decedent at the time of death.

◆ **Contract.** Certain parties and/or beneficiaries are named by a decedent in an estate planning contract. The decedent names a designated beneficiary who receives property. Contracts can pass through life insurance (where a primary and a contingent beneficiary are listed), a pension (where beneficiaries are also named), or a trust. Contractual beneficiaries supersede other beneficiaries with respect to the property in a will.

◆ **Trust.** A trust is a legal relationship used to split beneficiary interests from the management of a property. There are many different types of trusts. Some of the more popular trusts include the marital (type A), bypass or credit shelter (type B), qualified terminable interest property, or QTIP (type C), and estate (type D).

Marital trust (type A). A marital trust is established to hold property, usually for the life of the surviving spouse. It permits unlimited transfers to a surviving spouse. The manner in which property passes to a surviving spouse is quite flexible. Property can pass through an outright bequest to the spouse or by operation of law (see description below). Alternatively, one can arrange for the use of trusts.

The surviving spouse gets the income from the trust for life and can direct the disposition of the assets during life or at death. Type A trusts qualify for the unlimited marital deduction and are often used to ease asset administration or to permit a trustee to invest assets in the event that the surviving spouse is unable to invest or direct the assets. The trust's assets are included in the surviving spouse's estate.

Bypass or credit-shelter trust (type B). The bypass trust, also called a credit-shelter trust or nonmarital trust, is designed to take advantage of the unified credit for the first spouse who dies. The unified credit represents a federal credit that offsets any estate tax due on estates valued up to $1.5 million (in 2005). Estates greater than $1.5 million are required to pay estate tax. The bypass trust is used in conjunction with a marital deduction trust; because the decedent generally selects the remainderman (the eventual recipient of the property), the trust does not qualify for the unlimited marital deduction. The bypass trust receives just enough assets to absorb the unified credit remaining at the decedent's death ($1.5 million for 2005).

The income from the type B trust often goes to the surviving spouse. However, the survivor will have no power over the final disposition of the assets of the trust. A bypass trust may also give the surviving spouse a five-and-five power, which permits the survivor to withdraw principal up to the greater of 5 percent of the assets or $5,000 per year. A type B trust lets the surviving spouse receive an economic benefit from the assets, usually the income received from the trust, while taking advantage of the decedent's unified credit. However, the assets in a type B trust are not included in the surviving spouse's estate. It is called a bypass trust because the property, along with any appreciation and income accumulation, will bypass taxation in the surviving spouse's estate.

Qualified terminable interest property (QTIP) trust (type C). A QTIP trust is similar to a type A (marital) trust except that it allows you to provide a life income interest for your spouse while determining in your will who will take the property after your spouse's death. A QTIP trust qualifies for the marital deduction only to the extent that your executor elects to claim it. This provides added flexibility to the estate because it allows the executor to decide if there may be some tax advantage to be gained from paying tax in the first estate. This technique is useful for clients in second marriages who wish to leave property for the surviving spouse's benefit and then to the children of the first marriage.

Estate trust (type D). An estate trust permits income to accumulate without forcing annual income distributions. Assets transferred to a type D trust must qualify for the unlimited marital deduction, because the principal and accumulated income must be distributed to the surviving spouse's probate estate on death. It is only useful to the truly wealthy, because it permits the trustee to accumulate funds that would otherwise have to be distributed.

◆ **Operation of law.** Besides contracts, operation-of-law considerations also supersede a will. For example, as noted previously, holding property as joint tenants with right of survivorship (JTWROS) supersedes property passing through a will.

EXHIBIT 4.1

Budget Work Sheet

How to Prepare Your Monthly Budget

MONTHLY EXPENDITURES

Auto loan payment	$_____
Auto maintenance	$_____
Child care	$_____
Clothing	$_____
Contributions	$_____
Credit card payments	$_____
Dues	$_____
Entertainment	$_____
Food	$_____
Household maintenance	$_____
Income and Social Security taxes	$_____
Insurance	$_____
Personal care	$_____
Property taxes	$_____
Rent or mortgage payment	$_____
Retirement plan investments	$_____
Saving/investing	$_____
Transportation (gas, fares)	$_____
Utilities	$_____
Other	$_____
Total monthly expenditures	$_____

MONTHLY RECEIPTS

Wages or salary	$_____
Dividends (mutual funds, stocks, etc.)	$_____
Interest (CDs, savings account, etc.)	$_____
Rental and/or royalty	$_____
Other	$_____
Total monthly receipts	$_____

NET CASH FLOW

Total monthly receipts	$_____
Total monthly expenditures	− $_____
Monthly net cash flow	$_____

EXHIBIT 4.2

Net Worth Work Sheet
How to Calculate Your Net Worth

ASSETS	CURRENT VALUE
Business interests (proprietorships, partnerships, company stock)	$_____
Cash value of life insurance	$_____
Certificates of deposit	$_____
Other income investments (bonds, bond mutual funds, money market mutual funds)	$_____
Market value of home(s)	$_____
Miscellaneous (trust interests, inheritances)	$_____
Personal bank accounts (checking, savings, money market deposit accounts)	$_____
Personal property (jewelry, collectibles, cars, furniture)	$_____
Real estate investments	$_____
Retirement plan investments	
Individual retirement accounts (IRAs)	$_____
401(k) or 403(b) plans	$_____
Keogh plan	$_____
SEP	$_____
Profit-sharing plan	$_____
Pension plan	$_____
Stocks and stock mutual funds	$_____
Total assets	$_____

LIABILITIES	CURRENT VALUE
Car loans	$_____
Credit cards	$_____
Mortgages	$_____
Student loans	$_____
Other loans	$_____
Outstanding bills and obligations	$_____
Total liabilities	$_____
Net worth (subtract liabilities from assets)	$_____

EXHIBIT 4.3

Life Insurance Work Sheet

Life Insurance Needs Analysis Form

If amounts are entered for each category of need below, the resulting estimate should be viewed as a maximum amount of insurance that will meet all foreseeable needs of survivors. Note: All amounts should be expressed in current dollars.

LIFE INSURANCE NEEDS

Assets currently available to support family

Proceeds from life insurance already owned	$_____
Cash and savings	$_____
Equity in real estate (if survivors will sell)	$_____
Securities	$_____
IRA and Keogh plans	$_____
Employer savings plans	$_____
Lump-sum employer pension benefits	$_____
Other sources	$_____
Total assets	$_____

EXPENSES

1 Final expenses (onetime expenses incurred at death)

a. Final illness (medical costs will probably exceed health insurance deductibles and coinsurance, so assume that client will have to fund at least those amounts)	$_____
b. Funeral/burial costs	$_____
c. Probate costs (if unsure, assume 4% of assets passing through probate process)	$_____
d. Federal estate taxes (for most estates over $1.5 million willed to someone other than spouse)	$_____
e. State inheritance taxes (varies by state)	$_____
f. Legal fees, estate administration	$_____
g. Other	$_____
h. Total final expenses	$_____

2 Outstanding debt (to be paid off at death)

a. Credit card/consumer debt $_____

b. Car $_____

c. Mortgage (if it is to be paid off at death;
otherwise, include payments in life income) $_____

d. Other $_____

e. Total outstanding debt $_____

3 Readjustment expenses (to cover the transition period of immediate crisis)

a. Child care $_____

b. Additional homemaking help $_____

c. Vocational counseling/educational training
(for a nonworking or underemployed spouse
who expects to seek paid employment) $_____

d. Other $_____

e. Total readjustment expenses $_____

4 Dependency expenses (until all children are self-supporting)

a. Estimate household's current annual
expenditures $_____

b. To remove the deceased person's expenses,
multiply this figure by:

.70 for a surviving family of one

.74 for a surviving family of two

.78 for a surviving family of three

.80 for a surviving family of four

.82 for a surviving family of five

$_____ (Line 4a) x _____ (factor) = $_____

c. Deduct survivor's estimated annual income
from employment $_____

d. Equals current annual expenses to be covered
by currently owned assets and insurance $_____

e. To determine approximate total dependency
expenses, multiply by number of years until
youngest child becomes self-supporting:

$_____ (Line 4d) x _____ (years) = $_____

f. If support for dependent parent(s) is to be
provided, multiply annual support by the
number of years such support is expected to
continue:

$_____ x _____ (years) = $_____

g. Total dependency expenses (add Lines 4e
and 4f) $_____

5 Education expenses

a. Annual private school tuition in current dollars
(if desired) $_____

b. Multiply by number of years and children
left to attend:

$_____ (Line 5a) x _____ (years) = $_____

c. Annual college costs in current dollars $_____

d. Multiply by number of years and children left
to attend:

$_____ (Line 5c) x _____ (years) = $_____

e. Total education expenses (add Lines 5b and 5d) $_____

6 Life income (for the surviving spouse after the chidren are all self-supporting)

a. Annual amount desired (in current dollars) $_____

b. Deduct spouse's estimated annual income
from employment $_____

c. Equals annual expenses to be covered by
currently owned assets and insurance $_____

d. Multiply by number of years between when
the youngest child becomes self-supporting
and the surviving spouse begins receiving
Social Security benefits and other retirement
income, if any:

$_____ (Line 6c) x _____ (years) = $_____

7 Retirement income for surviving spouse

a. Annual amount desired in current dollars $_____
(less Social Security and any pension income)

b. Multiply by numbers of years of life
expectancy after retirement begins:

$_____ (Line 7a) x _____ (years) = $_____

8 Total funds needed to cover expenses:
(add Lines 1h, 2e, 3e, 4g, 5e, 6d, and 7b) $_____

9 Available assets $_____

ADDITIONAL LIFE INSURANCE REQUIRED

10 Subtract available assets (Line 9) from total
funds needed to cover expenses (Line 8). This
shortfall represents the estimated amount that
must be covered through life insurance. $_____

EXHIBIT 4.4

Client Risk-Tolerance Questionnaire

PERSONAL BACKGROUND INFORMATION

Date _____

Name _____

Address _____

City _____ State _____ Zip _____

Phone: Day _____ Night _____

Social Security or Taxpayer ID no. _____

Occupation _____

At what age do you plan to retire? _____

Spouse's name _____

INVESTMENT EXPERIENCE AND ANALYSIS

1 As an investor, where would you place yourself on the following scale? (Circle a number)

1	2	3		4	5	6	7		8	9	10

Minimize losses and fluctuations as much as possible	A balanced investment mix with some fluctuation and some growth	Maximize growth of assets with tolerance for risk or fluctuation

2 What is your age?

a. Under 25 years

b. 25 to 34 years

c. 35 to 44 years

d. 45 to 54 years

e. 55 to 65 years

f. Over 65 years

3 Do you expect to have large cash needs—such as buying a house, paying for a college education, having health-related expenses, retiring, or starting a new business—in the future? If more than one applies, check the earliest time period.

a. No, I do not expect to have such a cash need.

b. Yes, in 16 to 20 years.

c. Yes, in 10 to 15 years.

d. Yes, in 5 to 9 years.

e. Yes, in less than 5 years.

4 Some people want their investments primarily to grow in value and secondarily to produce regular income. Others primarily seek regular income rather than growth. These objectives may be long term (5 years or longer), medium term (2 to 5 years), or short term (up to 2 years). **Which statement best reflects your objective and its term?**

a. To have my investment grow in value over the years rather than to receive regular income from my investment

b. To have my investment grow in value, though I am investing for the medium term

c. To receive regular income from my investment, even though I am investing for the long term

d. To receive regular income rather than having my investment grow in value, though both are important to me because I am investing for the medium term

e. To receive regular income rather than having my investment grow in value, because I am investing primarily for the short term

5 People save money for several purposes. You should always have money set aside for emergencies, of course. But you also save for other reasons, from a dream vacation in the not-too-distant future to far-off retirement. **The main purpose for the money you are now considering for investment is to:**

a. Start or add to my retirement fund, which I do not anticipate using for 20 or more years

b. Start or add to a nest egg, which I do not anticipate needing for the foreseeable future

c. Start or add to a savings fund, which I may use for a rainy day in 5 or 10 years

d. Save up for a special purpose in the near future

e. Get a slightly higher return than I get in a certificate of deposit or savings account

6 How do you expect your annual income to vary over the next 2 years?

a. To increase substantially

b. To increase somewhat

c. To keep up with inflation

d. To decrease

e. To decrease substantially

7 Comparatively, how much income do you expect to have available for discretionary purchases, savings, and investment over the next 2 years?

a. Substantially more than I have now

b. Somewhat more

c. About the same

d. Somewhat less

e. Substantially less

8 Investment markets fluctuate. Though the long-term direction has been generally upward, there have also been periods of decline. **From a practical standpoint, not considering your views about taking risks, how easily could you replace investment declines with future higher income?**

a. Very easily

b. Easily, with some planning involved

c. It would be difficult

d. It would be very difficult

e. It would be impossible

9 Now consider your personal feelings about watching the ups and downs of the stock market. If you owned investments, how would rises and falls in the market affect you emotionally?

a. Short-term movements in the investment market would not affect me.

b. Short-term movements would affect me minimally.

c. Short-term movements would indirectly affect me.

d. Short-term movements would directly affect me.

e. Short-term movements would dramatically affect me.

10 What would you do with your investment if the market fell?

a. Not take my money out of the market, regardless of how

severe the decline

b. Consider taking my money out of the market only if the decline were substantial

c. Probably take my money out of the market if the decline were substantial

d. Take my money out even if the decline were not substantial

e. Take my money out no matter how small the decline

11 Which statement best describes your investment preferences?

a. I invest primarily to increase the value of my investment.

b. I invest to receive regular payments, even though that means somewhat smaller potential for my investment to grow.

c. I invest primarily to receive regular payments from my investment, and increases in value are of little importance.

d. My desire to preserve my investment is primary and outweighs my desire to have it increase in value or to receive payments from it.

I/We understand that the recommended portfolio for my/our account is based on the information I/we have supplied. Should there be any substantial changes in my/our financial situation or investment objectives, I/we will tell you.

_____

Signature   Date

_____

Signature   Date

Client Score Sheet

Client Name: _____

										SCORES
QUESTION 1:	1	2	3	4	5	6	7	8	9 10	_____
QUESTION 2:	a=6	b=5	c=4	d=3	e=2	f=1				_____
QUESTION 3:	a=10	b=8	c=6	d=4	e=2					_____
QUESTION 4:	a=10	b=8	c=6	d=4	e=2					_____
QUESTION 5:	a=10	b=8	c=6	d=4	e=2					_____
QUESTION 6:	a=10	b=8	c=6	d=4	e=2					_____
QUESTION 7:	a=10	b=8	c=6	d=4	e=2					_____
QUESTION 8:	a=10	b=8	c=6	d=4	e=2					_____
QUESTION 9:	a=10	b=8	c=6	d=4	e=2					_____
QUESTION 10:	a=10	b=8	c=6	d=4	e=2					_____
QUESTION 11:	a=10	b=8	c=6	d=4						_____
									TOTAL SCORE:	_____

	CLIENT'S SCORE RANGE
Aggressive-growth portfolio	**92–106**
Growth portfolio	**74–91**
Moderate portfolio	**56–73**
Income-and-growth portfolio	**38–55**
Income portfolio	**22–37**

EXHIBIT 4.5

Retirement Planning Work Sheet

*Please complete this three-part work sheet to determine the amount of **income** you will need in retirement and the **savings** you will need to reach your income target. After you complete this work sheet, meet with your financial planner to prepare a retirement plan. Annually you will want to update the information as your life situation and long-term goals change.*

SECTION 1: RETIREMENT EXPENSE FORECAST

This section helps you approximate the annual retirement income you will need to meet your postretirement standard of living. First you will calculate the approximate income necessary to maintain your desired living standard in today's dollars. In order to project annual living expenses during retirement, you must then multiply your living expenses by an inflation factor.

Annual retirement expense forecast

Current gross annual income [1]	$_____
Minus amount of annual savings [2]	– $_____
Subtotal (the amount you spend currently)	$_____
Multiplied by 80% [3]	$_____ x .80
Equals the approximate annual cost (in current dollars) of maintaining your current standard of living if you were retiring this year	$_____
—Multiplied by inflation factor from table below [4]	$_____
—Equals approximate annual cost (in future dollars) of maintaining your current standard of living when you retire	$_____

Explanations for the planner

[1] "Current gross annual income" includes all income from all sources.

[2] "Annual savings" includes, in addition to the usual sources of savings, reinvested dividends and capital gains, and any contributions to retirement plans that are taken from annual income.

[3] The general rule is that a retiree can maintain his/her preretirement standard of living by spending roughly 80% of preretirement annual income. Individual circumstances may dictate a higher or lower percentage. Ideally, you should prepare

a retirement budget that details expected expenses. This information can be obtained from the "interactive data-gathering stage" explained in Chapter 3. You may need a multiplier of less than 80% in some circumstances (for example, for clients who have paid off a mortgage, lowering their housing costs) or, in other circumstances, a higher multiplier (for example, extensive travel plans).

(4) The inflation factor multiplies the annual cost of living to account for price inflation at the time of retirement.

Inflation Factor Table

NUMBER OF YEARS UNTIL RETIREMENT	FACTOR	NUMBER OF YEARS UNTIL RETIREMENT	FACTOR
5	1.2	25	3.0
10	1.6	30	3.7
15	1.9	35	4.7
20	2.4	40	5.8

SECTION 2: RETIREMENT INCOME AND SAVINGS FORECAST

This section helps estimate the annual savings needed to generate future income to meet retirement expenses. The first calculation is for the first year of savings toward retirement (Line 7). Annual savings should be increased by 5% (or more) each year until retirement.

ANNUAL RETIREMENT SAVINGS FORECAST	CURRENT DOLLARS	INFLATION FACTOR(1)	FUTURE (RETIREMENT-AGE) DOLLARS
1 Estimated annual living expenses at retirement age (from section 1)			$_____
2 Annual pension income (projection at retirement age available from employer) multiplied by inflation factor (2)	$_____ x	_____ =	$_____
3 Annual Social Security benefits (projection at retirement age available from Social Security Administration)(3) multiplied by inflation factor	$_____ x	_____ =	$_____
4 Subtotal of projected pension and Social Security income (add Lines 2 and 3)			$_____

ANNUAL RETIREMENT SAVINGS FORECAST	CURRENT DOLLARS	INFLATION FACTOR[1]	FUTURE (RETIREMENT-AGE) DOLLARS
5 Shortfall (if expenses are greater than income) that must be funded out of personal savings/investments (subtract Line 4 from Line 1)			$_____
6 Multiplied by 17 [4]			$_____
7 Equals necessary savings/investments in future dollars by retirement age to fund retirement [5]			$_____

Explanations for the planner

[1] Use inflation factor table for the appropriate multiplier.

[2] Employers usually provide pension plan projections at retirement age expressed in current dollars. Multiply this number by an inflation factor to approximate benefits in future dollars.

[3] Social Security estimates are expressed in current dollars and therefore must be adjusted for inflation.

[4] As a general rule, for every $1,000 of annual income you will need to fund at retirement age, you will need to have at least $17,000 in savings/investments to keep up with inflation. If you plan to retire before age 62, use a factor of 20 rather than 17.

[5] Clients may be dismayed by the amount of savings needed to fund retirement. The number can easily exceed $1 million for younger persons and/or people with minimal pension benefits. Nevertheless, good savings habits combined with the power of compounding interest can usually close the gap between current resources and eventual needs.

SECTION 3: RETIREMENT SAVINGS ESTIMATOR

This section of the Retirement Planning Work Sheet can be used to forecast private pension and Social Security benefits at retirement and to approximate any additional savings or investment needed to fill a potential shortfall between those benefits and total income needs.

1 Amount of savings/investments in future dollars that need to be accumulated by retirement age to fund retirement (from Section 2) $_____

2 Minus resources that are currently available for retirement purposes [1] $_____

3 Multiplied by appreciation factor (refer to appreciation factor table below) [2] x _____

4 Equals estimated future value of retirement
resources that are currently available
(multiply Line 2 by Line 3) $ _____

5 Retirement funds needed by retirement age
(subtract Line 4 from Line 1) $ _____

6 Multiplied by annual savings factor
(refer to annual savings factor table below) [3]   x _____

7 Equals savings needed over the next year
(multiply Line 5 by Line 6) [4] $ _____

Appreciation Factor Table

NUMBER OF YEARS UNTIL RETIREMENT	FACTOR	NUMBER OF YEARS UNTIL RETIREMENT	FACTOR
5	1.4	25	6.1
10	2.1	30	8.8
15	3.0	35	12.6
20	4.2	40	18.0

Annual Savings Factor Table

NUMBER OF YEARS UNTIL RETIREMENT	FACTOR	NUMBER OF YEARS UNTIL RETIREMENT	FACTOR
5	.1513	25	.0088
10	.0558	30	.0054
15	.0274	35	.0034
20	.0151	40	.0022

Explanations for the planner

(1) Resources that are currently available typically include the current value of all investment-related assets that clients do not expect to use before retirement. Do not include the value of your clients' home unless they expect to sell it to raise money for retirement. Do not include any vested pension benefits if you have already factored them in on Line 2 of Section 2.

(2) The appreciation factor helps estimate what currently available retirement resources will be worth at retirement. The appreciation factor assumes a 7.5% after-tax rate of appreciation.

(3) The annual savings factor helps compute the amount clients need to save during the next year in order to begin accumulating the retirement funds needed by retirement. The annual savings factor assumes a 7.5% after-tax rate of return.

(4) The annual savings needed to accumulate a retirement nest egg assumes that clients will save on a regular basis.

CHAPTER 5

COMPLIANCE AND LEGAL ISSUES

JUST LIKE MANY other types of professional practitioners, financial planners must adhere to a strict set of rules and regulations. Planners who advise on investment and insurance in particular must follow the various regulations that oversee those areas. Rules governing these two aspects of financial planning practice will be the primary focus of this chapter.

The securities industry is regulated at both the federal

The Investment-World Alphabet Soup

◆ **BD (or B/D):** A broker-dealer is an individual or firm that charges a fee or commission for executing buy and sell stock orders submitted by another individual or firm. The broker firm can also act as an agent for a customer and charge the customer a commission for its services.

◆ **IAR:** An investment adviser representative is any partner, officer, director, or other individual employed by or associated with an investment adviser who (1) gives investment advice or makes recommendations, (2) manages client accounts or portfolios, (3) chooses investment recommendations or advisory services, or (4) supervises employees involved in any of these activities.

◆ **NASAA:** The North American Securities Administration Association is the oldest organization devoted to investor protection. NASAA represents the voice of fifty state securities agencies responsible for grassroots investor protection and efficient capital formation. Guidelines adopted by NASAA can be adopted by individual states.

◆ **NASD:** The National Association of Securities Dealers is a membership organization subject to Securities and Exchange Commission (SEC) oversight. Its members are securities firms. It was created by an amendment to the Securities Exchange Act of 1934 to promote fair trade in the securities industry. One of the NASD's subsidiaries, NASD Regulation, Inc., regulates the securities markets for the investors' benefit. One of its duties is to ensure that member firms and their employees comply with federal and state securities laws and regulations and the NASD rules.

and state levels. These rules govern how and by whom securities can be issued, registered, sold, and traded. At the federal level, the principal acts that regulate the industry are the Securities Act of 1933 and the Securities Exchange Act of 1934, which are discussed in detail later. The basis for industry regulation at the state level is the Uniform Securities Act, which each

◆ **RIA:** A Registered Investment Advisor is a financial services industry person or firm who gives investment advice about securities and is registered with the SEC and/or state securities administrator(s).

◆ **RR:** A registered representative is an individual who has been sponsored by a registered broker-dealer to take the securities exams required by the NASD and/or state(s) that are relevant to the products the individual will be selling. Advisers who are likely to buy or sell mutual funds, variable annuities, or variable life insurance should take the Series 6 examination. Advisers who need to buy or sell securities other than mutual funds should take the Series 7 General Securities Representative Exam. Once the RR is licensed, the broker-dealer (BD) holds the RR's securities license(s) and supervises the RR to ensure compliance with the securities laws. Through the BD, the RR can buy and sell appropriate securities. An RR might be a BD's employee or an independent contractor supervised by a BD. An RR's registration is only in effect while the RR is associated with the registered BD.

◆ **SEC:** The Securities and Exchange Commission was created by an act of Congress in 1934 as an independent, quasi-judicial agency of the U.S. government. It administers laws in the securities field and protects investors and the public in securities transactions.

◆ **UPIA:** The Uniform Prudent Investors Act updated trust investment law and trustees' responsibilities in recognition of the many changes that have occurred in modern investment practice.

state may or may not adopt in its entirety.

Insurance salespeople must be licensed with the state insurance commission in each state in which they do business. If financial advisers sell or recommend investments, they must adhere to broker-dealer regulations established by the National Association of Securities Dealers (NASD). Even if they furnish only investment advice, they must follow the investment adviser regulations set at either federal or state levels, depending on the amount of assets under management. An investment adviser must be registered and licensed with the NASD or the state(s) in which the practice is located.

So how does someone know which rules to follow? This chapter explains the various organizations, tests, and state and federal regulations important to financial advisers. The scope of a practice will determine which guidelines apply for each person.

Complying with the Law

REQUIREMENTS FOR SELLING INSURANCE

To sell insurance, people must be licensed by the state(s) in which they do business. Under the McCarron Ferguson Act, individual states are responsible for their insurance-practice regulations. The states take this even more seriously since a 1994 case in which agents in Florida were found to have engaged in widespread improper sales practices. The purpose of insurance regulations is to protect the public from being misled or deceived into making unwise and potentially harmful decisions affecting their finances and well-being.

Insurance salespeople who sell life insurance, disability insurance, annuities, and health insurance must pass a "Life and Health" state license examination. Those wishing to work with securities of any type, such as variable life and variable annuities, must register with the NASD. Those who sell home owners, automobile, or liability (umbrella) insurance must take a "Property and Casualty" examination. These insurance tests are not terribly difficult in most states, but the bureaucratic process of applying to take the exam can be cumbersome, with long delays. People planning to practice outside of their home state need to comply with the other state's reciprocity arrangements. That may mean taking another exam, getting a letter of good standing from the state division of securities, taking an ethics examination, or getting bonded (insured).

Steps in the NASD Licensing Process

1 Select a broker-dealer to be your sponsor.

2 Complete form U-4 (Uniform Application for Securities Industry Regulation or Transfer). This form is similar to an employment application and states that you will adhere to securities laws and regulations. Submit it to the broker-dealer. Check off the states in which you are applying for registration.

3 Fingerprints are taken at the testing site. The broker-dealer conducts background checks.

4 The broker-dealer registers the applicant by filing the U-4 and fingerprints with the NASD.

5 The NASD approves or disapproves the application and sends the broker-dealer a status report. Conduct unworthy of an investment adviser may result in disapproval. Once you are approved, you submit the status report to schedule the appropriate tests.

6 Take the appropriate securities exams. Results from the exam are recorded electronically and immediately given to the applicant.

7 The NASD sends the sponsoring broker-dealer a bill for your state registration(s).

8 Update your U-4 as necessary to keep it accurate.

9 If you leave your sponsoring broker-dealer, the firm must file a Form U-5 (uniform termination notice for securities industry registration) with the NASD. You provide a copy of the U-5 to your next NASD employer and obtain a new Form U-4 and fingerprints for the new broker-dealer to submit to the NASD.

REQUIREMENTS FOR SELLING INVESTMENT PRODUCTS

Those who sell mutual funds, variable annuities, and variable life insurance must sit for the NASD Series 6 Examination and for state life and health insurance examinations (see above). Of all the investment examinations, the Series 6 probably requires the least preparation time. Passing the Series 6 allows you to sell very specific types of products, such as mutual funds and some variable insurance policies. To sell mutual funds, variable annuities, and variable life insurance or stocks, bonds, and options, you need to take the Series 7 exam. This examination is much more difficult, comprehensive, and time-consuming than the Series 6. The Series 7 is a six-hour examination that tests knowledge of securities definitions, compliance laws, and other factors. The NASD permits people to retake the exam as many times as they wish after waiting periods ranging from thirty days to six months, depending on how many times the applicant has failed. Large brokerages usually fire employees who fail even once.

Someone who decides to take the examination must apply to the NASD. This agency reviews the application (U-4) and the form specifying which examination that individual wants to take (U-10). In addition to passing the Series 6 or Series 7, the candidate must sit for the Series 63 examination (Uniform Securities Agent State Law Examination), commonly called the "blue sky" test, since many advisers once sold unaware consumers "the blue sky." This state licensing examination covers the laws of the practitioner's state as well as national securities industry laws. After passing the Series 63 requirement and either the Series 6 or 7 exam, a person is qualified to sell securities to the public.

REGULATIONS FOR INVESTMENT ADVISERS

Professionals using the title of investment adviser are typically financial planners, pension consultants, or sports and entertainment representatives. Investment advisers must register with their home state if they manage less than $30 million and with the SEC if they manage more than that amount. At that point, the professional becomes a Registered Investment Advisor. The definition of investment adviser is in Section 202(a)(11) of the 1940 Investment Advisers Act:

…any person who, for compensation, engages in the business of advising others, either directly or through publications or writings, as to the value of securities or as to the advisability of investing in, purchasing, or selling securities, or who, for compensation and as part of a regular business, issues or promulgates analyses or reports concerning securities…

In other words, the definition of a Registered Investment Advisor is as easy as ABC: advice, business, and compensation.

◆ **Advice** pertains to information about securities, no matter how broad. In fact, the advice need not be specific. As a result, even if you provide only general asset allocation advice about categories of securities, or even suggest that a client buy a tax-free municipal bond, you have given advice and thus meet the first test.

◆ **Business** means you are "in the business" or that it constitutes a business activity of some regularity. In addition, if you hold yourself out as being in the business, meaning that you identify yourself as one who gives investment advice, for example, on your business card, you are deemed to be in the business and thus would meet the second test.

◆ **Compensation** means that someone has to pay you for that advice. It can be satisfied through a fee, a commission, or a combination thereof. The compensation can come from any source. It does not have to come from the person directly receiving the benefit of your expertise. In fact, referral fees from third parties, financial planners, and money managers all qualify. All of these examples would thus meet the third test.

EXCEPTIONS TO THE DESIGNATION AS INVESTMENT ADVISER

There are many exceptions to the definition of investment adviser, including the following:

◆ Institutions, such as banks, savings institutions, or trust companies

◆ Professionals, such as lawyers, accountants, engineers, or teachers, whose performance of these services is solely incidental to the practice of their profession

◆ Broker-dealers who offer investment portfolio advice as part of their business of being a broker-dealer and receive no special compensation for that service

◆ Publishers and employees of any financial publications (such as newspapers and magazines) that disseminate generic investment information to the general public

◆ Persons without an office in the state whose only clients are institutions

◆ Persons without an office in the state who do not direct business communications to more than five clients (other than institutions)

◆ Any person that the state administrator of the Uniform Securities Act decides not to include

EXEMPTIONS FROM REGISTRATION

The preceding list indicates those individuals or entities falling outside the act's definition of investment adviser and outside the parameters established by the SEC. An exemption, however, excuses someone who *is* an investment adviser from the need to register. Exemptions include the following:

◆ Persons who do no business in the state

◆ Advisers with a *de minimis* exemption—having fewer than five clients in any twelve-month period or fewer than a number set by the state. Clients consist of broker-dealers, financial or institutional investors (such as banks, insurance companies, or investment companies), or other investment advisers.

Registration Procedures

QUALIFYING FOR SEC registration as an investment adviser includes applying, passing an examination, and meeting ethical guidelines.

APPLICATION

Complete the application (Form U-4, if one has not been filed, and form ADV) and pay the appropriate designated filing fee (as set by each state). The application contains the following information:

◆ Form and place of business organization

◆ Proposed method of doing business
◆ Qualifications and business history of the applicant
◆ History of injunctions
◆ Financial condition and history
◆ Client brochure

EXAMINATION

Each state has specific requirements. Most states require the Series 65 Examination (Uniform Investment Adviser Law Examination) and the Series 63 Examination (Uniform Securities Agent State Law Examination). Advisers wishing to combine both exams into a single test-taking experience can opt for the Series 66 (Uniform Combined State Law Examination) in their place. In many states, attaining CFP certification can waive the Series 65 examination. To find out whether this is the case in your state, check with your state securities division. An applicant who has passed the exam does not have the right to transact business until a license or registration is granted.

MAINTAINING ETHICAL BUSINESS PRACTICES

Investment advisers (IAs) are required to act as fiduciaries and follow strict ethical guidelines when managing people's money. These guidelines were developed by the North American Securities Administration Association (NASAA) through a Statement of Policy (SOP), which defines unethical business practices of investment advisers and addresses the following:

◆ **Suitability.** IAs are responsible for making a reasonable inquiry of the client's financial situation, investment objectives, and needs before making any recommendations.

◆ **Discretionary authority.** IAs must receive specific prior verbal or written authority before placing orders for the account.

◆ **Excessive account activity.** IAs should not frequently trade on behalf of their clients without considering client objectives, financial resources, and character.

◆ **Unauthorized trading.** IAs cannot use their own discretion to place orders for clients unless the clients grant verbal or written authority.

◆ **Unauthorized third-party trading.** To place an order given by a third party, the IA must have prior written authorization from the client. This includes husbands not being able to place orders for wives, and vice versa.

◆ **Borrowing money or securities.** No borrowing of money or securities is allowed unless the client is a broker-dealer, bank, financial institution in the business of lending money, or person affiliated with the adviser.

◆ **Lending money.** No lending of funds is allowed unless the adviser is a bank, financial institution in the business of lending money, or person affiliated with the adviser.

◆ **Misrepresentations and omissions.** IAs cannot omit or misrepresent through exaggeration, falsification, or omission the qualifications of the adviser or its employees, the nature of the services offered, or the fees to be charged.

◆ **Third-party reports or recommendations.** IAs cannot provide clients with reports or recommendations prepared by third parties without disclosure of the source unless the advisers use the information as the basis for their recommendations.

◆ **Unreasonable fees.** Unreasonable fees are unethical even if the client agrees to them in advance.

◆ **Material conflicts of interest.** Any conflicts of interest that might influence the decision of a potential client to employ the services of the IA must be disclosed to the client before entering into an advisory agreement.

◆ **Performance guarantees.** IAs cannot guarantee specific investment performance, such as making a profit or backing an investment for clients.

◆ **Advertisements.** The laws prohibit untrue statements of material fact, testimonials, references only to specific past recommendations, guarantees of future performance, offering free services without the intent to perform, and references to charts, tables, formulas, or other devices used to forecast securities prices without spelling out the difficulties or limitations in their use.

◆ **Disclosure of client information.** IAs cannot disclose client information to third parties unless required by law or with the client's consent.

◆ **Custody or possession of client funds or securities.** Client funds must be kept safely through segregation and identification by client. Funds must be deposited into trustee accounts with prior notice given to client. Itemized reports must be provided quarterly, and the account should be verified by an independent public accountant's unscheduled audit.

◆ **Investment advisory contract.** All IA contracts must be in writing and indicate the services to be provided, term of the contract, amount of advisory fee or formula used to compute the fee, how refunds are determined for prepaid fees, whether the adviser has discretionary authority, and that the client's consent is required to assign the contract.

In 1996 the National Securities Improvement Act was signed. Title III of the Act, known as the Investment Adviser Supervision Coordination Act, became effective July 8, 1997. A key feature for RIAs is that the law ended the traditional double registration requirement; thus, an RIA is no longer required to be registered with both the SEC and the state. The law allows states to continue to register investment adviser representatives when the firm already has SEC registration. However, SEC-registered RIAs are no longer subject to their home state's record-keeping, disclosure, or net capital requirements. The law also created a national *de minimis* rule of five clients and provided that only the home state's rules concerning record keeping, net capital, and bonding could be applied to state-registered advisers.

MAJOR LEGISLATION REGULATING THE SECURITIES MARKETS

Congress has passed much legislation over the years to structure the securities markets in the United States. An adviser must become familiar with the following regulations that underlie this industry and affect the development of a practice:

◆ **The Securities Act of 1933.** This act deals primarily with new issues of securities. The intent was to protect investors in new securities by requiring issuers to register an issue with full disclosure of information when it is first sold to the public. It also requires that a prospectus (a written offer to sell a security) be given to buyers. The new issue must be registered in each state in which the underwriter (firm responsible for marketing the security) sells the security. False information is subject to criminal penalties and lawsuits by purchasers to recover lost funds.

◆ **The Securities Exchange Act of 1934.** This act extended the disclosure requirements to the secondary market and established the SEC to oversee registration and disclosure requirements. The intent of this act is to maintain a fair and orderly market for the investing public. It seeks to attain this goal by requiring organized securities exchanges to register with the SEC and to agree to be governed by existing legislation. In addition, the act addresses regulation of credit through the margin requirements set by the Federal Reserve Board; registration of insider transactions, short sales, and proxies; regulation of trading activities and client accounts; and net capital requirements of broker-dealers. The registration of securities in no way ensures that investors purchasing them will not lose money. Registration means only that the issuer has made adequate disclosure.

◆ **The Maloney Act of 1936.** This act extended SEC control to over-the-counter (OTC) markets. It provides for the self-regulation of OTC dealers through the NASD, which licenses and regulates members of OTC firms.

◆ **The Trust Indenture Act of 1939.** This act specifies that any corporate bond issue of more than $5 million and with a maturity date more than nine months in the future must be issued with a trust indenture, which is an agreement between the corporate issuer and a trustee on behalf of the investors. The trust indenture contains certain promises, monitored by an independent trustee, that protect the bondholders.

◆ **The Investment Company Act of 1940.** This act requires investment companies to register with the SEC and provides a regulatory framework within which they must operate. The act regulates the issuance of investment company securities by setting standards for the organization and operation of investment companies, the pricing and public sale of the investments, and the reporting requirements. Each company must state its investment objectives in the registration statement and prospectus.

Investment companies are required to disclose considerable information and to follow procedures designed to protect their shareholders.

◆ **The Investment Advisers Act of 1940.** This act requires individuals or firms who sell investment advice to register with the SEC. Registration implies compliance with the law. See the discussion of some important amendments to this act in the next section of this chapter.

◆ **The Securities Investor Protection Act of 1970.** This act established the Securities Investor Protection Corporation (SIPC) to act as an insurance company in protecting investors from brokerage firms that fail. SIPC is a nonprofit corporation, not a government-sponsored corporation, such as the Federal Deposit Insurance Corporation (FDIC). Members include all broker-dealers registered under the Securities Exchange Act of 1934, all members of national securities exchanges, and most NASD members. Each separate customer at a broker-dealer firm is covered for a maximum of $400,000 in securities and $100,000 in cash. Commodities accounts are not covered. Customers with claims beyond $500,000 are treated as general creditors of the excess amount. Note that an investor who has several accounts in his own name at one broker-dealer firm still has a maximum coverage of $500,000, because the protection is $500,000 per separate customer, not per account. Assessments are made against brokerage firms to provide the funds, with backup government support available.

◆ **The Securities Act Amendments of 1975.** These amendments abolished fixed brokerage commissions and a movement toward a national market.

◆ **The Insider Trading and Securities Fraud Enforcement Act of 1988.** This act expanded the definition of the liabilities and penalties for the illicit use of nonpublic information. Insiders (persons who have access to nonpublic information) may be held liable for more than just transactions in their own accounts. The act recognizes the fiduciary (the person legally appointed and authorized to represent another person on his behalf) responsibility of the insider to the issuer, the stockholders, and others who might be affected by trades made with insider knowledge.

Investors who have suffered monetary damage because of insider trading have legal recourse against the insider and any other party who had control over the misuse of nonpublic information. The SEC can levy a penalty of up to the greater of $1 million or three times the amount of profit made (or loss avoided) if insider information is used. Any individual who is a corporate insider and owns securities in that corporation must file a statement of ownership with the SEC.

◆ **The Telephone Communications with the Public Act.** This act, administered by the Federal Communications Commission (FCC), was enacted to protect consumers from unwanted telephone solicitations. It requires that companies performing telemarketing services, such as cold-calling, maintain a do-not-call list, institute a written policy available on demand on maintenance procedures for the do-not-call list, train reps on use of that list, ensure that reps acknowledge and immediately record the names and telephone numbers of customers who ask not to be called again, ensure that anyone making cold calls for the firm informs the customer of the name and telephone number or address of the organization, ensure that telemarketers do not call customers on this list for ten years, and ensure they only call between 8 a.m. and 9 p.m.

WHENEVER Congress passes a new law or makes significant changes to an existing law like the Investment Advisers Act of 1940, confusion and frustrating legal, regulatory, and procedural issues usually follow. This is not a surprising or unexpected result but rather a routine occurrence, since broader and different compliance responsibilities are often created as part of the new mandate.

The SEC—the federal agency charged with the responsibility of administering the law in question—is expected to issue clarifying regulations shortly after the enactment of new legislation so that individuals who are affected by the statutory changes may learn of and better understand their new responsibilities.

SEC ADMINISTRATIVE RELEASES

In late 1996 the SEC issued two extremely comprehensive and well-drafted pronouncements known as SEC Release IA-1601 and SEC Release IA-1602. These releases addressed many unanswered questions and clarified some areas of the amendments to the Investment Advisers Act. The SEC releases made changes in the following areas:

◆ **Eligibility for SEC registration.** The SEC devised a form known as Form ADV-T that has to be filed by every RIA in the United States to determine eligibility for SEC registration after the new law went into effect July 8, 1997. The RIA is required to list the dollar amount of assets under management as of a date within ten days of filing Form ADV-T. The form also requires the RIA to declare eligibility for SEC registration. Miscellaneous categories of eligibility are set forth on Form ADV-T. (Form ADV-S has been abolished.)

◆ **Determining the amount of assets under management.** "Assets under management" are defined as the securities portfolios for which an RIA provides continuous and repeated supervisory or management services. The 1997 releases define a "securities portfolio" as any account in which at least 50 percent of the total value consists of securities. Real estate, commodities, and collectibles are not securities and would not be included when counting up assets. Cash and cash equivalents are also excluded from the computation. The securities portfolio is determined no more than ten days before the filing of Form ADV-T. The accounts must receive "continuous and regular supervisory or management services" in order to qualify in the computation of the $25 million to $30 million minimum of assets.

In a significant development in the releases, if the RIA has nondiscretionary authority, these accounts will not automatically be considered part of the total assets under management. However, the SEC will consider including accounts over which an RIA has nondiscretionary authority if the RIA provides ongoing management services. The SEC release says, "The SEC believes that a limited number of nondiscretionary advisory arrangements involve assets under management on a continuous and regular supervisory or management basis.... Whether an adviser that does not have discretionary authority will be considered to provide continuous and regular management or supervisory services with respect to an account would depend upon the nature of the adviser's responsibility."

If the RIA attempts to qualify for SEC registration by asserting that assets under nondiscretionary management exceed the $30 million threshold, a special explanation must be supplied on Form ADV-T to justify the claim of continuous and regular supervisory or management services.

◆ **Transition between state and SEC registration.** The SEC wanted to avoid on-again, off-again, on-again registering, deregistering, and re-registering by RIAs whose assets under management fluctuate over and under the $25 million limit. Proposed Rule 203A-1 would permit RIAs having between $25 million and $30 million of assets under management to determine whether and when to change from state to SEC registration.

◆ **SEC registration required for advisers not registered by their states.** Under the 1997 law, advisers who "are not regulated or required to be regulated as investment advisers" in the state in which they have their principal place of business and principal office must register with the SEC regardless of the amount of assets under management.

The regulations interpret the 1997 law to mean that any person who meets the statutory definition of an investment adviser must register with the SEC if:

—the person has a principal office and principal place of business in a state that has an investment adviser statute but does not require registration, and the person is in fact not registered under that state statute; or

—the person has a principal office and principal place of business in a state without an RIA statute (only Wyoming, as of February 2002).

◆ **Regulations for adviser representatives.** The 1997 law provides that even when an advisory firm is registered with the SEC, the states can still license, regulate, and otherwise qualify investment adviser representatives of such a firm that has a place of business within that state.

The new regulations clarify which persons providing investment advice on behalf of SEC-registered RIAs would be subject to continued state registration and qualification.

The new regulations conclude that the term investment adviser representative as used by Congress means a person who is supervised by an investment adviser and who provides a substantial amount of investment advice to clients who are "natural persons" (not groups or firms). The term would therefore exclude supervised persons who provide advice to investment companies, businesses, educational institutions, charitable institutions, and other entities that are not natural persons. Those representatives, however, would still be subject to state regulation, even though the firm itself would need to be registered only with the SEC!

◆ **National "de minimis" standard.** The 1997 regulations provide clarification of a national *de minimis* rule by explaining how to count clients for purposes of the "fewer than six clients" rule. The new regulations remind us that *client* is not defined anywhere, and the SEC tells us that it will treat as a single client a natural person and (1) any relative or spouse of the natural person sharing the same principal residence, and (2) all accounts of which such persons are the sole primary beneficiaries.

A printout of this information can be requested for no cost from Text Library System (TLS), Middletown, Ohio (800-666-1656).

State Securities Regulations

BESIDES FEDERAL regulation, each state has laws that pertain to issuing and trading securities in the secondary market. These "blue-sky laws," which were devised separately by each state, gave way to the Uniform Securities Act (USA), which serves as model legislation for any state to follow. Many of the provisions are similar to federal laws regulating investment advisers, but there are some differences, such as the penalties for breaking the law. Federal law provides for up to five years in prison and a fine of up to $10,000. State penalties are lower, at three years and $5,000. Another difference is that advisers managing more than $30 million must register with the SEC, and those managing less than $25 million must register with the state, as discussed previously. Those in between ($25 million to $30 million) have the option of registering with either. A third difference is that SEC registration is effective until it is withdrawn, but state registration expires annually on December 31.

Protecting Yourself against Liability

PROFESSIONALS providing investment and insurance planning advice need protection from unintentional negligence in their practice and possible lawsuits. Many planners do not have adequate systems in place to collect client data or appropriate training to provide key information. Not all planners are good at managing client expectations. Unfortunately, some planners jeopardize their practices when concerns for compensation begin to take precedence over a client's best interests.

If clients lose significant wealth, even though it may not be the planner's fault, they may sue and generate enough jury sympathy to win a lawsuit. Protection from mistakes and unavoidable difficulties, therefore, is important.

There are two ways you can protect yourself. The first protection is through your business format (see Chapter 2). The second protection is through purchasing an errors and omissions (E&O) insurance policy.

ERRORS AND OMISSIONS INSURANCE

Many broker-dealers enter into contractual arrangements with a property/casualty insurer for protection against their negligence or that of their registered representatives. Self-employed planners should buy coverage through an insurance company. A person who is a registered representative of a broker-dealer or an insurance or investment company can acquire E&O insurance directly from the company.

The relationship between the broker-dealer and its registered representative is that of principal and agent. The principal may be held legally responsible for the acts of its agent(s). The mechanism by which the principal obtains insurance for the negligent acts of its agents, however, is quite different for broker-dealers than it is for most other professions. Broker-dealers will sponsor a "group" insurance program, typically requiring that all of its registered representatives purchase insurance as a condition of appointment.

The broker-dealer sponsors a group E&O insurance program to be certain that its registered representatives can demonstrate financial responsibility if their mutual client presents a claim. What the broker-dealer should understand, however, is that through the act of sponsoring the insurance program, the broker-dealer becomes the insurer of last resort if the program turns out to be insufficient. In other words, the broker-dealer implicitly warrants that its sponsored insurance program is adequate.

Imagine that the worst happens: an investor claim is brought against both the registered representative and the broker-dealer. The claim is settled against the broker-dealer, but because of some features of the policy, coverage is not available to the registered representative, who then pays dearly. The registered representative in turn initiates legal action against both the insurance broker and the broker-dealer. The registered representative points out the following:

◆ that the broker-dealer required insurance program participation

◆ that it informed its registered representatives of the many features of the program not generally available with other programs

◆ that the program summary was silent on the features of the policy that resulted in the denial of coverage to the registered representative

◆ that the registered representative believed that the coverage was adequate because it was so thoroughly approved and endorsed by the broker-dealer

◆ that the registered representative actually asked about the policy long before the claim ever arose and was roundly rebuffed by the broker-dealer's compliance department

This unpleasant legal scenario illustrates that the relationship with the insurer should be one of full and unqualified disclosure so that the registered representative may make an informed decision about coverage and so that the broker-dealer is protected from litigation.

SCOPE OF COVERAGE

The prevalence of group insurance programs provided through the broker-dealer stems from a time when most, if not all, of its registered representatives were employees and had been schooled extensively in the company's in-house training programs. The registered representatives initiated securities transactions and little else. But today's world differs significantly, as does the relationship between broker-dealers and registered representatives.

The typical registered representative today is an independent contractor and engages in many activities that do not directly involve the broker-dealer. As noted previously, such activities might include financial planning; asset allocation; investment management, either with or without discretionary authority; sales of life products including life, health, and disability insurance, as well as annuities; and a variety of other services including accounting or legal services, trust services, third-party pension plan administration, and actuarial services. Although no single broker-dealer-sponsored policy could possibly encompass all of these services, a policy narrowly focused on security sales will certainly fall short of the mark. The one-size-fits-all approach implicit in the design of these group programs sows the seeds of dissatisfaction, not to mention potential liability, for the sponsoring broker-dealer as well as for the investment adviser, particularly if the program is mandatory.

PRIOR ACTS COVERAGE

Group insurance programs have been made available only while a registered representative is a member of the sponsoring group, based on the assumption that the business and insurance relationship will span a career. But reality is quite a bit different. The movement of registered representatives from one broker-dealer to another, or from a commission-based practice to a fee-only practice, is becoming increasingly commonplace. The broker-dealer-based insurance does not trail along behind as the registered representatives adjust their practices. Worse still, that coverage may not be available at all for services rendered while the agent was acting as a registered representative of the previous broker-dealer.

AVOIDING LITIGATION

"Prevention is the best cure" is an appropriate adage for any financial planner wishing to avoid litigation. While taking care of clients' well-being, advisers should make sure to take care of their own. The following four guidelines can prepare you for future trouble:

1 Document communications and disclosures. Many life insurance agents, as well as financial planners who write insurance policies for their clients, do not fully appreciate the importance of documenting disclosures made to their clients. Errors and omissions claims are frequently won and lost over the ability of an agent to convince the court that the disclosures made to the client were professionally given and, if taken to heart by the client, might have prevented the client's injury or, at the minimum, would not have contributed to the loss.

Disclosure is the communication between the client and the agent regarding the technical activity involved in selling a policy, including the duties and obligations of both the agent and the client. If a court or arbitrator feels the agent has misled the client to think the company will pay claims not covered by the policy, the agent may become first in line to pay for what the court determines was promised. The issue may be ruled upon by a sympathetic jury, judge, or arbitrator weighing the oral representations of the client against whatever documentation the agent has retained after the passage of years.

Avoiding an errors and omissions claim should be an important concern in making a sale. Honesty and integrity shine through during a court hearing. A poor memory is apparent. The courts are required by law to give the financial adviser a fair hearing. However, it is the professional adviser's duty to have the documentation available to show the court that full disclosures were given, that the client needed the coverage or approved the purchased item, and that the questions raised by the client were answered fully and truthfully. Credibility is not accorded to the professional who relies on a halting memory unaided by documentation.

There are certain points in the sales process for insurance and securities that offer an excellent opportunity for document disclosure. When the adviser makes the presentation, a cover letter can summarize the client's needs and concerns and explain how the attached presentations will address the situation. The opportunity occurs again when an application is taken and again at policy or certificate delivery.

2 Keep records for five or more years. Lawsuits against financial planners and insurance agents are harder to defend against than many other negligence claims. Attorneys do not usually file lawsuits until just before the statute of limitations runs out. According to *Best's Directory of Recommended Insurance Attorneys and Adjusters,* the limit for commencement of action for insurance contracts is four years. The statute of limitations on tort claims is only one year.

However, a written contract, such as an insurance policy sold by an agent or planner, may be extended for longer periods because of later amendments or periodic service. This allows the facts to become faded or impossible to prove. Documentation, if available, will help reconstruct the chain of circumstances involved.

3 Make sure clients know their responsibilities and understand their decisions. Litigation frequently arises out of the failure of clients to fully disclose all of their past health history, including the full health history of their dependents. In the event of a moderate to large claim, any past treatment by a doctor or hospital may be fully investigated and compared with the original application.

Any misstatement of information regarding a client's past health history (preexisting conditions) on an application for insurance coverage will allow the insurance company to void the entire insurance coverage back to the date of the original application. The company can return all premiums paid less any claims payments made on the policy. It can also bill the client for the balance of any additional money paid out over the years for claims that were not offset by the premium.

Who gets handed the bill? The insurance agent is portrayed as the bad guy because he or she did not provide the coverage that the insureds thought they were buying or thought they were promised. The financial planner is represented as the person who advised accepting risk when history proves that to have been a poor choice.

If coverage is voided by the insurance company, the courts are very likely to look to the agent to pay the claim or claims. It is very important to document that full disclosure has been made with a signed and dated statement from the client.

The financial planner's disclosure requirements extend beyond insurance to issues of risk tolerance, retirement plans, and even career choices. Because the scope of a comprehensive plan is broader, the disclosure requirements are greater. Did the client really understand the principle of diversification? Did the client understand the principle of dollar-cost averaging? Did the client understand the trade-off between placing fewer dollars in insurance and more dollars into a qualified retirement plan?

4 Protect yourself with legal verification. In addition to answers on the application, a substantial amount of litigation arises out of what clients said they were told at the time the application was taken. An attorney can help draft wording that can be written on the proposals, similar to "No other coverage has been promised or implied other than the policy as written and endorsed and further described in the company's brochures and, if requested, a specimen copy of the policy. Questions regarding coverage must be submitted in writing with the application." Similar documentation could apply to disability and medical coverage.

This focus on documenting disclosure at the time an application is taken will not eliminate the litigation nightmare. In some cases a client denied benefits may initiate a claim that is withdrawn when the agent's documentation is reviewed. Good documentation will, in the event of a suit or arbitration, give legal counsel a more defensible position. It will also be a giant step forward in helping clients receive proper coverage, because they will understand that they must be very thorough in giving answers on the application.

The court's function is to grant relief to an injured party. Unless a financial planner or insurance agent has documentation signed by the client, the court will have to interpret the intent of the parties (agent vs. client). Without documentation accepted by both parties, the courts consistently hold the agent responsible for the implied agency relationship and assign responsibility to the insurance agent to sell a policy that will pay for the damages that the client incurs.

Where the basic intent of the sales and services are not documented or are not clear, the attorneys and courts have a basic responsibility to decide in favor of the injured party. What the insurance companies do not pay is shifted to the agent.

PROFESSIONAL LIABILITY COVERAGE

Those agents who do not believe in buying errors and omissions insurance are putting their and their families' financial future on the line. Agents who say they will buy errors and omissions coverage later may run up against the provision that known occurrences are not covered by any policy. If an agent has been put on notice of a problem, he or she cannot buy insurance to cover the problem.

Insurance is no substitute for good management practices. Both are needed by today's professional agent. Defense costs alone on a complicated case can run in excess of $100,000. Good management practices will help control claims and in doing so will help keep the cost of errors and omissions insurance low.

For free material on this topic, contact Text Library System (TLS), Middletown, Ohio (800-666-1656).

SEC AUDIT PROCEDURES

Section 209 of the Investment Advisers Act of 1940 allows the Securities and Exchange Commission to conduct investigations of violations and to bring actions to enjoin such activities. In conjunction with investigations, any person who without cause fails or refuses to attend and testify or to answer any lawful inquiry or to produce books or records is guilty of a federal misdemeanor and is subject to fine, imprisonment, or both.

A recent study released by the SEC reports that since 1981 the auditing of Registered Investment Advisors has increased by an astonishing 115 percent. Despite what many may believe and despite what had been reported previously, the SEC is not decreasing its level of audits.

Text Library System (TLS) of Middletown, Ohio, provides the following information about a typical SEC audit:

◆ **Initial contact from an SEC examiner.** Surprise visits from the SEC examiner are not unheard-of. Whether announced or unannounced, when an examiner appears, he or she must show appropriate identification. The RIA or the principal for the firm must cooperate with the examiner and must show the appropriate records.

Surprise visits currently appear to be the exception to the rule, although there is no guarantee that this trend will continue. Usually, as a practical matter, the SEC examiner will phone the office of the Registered Investment Advisor a few days before the investigation will be conducted. Even with a phone call in advance, the adviser has no more than a few days of lead time to prepare for the visit.

◆ **The audit process.** The examiner has the legal right to inspect all books and records of the Registered Investment Advisor as long as they relate in some fashion to "investment advisory activities." Although the SEC auditors have a manual that they may follow, every auditor's personality is different and every auditor will use his or her own methods and procedures. For example, some examinations last a few hours, and the examiner merely looks at a few random files to be sure that the "brochure rule" has been complied with and the required copies are placed in the clients' files.

However, other audits last three or four days, while the examiner goes through all seventeen of the record-keeping steps and goes through almost every file. There is no way to predict the extent or scope of an SEC audit. However, if there have been complaints against the RIA, it is clear that the examination will be an exhaustive one.

◆ **Follow-up procedures.** Following the completion of the audit, the SEC examiner will draft a short letter highlighting the outcome of the investigation if problems or issues raised during the examination remain unresolved. This is referred to as the Deficiency Letter.

In the event that the deficiencies or infractions that have been found are relatively minor, the examiner will merely point them out to the RIA in the letter and request that the RIA advise the SEC of what steps will be taken to correct the problems.

If the problems are more numerous and/or severe, however, or if the RIA refuses within a reasonable amount of time to correct the discovered violations, regardless of how minor, the appropriate SEC regional office could institute a compliance proceeding, which could enjoin "violative activities" or place limitations on the RIA's activities. It is unlikely or rare that this would happen. However, it is possible.

◆ **Your response is required.** If you receive a Deficiency Letter you should take immediate action to correct the situation. Then write to the auditor and provide documentation of your response to each matter. That should conclude the audit.

Be certain to amend your business practices to avoid the same problem from recurring. Should you be audited in the next few years, you can be certain the auditor will have the file and will check on your continued compliance.

CHAPTER 6

BUILDING THE PRACTICE INFRASTRUCTURE

YOUR DECISION to start a financial planning practice can be the opportunity of a lifetime if you take the time to carefully plan and build the infrastructure of your business. Entrepreneurs pride themselves on the humble origins of their ventures. How often do we hear that a successful start-up began in someone's garage? Not so in financial planning. There are fundamentals the financial planner must include to build a solid business.

There is simply no substitute for a strong business foundation in professional services. You will need to address some basic questions. What image should my practice project: young and dynamic, or established and conservative? Should the practice mirror others in my region, or should it have a unique story and an organization to match? These issues and others the start-up financial planner must face are worked through in writing a business plan.

The Business Plan

THE NEED FOR A BUSINESS PLAN

Financial planners are motivated by a desire to help people achieve life goals. Like the plans they create to help others, a good business plan will enable financial planners to achieve their own life goals.

A business plan, like the scientific method, is both a process and a tool. A rigorous approach to practice planning forces the aspirant to temper enthusiasm with the harsh reality of making a living without the resources and security of a big company. The business plan forces us to think about the realism of our goals, the depth of resources we need to build the practice, and most important, the blueprint for achieving success.

The ultimate purpose of a business plan is to have a goal-oriented, smooth-functioning, and lasting business. The first step is to confirm that long-term personal goals are compatible with the entrepreneurial style of a self-employed service provider. The preparation of a business plan is somewhat like oral exams for a Ph.D. The exam itself is not as much of a challenge as the preparation. If you can get through the planning process and not get unnerved by the complexity of the task and the risk of going solo, you have a very good chance to endure the first year of practice. Thus, the business plan builds fortitude and self-confidence in addition to producing a design for your practice infrastructure.

THE DO'S AND DON'TS OF A BUSINESS PLAN

◆ **Do not use language that oversells your plan to yourself and to the reader.** Never use hyperbole: the terms *fantastic, exceptional,* *world class,* and *paradigm shift* are substitutes for sound thinking and are immediate alarms to the astute investor, partner, or employee.

◆ **Do use as few words as possible.** Anyone can write a twenty-five-page business plan, but only someone who understands the essence of the practice-to-be can explain it in five pages.

◆ **Do include numbers.** A business plan springs to life when the goals, strategies, and tactics are translated into believable numbers. Do the differentiating characteristics of the proposed practice support reasonable revenue growth and operating expense? Is the magnitude of business revenue consistent with the target population, products, and pricing? Spend some time explaining the assumptions that underlie your financial data. This is a sure way to add credibility to your calculations.

◆ **Do answer all the likely questions from investors, partners, and employees.** Often, a simple, unresolved inconsistency in a business plan can divert the reader's attention from your message. Readers' questions may include the following:

—Is your business idea unique?

—Is there a sufficient market for your specific service?

—Are your financial projections conservative yet adequate for business growth?

—Do your experience and skills match the challenges of the business plan?

ELEMENTS OF A BUSINESS PLAN

A business plan follows a logical sequence of topics from macro to micro. The largest scale issue is the marketplace and competition. The business plan starts from the market's opportunities and challenges and closes with fine detail on steps to be taken to implement the business. A business plan has the following elements.

—Executive summary: one page that explains why the business will succeed

—Company description: a profile of the financial planning practice

—Industry analysis: market trends that make the business attractive

—Target market: who will buy the business's products and services

—Competition: from whom you will take market share and why

—Marketing plan and sales strategy: the cycle beginning with prospect awareness and resulting in revenue

—Operations: where the business will be located and equipped

—Management and organization: staffing

—Long-term development and exit plan: how the practice will look at the point of maximum value

—Financial data: multiyear profit and loss (P/L) and cash flow statements

—Appendix: supporting data

◆ **Executive summary.** This is the single most important *and* most difficult part of your business plan. A reader must easily grasp the uniqueness, soundness, and potential of your business. The executive summary must not the leave the reader with doubts. It is your statement of vision, aspiration, and capability. If you cannot prepare a clear, concise, and compelling condensation of your business in one page, the reader will drag through the rest of your plan. The executive summary persuades a reader to spend time learning about you through words. State the mission of your enterprise concisely and simply. Write the executive summary after you have completed the core of your business plan. A good test of whether your business plan is clear is to have a friend or colleague read your executive summary and repeat its salient parts.

◆ **Company description.** Most business failures occur because the principal misreads the market or disconnects with customers, which illustrates a misperception of the business. The parameters of the business must be clearly defined before effective marketing can be planned. This section of the business plan states the basics: company name, management titles, business location, product and service package, fee structure, and legal form. This section should also amplify the mission into the objectives and underlying business principles of your company.

◆ **Industry analysis.** This section includes a description of the overall financial services industry. Although you will not compete with large, fully integrated investment and accounting firms, you do need to consider how these large competitors operate and how they could affect your business. Focus your thinking on the segment(s) of the industry defined by your products, services, target clients, and geography. Carefully note which of those areas could be expected to provide the most growth potential, given your capabilities. Remember that in market segments with many like competitors, entry is relatively easy, and competition is based on price. Conversely, in market segments with a few dominant competitors, entry is more difficult, and competition is based upon differentiation. You need to decide whether you are going to compete on price (and thus require a high volume of clients) or differentiation (and thus need fewer clients). In the financial services industry, with plenty of suppliers and distributors, the cost of entry is lower, which is good. But your business plan must address how you will stay in business.

◆ **Target market.** The type of customers you wish to work with will determine your overall product and service mix and thus affect your success. Moreover, if you are planning to use the business plan to secure financing, defining the nature and size of your market is a requirement. Bankers or backers want to know that there is enough market available to allow you to compete. A tighter market means more risk and more difficulty raising money. Market research may also lead you to change your thinking about advertising, packaging, location, sales structure, and even the features and benefits of your service program.

◆ **Competition.** Every business has competition. There are 250,000 people who define their work as financial planning. Seventy thousand, or 30 percent, have some type of financial planning credential. Generally, the certified planner will have an easier time attracting cold-call prospects. Practically, the credential is no guarantee of success. Respect your competitors. Do not underestimate their ability or overestimate yours. Know what the competition does well and what its weaknesses are.

Prepare a competitive table. Across the top, name the types of financial planners you will compete against (or better, the market leaders), ending with your company. Down the side, list the important competitive characteristics that differentiate them: price, reputation, professional network, experience, product/service depth, business location, and so on. Within the grid, mark the planners as high, moderate, or low competition with an *H, M,* or *L.* If your competition scores in the moderate to high range, you will need a more potent competitive profile. Play your strengths against your competitors and bolster your weaknesses.

◆ **Marketing plan and sales strategy.** Marketing is designed to increase client awareness and deliver an effective message about your service. Sales strategy, on the other hand, is the process of leveraging marketing to procure clients. Successful marketing is the key to maintaining a steady flow of new interest in your business during start-up. Referrals will take over as your primary marketing tool once you are established. Your marketing plan should define how you will make clients aware of your service and what special message you are trying to convey about yourself, your product, and your firm. Marketing does not need to be expensive or massive, but it should be focused and disciplined. A more detailed description of how to develop your marketing plan follows in Chapter 7.

◆ **Operations.** Ten percent of success comes from a great idea. Ninety percent of success comes from properly executing a great idea. The operations section of your business plan explains how you will implement your idea: the day-to-day functioning of your company. Do not assume that the most basic business activities are dull, unavoidable details. Each aspect of your business system is worthy of evaluation and improvement. Spend time preparing a basic standard operating procedures (SOP) manual. This manual should describe the specific details of the processes by which you produce, distribute, and maintain your services. Even though you may start off alone, you will not want to take the time later to write an SOP manual once employees come on board.

◆ **Management and organization.** People inside the organization ultimately determine your success. In fact, bankers and investors evaluate the business risk of a new venture based largely on the strength of the people involved. Lenders often read the management section of a business plan first. Carefully consider the people you associate with your business. Whether advisory board members, consultants, or employees, these people affect your credibility. Some prospective clients may be impressed with a large organization. However, the astute client knows that he or she is paying for your overhead, not your thinking. Create as small an organization as possible. Impress investors and prospects with fewer, better people.

◆ **Long-term development and exit plan.** What is your organization's ultimate destination? How do you want your business to look in five, seven, or ten years? This section of the business plan helps you draw the road map to your destination personally, professionally, and financially. Spell out specific terms you would like to hear when your company is judged: community spirited, best in the state, most often referred, most partners, high ethics, good value, and so on. These milestones will help keep you on track and let you measure your progress. In developing your long-range plan, make sure logical annual steps or growth events link to your end point.

◆ **Financial data.** Many times this section is the toughest for the planner. How can one realistically predict the future with the accuracy of numbers? Yet, as mentioned before, all strong business plans are definitive and measurable. Thus, you need to come up with definitive and measurable results. This exercise has two benefits. First, your assumptions about revenue (volume and price) and operating expenses and collections (accounts receivable) must fit together to yield profit and cash flow to sustain the business. A good business plan is seen in the flow of the numbers (and in the execution). Second, investors will want to hear you talk about the financial data. A good marketing plan is made stronger by an articulate financial summary.

The profit and loss statement (P/L) and sources and uses of funds statement (cash flow) will reflect the quality of decisions you have made and the impact of decisions you have laid out in your plan. For example, your product/service portfolio and pricing decisions are reflected in your revenue estimates. Your advertising mix is reflected in your cost of operations. Your compensation model and the quality of the customers you retain are reflected in your cash flow. A third financial tool you will need is a balance sheet. Your accountant (or accounting software package) is the source of your financial data.

◆ **Appendix.** The appendix should be designed to reinforce the business plan's content. Avoid giving too much detail in the body of the text. Rather, the text should state your conclusions and the reasons for them. The appendix should give the specifics, the examples, and the background data sources that support, confirm, or reinforce your conclusions throughout the business plan.

Building Your Infrastructure

ONCE YOU have completed your business plan and done a reality check with trusted colleagues, you should turn to planning the workings of the business: the infrastructure.

ESTABLISHING YOUR COMPENSATION STRUCTURE

Clients who see the need for engaging your services for personal financial planning work will not be uncomfortable paying you your worth. They know you are a professional and must be paid for your expertise. The greatest problem you may encounter is undervaluing your worth—in other words, charging too little. Remember that your clients will not come around annually and pay you the cost of a new plan. Rather, they will pay for this service up front and will visit with you on an annual basis for a periodic checkup or update. This update is minimal to the cost of the initial plan. Therefore, you must account for the importance of your meeting with the client up front.

The compensation structure selected by a planner is often a reflection of the type of practice provided. It represents an image, both professional and personal, that is portrayed to the client. It also represents the types of clients you wish to pursue. The compensation structure should be addressed when you set up your business, since you will commit to one method going forward. It is not something that changes frequently. You will revisit the issue periodically as your practice matures. But it is crucial to establish a compensation structure from the beginning that you feel comfortable with. There are no right or wrong compensation methods. The selected method must be evaluated on its merits for the type of practice you desire to run. In your review, you will find yourself favoring some methods and not others. You may also feel that some methods are more in line with your ethics than others. In any event, you must focus on what you want to achieve from your practice.

There are five methods of compensation that financial planners can use to charge their clients. They are commission only, fee only, fee based (fee and commission), fee offset, and assets under management.

1 Commission. Planners working on commission receive payment from a third party, usually an insurance or investment company. The planner's fee, of course, is bundled into the amount the client pays the third party, but the actual payment comes directly from the third-party vendor. The payment can take the form of a lump-sum payment made at the time of sale to the client or of a long-term "trailer," in which the planner is compensated every time the client makes a payment on the vendor's product. Commission payments can continue for many years. Some planners discourage this form of compensation because it can skew a planner's objectivity and independence. However, the bottom line is doing what is appropriate for the client, always and forever. Do that, and this type of payment will not present a problem.

Many planners entering the financial planning business work on a commission basis, because it is the easiest way to enter the business and probably the quickest way to earn a living. Commissions (whether alone or in combination with fees) still represent the dominant form of compensation structure in the industry. That is because its origins are in the insurance and stockbrokerage industries, in which that mode of payment has been the most common. Commissions make sense if you are providing specific product recommendations and want to see the implementation through. The payouts are large, and you can make a comfortable living from your practice.

However, clients may perceive an inherent conflict of interest, since your income stream is tied to purchases of product from you. Usually when planners have been in the business for a number of years, they feel a desire to upgrade their practices away from commissions for this reason. This task is difficult for most planners, because they must deplete their income stream—those recurring commissions—

and go cold turkey until fees are earned. This approach could take some time but may be worthwhile in the long run.

Transitioning to fees. For you to be successful in making a transition with your existing clients, they must buy into the idea of paying separately for a service that in their minds has been received for free for many years (since the commissions received by you were included as part of the payment they made to the product sponsor). This is not to say that your clients did not realize that they paid you. To the contrary, they recognized that but probably paid little attention to it, because they were not writing the check directly to you. They paid those premiums to the product sponsor, who in turn paid you some of that money. Because commissions are built into a life insurance premium or an investment product, many clients view them as a cost of doing business. Making the transition to fees separates the money paid to you and to the product company, and it can take months or even a year or two for you to make a similar income through fees.

2 Fee only. Fees are direct charges to the client. They can take one of two forms. In the first, the planner charges the client by the hour (an hourly fee arrangement). For example, planners typically charge anywhere from $100 to $400 per hour. You should provide clients with an estimate of how much time you will spend with them so that they can reasonably estimate the fee. The second type is a flat fee that depends on scope of the project (a flat-fee arrangement). For example, planners usually charge $2,000 to $5,000 for a comprehensive financial plan. The planner bases the fee on how many hours it will take to complete the assignment. If the planner determines it will take ten hours to put together a plan at $300 per hour, the flat fee is $3,000. If the plan actually takes longer than ten hours to complete, the planner should eat the difference and not underestimate the time required for the project the next time it is undertaken. Some planners prefer this method since it appears to eliminate any conflicts of interest stemming from accepting payments on product recommendations. Also, planners want to be thought of as professionals—in the same light as CPAs and attorneys, who generally have a fee-oriented practice.

How to charge for services is determined somewhat by what you do for your clients. If your services are relatively uniform for all clients, a formula fee works well. The formula can be based on any number of factors, such as client income, investment assets, or net worth. You may even base the fee on the complexity of the client's situation. The main advantage of this method is the simplicity of determining a fee and the ease of billing. The main disadvantage is that the formula can result in a fee that is grossly disproportionate to the actual cost of delivering the service. If the formula results in a fee that undercharges the client, then you can go broke. The flip side is that you could unintentionally overcharge and eventually lose a client due to the cost exceeding the value being received.

Charging by the hour works well when the services you provide vary from client to client. The primary advantage is that you have the ability to handle each of these different client situations. The primary disadvantage is the effort involved in keeping time records and the possibility that your clients may dispute a particular activity or the time recorded to complete your work for them.

Going fee-only is the trend in the profession. Because planners who practice on a fee basis feel no pressure to sell a product, they may come across to the client as being more objective. This professionalism makes them feel that they are doing a more satisfactory job for the client. However, this payment structure is not all positive.

For starters, it takes time to convert to a fee-only basis, and some planners may argue that it is tough to make a living solely on this compensation method. Another concern is that planners have little incentive to see through the implementation of the plan since they are not getting paid specifically for the follow-up. A third drawback is the possibility that the total cost of doing the planning for the client will be higher that what was initially quoted, especially if there is a commission earned by an outside party. You may quote a fee and find that it is too low. You must honor your word, however, because the client has trusted your professionalism and expects to pay a set amount.

If you provide ongoing services for a client, you may want to quote a periodic retainer. Just calculate the number of hours you think you will spend at your normal billing rate. The fact that a fee is earned for service rather than a commission eliminates an apparent conflict of interest. Your clients may come to expect fees for quality advice. This, however, is not always the case.

3 Fee and commission. A combination approach provides for you to receive both fees and commissions from the client. It is easy to double bill clients under this method. To avoid this problem, make sure that services are completely separate and charge individually for each.

The total amount of compensation you receive could be perceived as being excessive to the client, because it appears that you are paid twice for the same work: you get a fee for meeting with the client and then receive monies on the recommendations you suggested. You may view this differently, perhaps, since you are getting paid for doing two separate jobs—that is, providing a plan and receiving a commission for the implementation of an insurance or investment product. It can also make you more alert to the types of products available in the marketplace.

This double billing basically indicates that you want to be paid for everything you do. Some professionals suggest avoiding this approach since it tends to provide less value to the client and does not work well to build long-term clientele.

4 Fee-offset. A fee-offset compensation program essentially reduces the amount the client is ultimately responsible for paying to the planner by substituting commissions paid by third-party vendors for the client's direct outlay of funds. For example, if the planner charges the client $2,000 and the planner recommends an insurance product that has an $800 commission to the planner, the planner then receives only $1,200 directly from the client. The client pays the remaining $800 as a commission on the insurance policy. The planner still receives the payment to complete the work, yet the client gets a discount. This method usually provides the best of both worlds for the planner and the client. This approach is good if you want to guarantee yourself a certain dollar amount from the client. In essence, you are providing the recommendations and have included the pricing in your up-front fee, so you know how much you are making at the outset of the engagement. It works for clients, because their fee is capped and can even be reduced if they buy additional products you implement. They pay you the net amount (gross fees less commissions). The downside is that this practice may not be legal in all states. Some states consider this rebating and will not permit it. Check with your state investment and/or insurance commissioner.

5 Assets under management. This type of compensation involves receiving a payment from a client based on the assets under management or control. The planner is paid some percentage of the assets or a flat fee for directing the client's assets through several investments, usually in a long-term arrangement. Many planners charge their clients 1 percent as a management fee. If a client has $1 million invested, the planner would receive an annual management fee of $10,000. The fee is deducted from the client account at the beginning of each quarter.

You can also charge for managing your clients' assets if you like receiving a quarterly annuity from your clients. This method provides you with the most stable income stream of any of the above methods. Once you build an acceptable level, such as $10 million under management, and charge a fee for managing those assets, such as 1 percent, you can receive an income of $100,000 per year.

There is an increasing desire to move into this part of the profession because most planners believe that their clients lack the expertise to properly allocate their own investments. If clients want to reach their desired goals, such knowledge is critical. However, many planners begin to focus on this area at the expense of other vital financial planning areas. Nothing can be achieved on behalf of your clients' well-being if the insurance and cash flow arrangements are not adequately planned first; only after these infrastructures are in place would an asset management service be warranted.

However, this method does have its drawbacks. First, if your clients have a substantial amount of assets in retirement accounts or in real estate investments, these assets are outside the actively managed accounts. You must consider these assets when doing asset allocation, yet you may not be able to bill for actively managing these accounts. You may be able to get around that by charging a higher setup fee for these types of situations.

Second, if you promote return as a way to attract clients, your practice will be short-lived. That is because it is nearly impossible to outperform the market over the long term. What you need to do instead is to manage your clients' expectations effectively. Planners using this approach must provide value to clients by educating them that investing is a long-term process and not a quick fix, which basically states to the client that you can pick and choose the best investments for them and their investment goals. This provides a safe harbor from fluctuating markets and keeps the income stream intact.

Industry trend in compensation. The trend in the industry is toward compensation through fees or assets under management. Planners enjoy the responsibility of seeing their clients' assets grow. They enjoy selecting investments and taking a balanced approach to the clients' financial futures. Most planners start out with small minimum balances, such as $100,000, and increase those minimums as they obtain new clients. The problem then often becomes one of time management—how to deal with all the clients you represent. Planners can then limit whom they will accept, for example, not taking on new clients without at least $500,000 in investable assets.

These planners find it more cost-effective to bill at an hourly rate for different levels of service rather than relying on the sale of a product to cover those costs. For example, assume you work with the client and charge a base fee of $1,700. You could allocate your time to your coworkers and essentially cover their pay through client billings as shown in the box at right.

Choosing the right compensation structure for your practice. Since determining your compensation structure is so important, you may not be ready for that decision right away. You may in fact engage in some trial and error until you arrive at a method that is both comfortable for you and fair to the client. Yet choosing the right fee structure enables you to reasonably estimate how much revenue the firm will take in, which is essential for growth and expansion. You should continually revisit the issue, since economic conditions may change or your practice may take a new direction.

Itemized Breakdown of Client Invoice

2 hours of your time with the client during the interactive goal-setting and data-gathering stage @ $200	$400
6 hours of assistant's time inputting financial data @ $100	$600
2 hours of your investment adviser's time @ $150	$300
2 hours of your time with the client explaining the plan, providing recommendations, and developing an implementation plan @ $200	$400
TOTAL FEE	**$1,700**

CHOOSING YOUR LOCATION

In real estate and in business, it is often location that determines value and success. Location, though to some a seemingly superficial consideration, may be the most important aspect of any business. The right location often depends on the type of practice you want and vice versa. Will you go after high-net-worth clients? An office park might serve you well. Or will you serve more modest-income clients? Consider a local shopping mall, a converted residence zoned for business, or even your primary residence. An office in a business townhouse development can provide a homelike feel, rather than a pure business environment. It lends itself to clients stopping in unannounced to say hello or catch up on today's marketplace. Some planners view a marble floor, big office building, and plush offices as signs of being ultraprofessional. There is no right approach, other than housing your office to fit your professional approach and your personality.

BUILDING YOUR TEAM: INTERNAL STAFFING

Your practice is only as good as the people who run it. It is impossible for you to do everything required in a successful business. You need to attract, hire, and retain the best people you can afford. More simply, you cannot afford not to. If a job does not involve presenting to clients, making investment decisions, or handling significant client issues, delegate to staff members. Delegation does not indicate you are losing control of your business. In fact, it can mean you are more effectively controlling operations.

You will at least need an office manager who handles basic accounting and key administrative tasks. Next to the professional, the second most important person in a start-up is the office manager. In new or small firms, the same person can do bookkeeping and administrative tasks. For larger firms, it may be a good idea to organize staff by specialties.

You may also want to consider a paraplanner. A paraplanner operates like a paralegal. This trained assistant has completed a basic financial planning course, ideally holds a certificate in accounting, is skilled in spreadsheet preparation, and assists the planner with back-office development. The paraplanner inputs the data from the client interview worksheet, ensures that the planner has easy access to stored information, makes sure follow-up on client issues is provided in a timely fashion, and answers general questions from prospects and clients. This lets the planner concentrate on client contact and project management. The paraplanner is your right-hand person. He or she must be confident solving client issues before they become problems. For example, a paraplanner knows that when you are meeting a client for the first time, you should have all the information you need in advance. Your paraplanner should think one step ahead of you, and good ones are worth their weight in gold.

Delegation to a staff member can be performed consistently by following standardized procedures. A procedures manual (see the following section) outlining what gets done and why and who does what and when provides for uniformity within the office.

HIRING STAFF

It is very difficult to find, hire, and retain the right staff. Advertising is easy; however, predicting the success of an applicant in your business is very hard. You, like all managers, will make hiring mistakes. Your goal should be to keep errors to a minimum and learn from each hiring experience.

◆ **Searching.** Where do you look for employees? Begin by contacting the placement office at a local university or paraprofessional institution. You can get access to very recent graduates and alumni. Many placement offices have interns as well, who can perform project assignments or work part-time. Second, call your local Financial Planning Association (FPA) chapter. Many times they have planners, paraplanners, students, and others who are seeking work listed in a job bank. This is a good way to find qualified help. Third, many CFP students are looking for practical on-the-job training opportunities as well as cash for tuition and living expenses. Use the many job websites to find candidates as well.

◆ **Interview preparation.** When you interview a job candidate, you should prepare questions *and* answers in advance. It is fairly easy to determine that a candidate has the technical skills you seek. It is much more difficult to predict personal chemistry and a candidate's ability to work unsupervised while you are out selling. The following queries will help you assess a potential employee's interest and ability.

—Have you worked in a service industry before? How did you like it? What helped you to be successful?

—Why would you like to work in financial planning?

—What type of working environment do you like?

—Where do you see yourself five years from now?

—Do you like doing detail work on specific projects, or do you prefer new projects with little definition?

—Do you enjoy dealing with clients?

—Do you enjoy telephone work?

—Are you able to travel on occasional overnight assignments?

—Describe yourself in three adjectives. How do others see you?

—What kind of compensation plan are you looking for (salary, commission, bonus, or hourly)?

◆ **The interview.** The purpose of the interview is to provoke discussions on the above questions and leave room for spontaneous
exchange. Your goal is to determine whether the individual (1) has
the skills necessary to become a contributing force within the office
and (2) will fit into the office environment today and tomorrow.
You will see the people you hire for forty hours every week, so think
carefully. Many planners emphasize whether someone will fit in
over depth of experience on the theory that skills can be taught but
personality is innate. Decide what criteria you will use, and develop
your own checklist of questions and responses to ensure that you
have a basis of comparison to make the best hiring decision.

◆ **Making the decision.** Are this person's attitude and skills
relevant for the type of environment and practice you wish to
promote? After the initial screening process, bring in the most
qualified candidates for a group interview with the rest of the staff,
a consultant, or colleague with good staffing judgment. This provides a second opinion and lets the staff consider group chemistry.
Once a candidate has finished interviewing, assemble your team
and get immediate feedback. How does your current staff or colleague feel about adding this person? Weigh your staff's opinion
heavily; they will spend the most time with the new hire. For best
post-hire results make sure your staff has adequate input on the
new people who will affect their quality of work. Once you have
made your decision, draft an offer letter and mail or fax it to the
candidate. You should decide if you want the offer contingent on
references, background check, and health or drug test. Make sure
you tell all candidates up front about preemployment screening.

◆ **Office procedures manual.** An office procedures manual serves
two functions. First, it spells out exactly what your business does,
what needs to be done, and who needs to do it. Second, it serves
as a reference source for all client information. Client addresses,
phone numbers, fax numbers, and e-mail information are incorporated into the document so that if a staff member needs to
look up client information, it can be found in this single source.
The document also defines office procedures from the first time
you correspond with a client to the first office visit to the delivery
of a financial plan.

For example, if you work from referrals, once the referred prospect calls you, you send a prepackaged new client information kit. This kit contains a client data form, a color brochure, SEC form ADV, Part II (or similar NASD-required brochure defining your investment advisory practice, if pertinent), a description of the personal financial planning process, and biographical information on the firm's principals and staff. The manual describes how to make a follow-up call to a prospect to set an appointment, how to send a letter stating all the items the client should bring to the office, and how to send a payment schedule. After the client comes into the office for the preliminary interview stage (the first *P* of the PIPRIM process discussed in Chapter 3), a staff person sends an engagement letter. These procedures should be clearly spelled out in the manual so any new staff member can easily understand them and implement them with minimal assistance.

◆ **Using consultants.** Sometimes it makes sense to outsource work. In fact, the Trendsetter Barometer survey conducted by Coopers & Lybrand, LLP, shows that 83 percent of America's fastest-growing companies have turned to outsourcing for one or more functions. The benefits of outsourcing can be significant. First, it is less costly. Consultants do not receive benefits and need not be paid during slow periods. Second, a specialty consultant can help you solve immediate problems, expand your reach to prospects, and acquire new skills for the staff. Third, outsourcing can allow you to handle work overflow. If business becomes very brisk, a consultant can be the difference between accepting and declining work.

However, there can be problems with outsourcing. First, the cost of hiring a specialist is usually higher per project or per hour than that of a full-time worker. Second, consultants may not be available if you need things done in a hurry, because they are constantly looking for and working on other jobs.

◆ **Staff compensation.** How can you pay your staff competitively, promote teamwork, and reward individuals for outstanding efforts? Talented employees who are not satisfied with compensation and/or work conditions tend to perform the minimum and never get to the creative problem solving and innovation you need to grow your support organization along with your business. If you assume your office operation is simply administrative, procedural, and repetitive then you need people and compensation to match. However, if you are looking for an office team that can grow with your business plan, search for new ways to serve clients, and improve operations, then you need a different employee profile and compensation plan. The more dynamic the business plan, the more dynamic the organization and compensation plan.

Compensation thus depends largely on the type of work your employees will do. Ideally, as noted previously, you and the principals will manage face-to-face relations with clients, design financial products, and implement marketing tactics. The balance of activities will be the domain of your office staff. You will have to oversee and delegate at the same time. This delicate balance can be very difficult, if not frustrating. A shift to either end of the continuum can mean loss of control or too much control. Clear task definitions and performance standards are the best ways to insure consistency. Here are the tasks your office staff should manage:

—Computerized client information system
—Client contact program
—New client proposal preparation
—Office equipment needs assessment and maintenance
—Central calendar management
—Telephone inquiries from prospects
—Behind-the-scenes problem solving
—Implementation of direct marketing programs
—Accounts receivable

Some of the most important work your office staff will manage will be client confidential. State or federal licensing may require some information and client functions to be held confidential. However, you must decide who on your staff will have access to what information. It is much more difficult to remove access to information than to set restrictions from the beginning. Take time to consider sensitive issues in your business plan.

Compensation models should include base pay and some sort of incentive for personal excellence and business success. With this notion in mind, here are some common approaches:

—Administrative assistant: base salary of $25,000 to $35,000 and annual incentive bonus of 5 to 7 percent of base salary

—Office manager (oversees administrative assistants and part-time staff): base salary of $50,000 to $75,000 and annual incentive of 7 to 10 percent of base salary

—Salesperson: base salary of $20,000 to $25,000 and commission of 100 to 110 percent of base salary on a sliding scale linked to sales growth

—Fee-only financial planning support: base salary of $35,000 to $50,000

The compensation models you choose will depend on the profile of the staffing your business plan requires, competition for staffing, and your compensation and ability to pay. The more dynamic your compensation design, the better the quality of people you will attract and retain. Structure your plan so compensation grows with personal and business success.

DEVELOPING A BUSINESS ADVISORY BOARD

The details involved in setting up your business can occupy too much attention. You need to keep your focus on the larger issues at the same time. One of the larger and enduring issues is the implementation of your mission. It is very difficult to blend the big picture with the details of starting a professional services business. An advisory board of complementary professionals can give you what they have learned about how to balance the short term and long term. The entrepreneur will make mistakes. An advisory board will reduce the mistakes and mitigate the consequences.

Your board is a reflection of you and vice versa. Select the best people you can attract. In doing so your business plan will receive instant credibility and will improve over time. Why would top people in marketing, banking, or general management want to help you? First, not because you are a good salesperson. Quality board members do not want to be "sold" a business plan. Most often board members are dedicated friends, established businesspeople who enjoy being mentors, or people who want to add board membership to their own experience base. You do not need to compensate board members. An annual dinner, social outing, mention in a community newspaper press release, or biographical mention in a professional practice information brochure are ways to thank your board.

Your advisory board should be small enough to meet regularly but large enough to represent the disciplines you need to guide you. Seek people with recognized skills and a record of success in direct marketing, general management, financial products, and banking as a start. The above blend of professional expertise would create a board of five members including you. If possible, try to include one person who is outside your region. This will bring a more "global" perspective to your practice.

Your advisory board should meet once a month for an hour during the first year to follow the implementation of your business plan and help you anticipate problems and opportunities. Your out-of-state board member can be teleconferenced into the meetings. Another option is to alternate formal sessions with breakfast meetings to discuss immediate issues needing guidance. A subset of your board could meet to discuss marketing, collections policy, or financing. Always prepare an agenda for the board so they can think about how to help you.

At the first advisory board meeting, focus the discussion on the mission of the company and the business plan. At later meetings, select one central theme to explore and resolve. Meetings should always be close-ended, meaning an action plan has been created. In January focus on client service, February on pricing, March on alternative distribution channels, and so on. When critical issues come up, like a supplier going out of business or a new competitor in the area, call for an impromptu meeting, fax or e-mail your thoughts to the members, and solicit ideas. Your advisory board is motivated to see you succeed: do not be concerned about *over*working them, do be aware of *under*working them.

Interdependence of the Business Plan and Business Infrastructure

IF THE BUSINESS plan is the heart of your enterprise, the infrastructure is the brain, arms, and legs of your enterprise. Each depends on the other for a thriving organism. Creating the business plan forces you to think your idea through to the details. It is the blueprint you, your investors, your board, and your employees will use to measure progress. No business can succeed without a plan, because no entrepreneur can know how to react to business problems and opportunities fast enough to make the right choices. Business plans help managers anticipate and prepare for the future with logical, resource-efficient contingencies. Although you may want to surprise your competitors, you do not want to surprise your investors, clients, or accountant with unanticipated business setbacks. Prepare for the worst and work for the best.

EXHIBIT 6.1 presents a sample business plan. This simple plan provides a model or starting point for preparing your mission and strategy and for what to include in the plan (see pages 206–213).

Following the body of the plan, the appendix will include supporting information; market research citation; assumptions about economic and population trends; calculations used in your income statement, such as revenue growth; and so on. The appendix should include new information unrelated to the business plan. Rather, it should clarify, support, or reinforce the arguments and statements you make in your business plan. Detailed information about shareholders, advisory board members, and employees should also be included here. You may elect to explain the rationale for your business strategies, previously summarized in the plan, and explain why alternative approaches were evaluated and rejected. This shows the reader, and most important, potential investors, that you openly and competently evaluated your business plan. However, do not depend on your appendix to explain your business plan. Many astute investors will try to make a "no" judgment after the first page and reserve "yes" until they have analyzed the entire plan, interviewed the principals, and checked the numbers.

EXHIBIT 6.1

Financial Planning Company Business Plan

EXECUTIVE SUMMARY

◆ **Company description.** Financial Planning Company (FPC) is a Colorado-based company providing fee-based financial planning services to individuals. Sixty percent of the firm's stock is owned by Brian Jones and 40 percent of the company's stock is owned by Nancy Mandone.

◆ **Mission statement.** FPC's mission is to provide fee-based financial planning services to individuals with incomes between $50,000 and $100,000. The firms will generate income from financial products provided to clients and from financial information service subscriptions over the Internet.

◆ **Products and services.** FPC provides fee-based comprehensive and modular financial planning services for middle-income clients. Hourly fees of $150 are billed to clients. Financial plans generally take twelve hours to complete. FPC is also licensed to receive insurance and securities commissions from sales of recommended products.

◆ **Target markets.** FPC will target the Greater Denver metropolitan area. Metro Denver has a population base of over 2.3 million persons of which 50 percent are in the $50,000 to $100,000 income range.

◆ **Marketing and sales strategy.** FPC will differentiate itself from other financial planning firms by educating its client base to become more aware of financial planning issues and by providing added value information services.

◆ **Competitors and market distribution.** There are sixty providers of fee-based financial planning services in the Denver metropolitan area. Thirty are solo practices, ten are multiple-partner single-location practices, and ten are multiple-location firms.

◆ **Competitive advantages and distinctions.** FPC's major competitive advantage is its ongoing educational approach. By educating prospects to make the right choice in financial strategies and financial assistance, FPC will attract a higher quality clientele with long-term relationship potential. FPC will be the first firm to offer an interactive website that allows prospects to assess their readiness for financial assistance, and presells FPC's solutions. In addition, the firm intends to expand its practice locations to provide "neighborly" service compared to the "downtown" image of competitors.

◆ **Management.** President Brian Jones has been a practicing financial planner for more than fifteen years. He specializes in working with middle-income families and their concerns.

◆ **Operations.** FPC conducts business at 123 Jefferson Street, Denver, Colorado.

◆ **Financials.** Annual revenue projections for the current year are $250,000. In 2006, we expect revenue to surpass $350,000. In 2007, we expect revenue to exceed $500,000.

◆ **Long-term goals.** FPC's long-term goals are to open an office in Colorado Springs in 2006, Fort Collins in 2007, Greeley in 2008, and Phoenix in 2009. Each location will be managed by an equity partner.

◆ **Funding and exit strategy.** FPC will require initial capitalization of $170,000 for year one. These operating funds will be attained through commercial notes secured by the principal's assets. The owners of FPC expect to sell 70 percent of their equity to new partners by 2010.

COMPANY DESCRIPTION

◆ **Company mission.** FPC's mission is to be the leading "neighborhood" fee-based financial planning service for middle-income clients earning $50,000 to $100,000.

◆ **Services.** FPC provides comprehensive and modular planning services for a flat fee. When appropriate, the firm may also recommend and sell various investment and insurance products. FPC will retain an ongoing relationship with clients, with whom FPC will meet at least once a year. The firm will also perform hourly financial planning services for clients with specific and immediate financial needs. FPC will also offer an affordable, value-added financial services newsletter, free to clients and subscription to the general public. The newsletter will be printed as well as an Internet product.

◆ **Legal status.** FPC is a Colorado-based company providing fee-based financial planning services to individuals. Sixty percent of the company's stock is owned by Brian Jones and 40 percent of the company's stock is owned by Nancy Mandone, a nonoperating partner. FPC is a Subchapter S corporation.

INDUSTRY ANALYSIS

FPC will be well positioned to take advantage of the significant opportunities presented by the intergenerational transfer of wealth. With $6 trillion dollars expected to change hands over the next ten years, FPC sees the need for retirement and estate planning services for people who may be intimidated by financial planning or may think such services are not affordable. FPC has not seen other fee-based financial planning firms taking the education-first approach toward working with neighborhood communities.

◆ **Barriers to entry.** Many planners in the Denver market are selling the same products and services, competing on a price basis with high center-city overhead. The "commoditization" of the market could mean confused and underserved consumers, intense price competition, and shrinking margins. Consumers are likely to want more service from their advisers rather than the same service at a lower price. FPC's strategy will be to attract prospects with an educational approach to personal financial management and to retain clients with complementary financial information giving helpful hints to increase buying power.

◆ **Current environment.** The current environment supports the need for additional fee-based financial planners entering this marketplace. With 130 million households in the United States and approximately 100,000 licensed or registered financial planners, the ratio of targets to planners is 1,300 to 1. Thus, the market is far from saturated. Assuming the Denver market reflects national demographics, there are many consumers who will need FPC's help. Focusing on the vast middle- to upper-middle-income market, FPC will have a growing market to tap.

◆ **Long-term opportunities.** Short- and long-term growth potential for FPC appears very positive. We expect that consumers will recognize the value and accept the additional expense of working with licensed financial planners and will respond to FPC's educational approach to promoting the importance and ease of professional assistance.

TARGET MARKET

FPC will target households in the Greater Denver metropolitan area that fit the following profile:
—Head of household age: thirty-five to sixty
—Income range: $50,000 to $100,000
—Occupation: small business owners, professionals, salespeople
—Location: Metro Denver
—Socially and environmentally responsive
—Family and generationally oriented
—Internet capable

COMPETITION

FPC's primary competitors include the following fee-based financial planning firms:
—PTH Financial: 1998 start-up, one downtown office, investment-services focus
—Denver Planning Associates: 1985, suburban location, bilingual, retirement-planning focus
—CKP Services: 1973, two locations downtown, full service, well regarded, not marketing
—Johnson Financial Planning: 1997, one suburban location, full service, multigeneration focused
—Aspen Planning: 1991, affiliated with Aspen Real Estate Associates, investment-planning focus

FPC recognizes the strengths, weaknesses, and resiliency of these major competitors. The firm does not intend to target their current customer base but rather pursue the untapped market of consumers who have resisted, overlooked, or shied away from professional services. FPC intends to educate its clients to select appropriate investments to meet long-term goals and objectives.

◆ **Market share.** None of the competitors listed above has significant market share. This is due to the large number of fee-based financial planning firms in the marketplace.

◆ **Competitor strengths.** FPC's major competitors have excelled in the following areas:

—A total of twelve salespeople soliciting prospects. No single firm has more than three salespeople.

—Several firms have affiliations with local accounting, legal, and investment firms. These relationships provide clients with ready access to complementary professional services.

—Several owners are prominent in local environmental issues, school boards, and community service. These commitments add credibility and access to new targets.

◆ **Competitor weaknesses.** FPC's major competitors have neglected the following opportunities:

—The Internet: No firm uses the Internet for interactive communication with prospects or clients, although several have websites.

—Community focus: The more established firms promote their upscale, downtown location, which attracts high-income prospects but ignores the needs of middle-income individuals and families.

—Pricing: Most competitors follow the same pricing scheme, offering free initial consultations, various forms of money-back guarantees, and referral incentives. This motivates prospects to think price, not value. Although FPC recognizes the attraction of price, the firm will strive to attract fewer but more loyal clients with long-term family needs.

MARKETING PLAN AND SALES STRATEGY

FPC intends to attract prospects and retain clients through the following marketing and sales approaches:

—Press releases: Business founding and advisory board formation, community events, staffing appointments, and promotions

—Brochures: Professional services brochures, special topic literature

—Consumer events: Shopping center openings, community social events, seniors' events, civic group meetings

—Direct mail

—Newspaper advertising and articles in special supplements (retirement planning, education planning, and estate planning)

—Internet: Interactive website allowing prospects to answer a ten-question financial profile, ask a "wizard" questions about financial planning, and communicate directly with the firm via e-mail

OPERATIONS

FPC operates from 123 Jefferson Street, Denver, Colorado. FPC also maintains an electronic location at its Web-based customer training center. This virtual center makes it easy for clients to access our financial information and services products from home. We believe the Internet offers prospects a low-risk method requiring low commitment to learn about financial planning and FPC. Further, the training center lets prospects and clients pose questions to FPC professionals in a chat-room environment.

MANAGEMENT AND ORGANIZATION

FPC President Brian Jones has been a practicing financial planner for more than fifteen years. He specializes in working with middle-income families and their concerns. He is a graduate of Hofstra University and is a CPA. FPC intends to hire an office manager in year one and a salesperson in year two and build a clientele in target suburban locations.

LONG-TERM DEVELOPMENT AND EXIT STRATEGY

FPC will grow steadily over the next five years. By 2010, FPC plans to have a 5 percent market share of families with incomes between $50,000 and $100,000 who today are not using professional planning services.

◆ **Strategy for achieving goals.** FPC will consider accepting partners in the Denver area and selling franchises in particular locations in the United States with demographics similar to those of the Denver area.

◆ **Risks.** The greatest risks of expansion are the chance of diluting FPC common stock and the fixed costs associated with increasing the number of FPC offices.

Income Statement

FINANCIAL DATA	2005	2006	2007
Gross revenue	$250,000	$350,000	$500,000
Operating expenses			
Salaries and wages	$100,000	$140,000	$200,000
Employee benefits	$10,000	$14,000	$20,000
Payroll taxes	$15,000	$21,000	$30,000
Professional services	$2,000	$2,500	$3,000
Rent	$12,000	$12,600	$13,200
Web development	$2,000	$2,500	$3,000
Depreciation	$1,500	$1,800	$2,100
Insurance	$2,000	$2,200	$2,400
Utilities	$4,000	$4,400	$4,800
Office supplies	$500	$630	$700
Marketing	$5,000	$5,500	$6,000
Travel/entertainment	$5,000	$5,800	$6,600
Bad debts provision	$2,500	$3,500	$5,000
Total	$161,500	$216,430	$296,800
Net income			
before taxes	$88,500	$133,570	$203,200
Provision for			
income taxes	$17,700	$26,714	$40,640
NET INCOME	**$70,800**	**$106,856**	**$162,560**

Balance Sheet

CURRENT ASSETS

Cash	$30,000
Accounts receivable	$10,000
Prepaid expenses	$5,000
Total	**$45,000**

FIXED ASSETS

Building	$250,000
Equipment	$50,000
Furniture	$60,000
Total	**$360,000**
Total assets	**$405,000**

LIABILITIES

Accounts payable	$25,000
Accrued payroll	$15,000
Taxes payable	$5,000
Short-term notes payable	$20,000
Long-term notes payable	$150,000
Total liabilities	**$215,000**
Shareholders' equity	**$10,000**
Retained earnings	**$180,000**
TOTAL LIABILITIES AND OWNERS' EQUITY	**$405,000**

CHAPTER 7

MARKETING YOUR PRACTICE

The Nature of Marketing and Sales

IN THE PREVIOUS chapter you saw how to prepare a business plan and build a practice infrastructure. In short, you were introduced to *spending* money to get your business going. In this chapter, the art of *making* money is introduced: marketing and sales. Making money the right way is an art. Almost anyone can advertise, put a sign on the front door, and start a business.

Marketing and sales is the process of attracting the right customers with the right message and the right products and services. The proof of marketing success is client growth and retention. How are these measured?

◆ **Increasing prices.** Have you been successful in increasing your prices for the same product or service over time? If so, this means you have provided more value to customers for the same products and services than your competitors have.

◆ **Increasing margin per client.** Are you leveraging your marketing investment in new clients such that it costs less over time to attract and retain customers? If so, this means you have used an effective mix of marketing tools to get your message across to the right customers.

◆ **Increasing referrals.** Are you getting an increasing number of unsolicited inquiries about your firm? While you cannot be sure that new inquiries come from satisfied customers or are driven by advertising, you will know something is wrong if no one calls. You should have your front-office staff track new inquiries carefully and note call rates before and after promotional events. If the incoming call rate is increasing each month and positive blips occur around the time of a promotional event—usually within thirty to sixty days—then you are getting the combined benefit of word of mouth and marketing.

◆ **Increasing retention.** One can argue that client retention is a function of the quality, value, and ongoing care you provide to your clients. However, client retention is also a function of your ability to design and communicate new products and services. The speed with which new products and services are adopted by clients is a measure of your marketing acumen.

What Is a Marketing Plan?

MARKETING IS the process of finding and creating customers for your products and services. Sales is the process of transforming an interested prospect into a committed client. Your marketing plan is a written document that describes your targets, your message, the ways you plan to communicate your message, the costs involved, and the expected results. In essence, a marketing plan is a road map that helps you figure out the best way to reach your clientele. It helps you to understand your business thoroughly by requiring you to think and write about how to differentiate your services. If your message is not clear and different from the competition, no amount of hard work will yield increasing prices, margin per client, referrals, and retention.

A marketing plan should be easy to comprehend, easy to follow, and based on a logical sequence of steps. Almost anyone—prospect or friend—should be able to understand, recite, and follow your plan. Ask your advisory board to add a professional touch to any rough edges or to mention opportunities you may have overlooked.

Elements of a Marketing Plan

YOUR MARKETING plan will be a subsection of your overall business plan (see Chapter 6). Use the following basic elements to organize your thinking on marketing your start-up professional financial planning practice.

◆ Executive summary
◆ Market analysis and objectives
◆ Developing marketing targets: attracting prospects, turning prospects into clients, retaining clients, building referrals, and niche positioning
◆ Developing marketing tactics: understanding the four Ps
◆ Creating strategic alliances
◆ Marketing budget
◆ Action plan
◆ Auditing the results: quantitative methods (keeping a scorecard) and qualitative methods (client satisfaction survey)

Executive Summary

THE PURPOSE of the executive summary here is the same as in the business plan. It provides the reader a succinct, cohesive overview of the rationale, tactics, cost, and expected results of the marketing plan. As with the executive summary of your business plan, the opening section of your marketing plan must convince the reader of the logic and probability of the marketing plan. The reader will not go further into the plan if the executive summary does not hold together. Here are the common pitfalls of an executive summary:

◆ **Market opportunity is too narrow to build a business or too large to effectively compete.** For example, providing mutual fund investment consulting is too narrow as well as being adequately served by other professions.

◆ **Target market is too vague, too large, or too small.** A description of a target audience of consumers " in need," or consumers with gross incomes over $50,000, or consumers with disposable incomes of 15 percent to 20 percent of gross, is ill-defined.

◆ **Market messages are too loud.** There is a tendency to overwhelm the marketplace with noise rather than message. People tune out noise—aimless slogan marketing—and tune in crisp messages that align with real consumer needs.

◆ **Marketing tactics are grandiose.** It is very easy for an entrepreneur to feel so strongly about his or her business idea that emotion overrules marketing spending. Take, for example, the majority of dot-com companies in the late 1990s. Many of these companies billed themselves as having great potential—only to realize losses into the early 2000s. Ultimately, many ended up going out of business. The lesson here is not to make big promises early on; they may not pan out.

◆ **Marketing results are not measurable.** Ask a marketing manager to design a method to measure results, and you often hear groans and complaints. It is easy to get lulled by the hype and forget that marketing competes for company resources like any other investment. Return-on-investment analysis (ROI) is just as necessary for marketing as it is for adding another planner to your staff.

As suggested in Chapter 6 in reference to the business plan, write the marketing executive summary after the rest of the plan has been completed. You will maintain a better overall perspective after having defined the details.

Market Analysis and Objectives

ANALYZING THE market and setting objectives make up one of two core sections in your marketing plan, the other being determining your marketing tactics. In this section, you describe very simply why your company should exist. What is the market opportunity that current suppliers of financial planning services have failed to satisfy? What business do you want to be in? For example, a colleague in the clinical laboratory business has pointed out that his business is not running diagnostic tests on blood and urine samples. His business is providing medical information to improve patient quality of life.

Your mission statement is the starting point for marketing. It should describe why your organization will exist—what purpose it will serve. Later in your marketing plan you will take the next step and explain how your firm will fill this void permanently and profitably.

How do you conduct market analysis and arrive at marketing objectives for your practice? The first step is to do a needs assessment. Within your mission, what are the needs in the marketplace, both satisfied and unsatisfied? Make a list of financial planning needs of major consumer groups that are adequately satisfied with high-quality service and at a fair price in your region. These are the areas you will want to avoid initially. Why go after satisfied customers when there are so many that are not satisfied? Now make a second list of consumers whose needs you believe are not being satisfied. Who are these people, and what do they want? How do you find out? Ask your colleagues in allied professions: law and accounting. Look for articles and syndicated columns on personal finance in newspapers and magazines. Listen to radio talk shows. The more homework you do, the more tightly defined your market analysis will be.

Next, how do you quantify unsatisfied needs? This means determining how many people in your geographic capture area have the financial planning needs you have identified. This task is very difficult and unscientific. First you need to develop a demographic profile of your capture area. Your capture area is defined as the region or regions you plan to serve. This may be determined by a distance from your office—for example, within a 100-mile radius. It may include municipalities or communities that surround your office, perhaps ten areas you know. Starting with a rough map of your territory, you need to find out how many people live in the capture area and what percentage of these people might have the unsatisfied needs you have identified. Your local reference librarian can help you with census information. Also, try one of the Internet search engines to research demographics. Your state department of human resources, which typically gathers demographic information, may have a website.

Once you have an estimate of the people living in your capture area, how many could be interested in fulfilling the unsatisfied financial planning needs you have targeted? This is where any notion of scientific inquiry ends. You simply will not know until you start to ask. However, it is possible to sketch the population you are trying to reach. If your needs assessment suggests that people have sophisticated and multifaceted financial planning needs, then education level and income may be relevant markers to measure. If your needs assessment suggests an opportunity for working with medium-income families who do not have a financial adviser, look at areas where there are no brokerage firms, community newspapers do not carry advertisements for CPAs, and savings and loan associations are common. These areas are likely to be populated with a higher concentration of people meeting your income and education profile. But how many of these people will want the unique services you think will fill a void?

In Chapter 6 it was estimated that there are some 1,300 families to every financial planner in the United States. If this suggests an underserved national market, then your capture area should have about the same ratio. If there are ten major competitors in your capture area (defined by specific demographics and geography), you would all share a market potential of 13,000 families to be consistent with the national ratio. Since you are not national, how many families are there statistically in your capture area? Assume your library work leads to an estimate of about the same number in your local market. Then your capture area is underserved as well. How many of these 13,000 families do you need to win in year one to fulfill your business plan? (Note: 13,000 families would be about 45,500 people, the population of a medium-sized suburban town or community.) Here, you work backwards from your revenue goals. In your business plan you have already assumed a revenue goal for year one. This was logically based on an estimate of the number of prospects you can turn into clients times an average fee per client. If you assumed one hundred clients in year one, what percentage penetration of the total capture area would that be? This would equal less than 1 percent of the market (100/13,000 = .008). In general, you should estimate no more than 1 percent market penetration no matter how unique your product or service or how clever your marketing plan. One percent of 13,000 families is one hundred thirty available customers, and that would leave you room to increase your business. Fewer available families would mean more competition, pressure for higher differentiation, and more expensive marketing.

Remember, this long calculation is based on many assumptions and is only a starting point, a rough estimate. You would be wise to visit the communities you plan to serve to hand out a short and simple prestamped survey to quantify local needs. Look for signs of unsatisfied need in local newspaper articles, ask friends and colleagues, listen to the radio—in other words, keep your market research radar operating all the time.

What About the Competition?

THE MARKET analysis above assumes a static competitive environment. Do not expect the established competitors to welcome you to their market. The best way to solidify your market research estimates is to do a SWOT analysis.

SWOT ANALYSIS

Assessing your strengths, weaknesses, opportunities, and threats is a method to determine how your company (defined by your business plan) is likely to fare against competition. The goal is to predict where your company will excel and where you may have trouble competing.

A list of comparative strengths will help you plan a differentiation strategy, while a list of weaknesses shows you where you may have to make adjustments and investments in strategy. A list of competitive threats and opportunities may help you predict how and when your competitors will respond to your entering the market. Look at the top three or four competitors' strengths, weaknesses, opportunities, and threats, and have a contingency plan ready in case they decide to outmarket you. The size of your capture market is directly related to the degree of advantage your competitors allow. Strike early.

EXHIBIT 7.1 (see pages 239–240) is an example of a SWOT analysis for Financial Planning Company (FPC). The management of FPC would use this SWOT analysis to build a contingency marketing plan to respond to competitive threats and opportunities as they may emerge in the future. In your own marketing planning, if you feel the probability of a competitive action to be extremely high, do not wait; take preemptive action. In the case of FPC, the owners should launch their Internet site but have second- and third-generation technology ready to implement by the end of year one.

Marketing Objectives

YOUR MARKETING objectives define the strategy and tactics you will follow to create demand for your products and services. This demand will result, ideally, in the revenue growth numbers in your business plan. Marketing objectives should be organized in the following three categories: (1) marketing outcomes, (2) targets, and (3) communication tactics.

Setting marketing objectives for your firm is analogous to helping your clients establish their financial objectives through PIPRIM, as presented in Chapter 3. Use the same process to think through your marketing objectives.

EXAMPLES OF MARKETING-OUTCOME OBJECTIVES FOR FPC
◆ Reach 50 percent of the capture population with an impression of FPC as the community financial planning service for East Denver–area families by the end of year one (assume 50,000 families x .5 = 25,000 families).

◆ Motivate 10 percent of the families reached by FPC's marketing message to inquire about financial planning services by the end of year one (25,000 families x .10 = 2,500 families).

◆ Convert 5 percent of inquiries into clients by the end of year one (2,500 families x .05 = 125 families).

EXAMPLES OF TARGET OBJECTIVES FOR FPC

◆ Build a demographic profile of three communities in East Denver by the end of the second month of year one.

◆ Prepare a list of 25,000 families within the three East Denver communities by the end of the third month of year one.

◆ Schedule a public financial planning presentation in each of the three target communities in the first six months of year one.

EXAMPLES OF COMMUNICATION OBJECTIVES FOR FPC

◆ Prepare a cover letter and professional brochure to promote the community financial services message to middle-income families who have no experience with professional planners. Complete mailing by fourth month of year one.

◆ Interview and hire a freelance Web designer to set up a first-generation website with e-mail question-and-answer capability by the end of the third month of year one. Complete the design for second- and third-generation websites by the ninth month of year one.

Developing Marketing Targets

WHO ARE the target audiences you are trying to reach, convert, and retain? What message are you trying to communicate to these target groups? In general, there are four categories of people you want to reach: prospects, inquirers, existing clients, and referrals.

PROSPECTS

Prospects are, by definition, consumers who do not know that you exist and may not think they need planning products and services. This group is the faceless public. You know they are out there, but you cannot distinguish them. Promoting your firm to this group is classic shotgun marketing. It requires a very general message, stated in common and unintimidating words. Here are four simple rules on how you can attract prospects.

1 Position yourself as a specialist. You cannot be all things to all people. It is virtually impossible to keep up-to-date in all planning areas. You are destined to become a specialist. Get very good at one aspect of financial planning and make yourself known as the firm that specializes. There is more demand for an adviser who is the best on a specific topic—such as retirement, investments, insurance, or income tax—than for a generalist who gives up high-margin business to a specialist. Consider the planner who enjoys working with seniors. Seniors have wealth, have the time to get involved, and know many other people with similar financial needs. One planner decided to dedicate his practice to clients fifty years old and over who are AARP members. He then immersed himself in the issues concerning older adults: Social Security, Medicare, Medicaid, early retirement options, estate-planning matters, health insurance, fear of aging, and other issues affecting quality of life. He is now an expert on the needs of this special group and is in high demand for speaking engagements. He is known among seniors in his capture area as the first call to make for help.

2 Differentiate yourself from your competition. Make sure consumers see your services as different from those of competitors. Positioning yourself as a specialist will help to do this. So will taking an inventory of opinion in your capture area. Ask people the following questions:

—What would make you visit a financial planner?

—Do you believe a financial planner can assist you?

—What would motivate you to place your finances in the hands of a professional planner?

3 Package your services to meet the specific needs of your target market. You may decide to bundle your services in a way that encompasses all the primary needs of your chosen market. For example, if you provide a comprehensive financial plan, income tax return preparation, and money management services all for one price, that might attract more clients. Most consumers appreciate one-stop shopping, including for financial services. You can still price your services individually for clients who wish to purchase them separately.

4 Reevaluate your position regularly. Never be satisfied with where you are professionally. Complacent advisers do not expand their businesses or change with the times. Imagine if General Electric never made anything but washing machines, or IBM never expanded beyond the mainframe computer. Merrill Lynch is challenging its traditional broker distribution system by employing the Internet to transact customer business. Along with your clients, you, too, will need to change with the times.

ONCE YOU KNOW what you want to say to prospects, consider how you are going to reach them. Direct mail and seminars are two cost-effective methods.

◆ **Reaching prospects with direct mail.** There are so many people in the prospect category that you are forced to blanket a community with a single message and hope enough people will be attentive. Direct mail, the most common prospecting tool, usually generates a 3 percent to 5 percent response rate. You can maximize your response rate by adhering to a few simple principles:

—Deliver one message and repeat it often.

—Make the reader feel competent, not stupid, about taking action.

—Use pictures of friendly people helping friendly people.

—Use color in the text to amplify your key point.

—Deliver your message in less than one minute of reading time.

—Make it easy for the reader to respond: include a tear-off card or an 800 number.

—Ask the reader to pass the information on to a friend or family member.

◆ **Reaching prospects with seminars.** Seminars are presentations made to a group of prospects who have similar interests and needs. These workshops can vary in length from fifteen minutes to eight hours and can come in a variety of formats, from live presentations to audio/phone teleconferences. Seminars are successful if they generate appointments from participants who want to find out more about the topic. Seminars are also successful if they help you build a trusting relationship with prospects, some of whom will get to know you and a few of whom will seek your services. Those trusting relationships also give rise to referrals (as explained below), the ultimate revenue ticket.

Seminar participants should experience comfort, understanding, respect, emotional uplift, and the desire to change.

Comfort. Do the participants like you? Are they threatened by what you have to say and therefore feel uncomfortable? If so, they may never come to trust you enough to become clients. People generally do business with people they like and admire. Creating a comfortable connection should be your top seminar priority.

Understanding. Do the prospects really understand your message without distortion or confusion? Did you make it clear and fun? Did you demystify the topic?

Respect. Help prospective clients see that you are a confident, knowledgeable planner and can help them in their financial lives.

Emotional uplift. Effective seminar leaders hit a positive chord with participants, leading them to feel slightly dissatisfied with their current financial strategies. You do not want them to feel guilty or hopeless, but you need to help them realize that there may be a better way to preserve wealth. If they leave your seminar still unchallenged intellectually and emotionally, they have no incentive to call you.

Desire to change. You want seminar participants to act as quickly as possible. You must outline an action plan for your audience. They will follow it if they become motivated to act. Demonstrate your expertise and ability to make things happen by showing them you can help them. For them to be successful, they must step out of their comfort zone and risk change.

Below is a simple checklist for effective financial planning seminars:

—Educate, do not sell. Product pushers turn off an audience.

—Interact with the audience. Get your audience involved—the more, the better.

—Keep it simple; use terms everyone can understand. Keep concepts at the lowest common denominator.

—Use analogies familiar to your audience. Discuss stories the audience can relate to, especially if it is an industry trade group, such as doctors.

—Show up early, stay late. Give the participants a chance to talk with you before and after the meeting. They may even ask you to cover a specific topic that is important to that group.

—Use evaluation forms. Learn from your seminar participants. Find out what you are doing right and wrong. Make changes in your content and style. Aim for perfection with 100 percent inquiry.

INQUIRERS

Inquirers are the prospects you have successfully motivated with your message. These people probably know they should do better financial planning but are uncomfortable facing the future, mistrust "salesmen," or think they have too little money to plan with. If someone calls you, for whatever reason, the inquirer has decided to take action. Be impressed with the significance of this decision and handle the inquirer with patience and understanding. When the inquirer calls, whether motivated by direct mail or an article about you in the local paper, have your team ready to deliver a tight script. Emphasize the "privilege" of talking to the inquirer, that his or her concerns are common, and that you or other principals have experience in helping people in the same situation. The challenge is to get the inquirer to take the next step and come in to your office for the preliminary meeting discussed in the PIPRIM client management system. As a general principle, attempt to make contact with prospects six times before moving on. These contacts might consist of a follow-up letter, a seminar invitation, a newsletter, a phone call, an audiotape, or even a questionnaire.

The task of turning inquirers into clients is handled in depth in the PIPRIM process described in Chapter 3.

EXISTING CLIENTS

Existing clients make up your exclusive human-asset base. Your goal is to retain this valuable asset. Remember that your client base is a huge investment in time and money and is the easiest target for price-gouging competitors. There are three goals to keep in mind with your existing client base: (1) keeping clients happy, (2) selling them more products and services, and (3) encouraging referrals.

The issue of client communication is covered extensively in Chapter 8. At a minimum you should make an "impression" (direct contact) with each client at least three times per year. This could include one or two telephone calls, sending the client an article about your firm in the local newspaper, and a personal meeting, if only for coffee. Your task is to make the client feel important but not used. Make sure your clients have no reason, least of all price, to switch planners. You must teach your clients that value is the measure of a financial planner. Always deliver more than your client expects and you will create an impermeable barrier to competition. Happy clients are open to new financial solutions, so do not hesitate to bring new ideas to their attention. They expect it. Finally, let your clients know that you would be grateful for referrals. They expect this, too. You need not offer an overt "payoff" for referrals, but make it fun for your clients. If you can afford it, put each referring client's name into a drawing for a complimentary (be sure to use that word, not "free") dinner, gift certificate, or donation to a favorite charity or civic group. Keep the incentive upscale and clients will feel delighted, not pressured, to help you.

Like stocks in a portfolio, not all clients are worth keeping. High-maintenance clients who generate little revenue are unprofitable. You need to separate your clients into categories A, B, and C. Your A clients are those who believe in you, consistently respond to new ideas, and have income growth potential. B clients are loyal but have less inclination to try new ideas and have some income potential. C clients are long shots. They may have long-term potential, but they are slow to act and generate little income. Your C client list needs constant churning. Use the "up or out" method to move clients. If a C client fails to move up to a B in a year, then move the client out. Cultivate your As and the top half of your Bs. Keep your cost of servicing low by working hard to build a small, loyal, and growth-oriented clientele.

REFERRALS

Referrals, like retention of existing clients, is a measure of your marketing success. The higher the rate of referrals, the more you should believe in your marketing program and client satisfaction.

The referral is a special person. He or she is somehow attached to your client as friend, colleague, or family. This sense of trust is very delicate. If the referral's experience with you is less than what your client in a sense promised, both of you are embarrassed. Remember, an unhappy customer tells thirteen other people. In a small community disappointment travels fast.

Nevertheless, the best way to obtain new clients is through referrals. In fact, when your business begins getting referrals, it can grow exponentially. When you first start out, the easiest way to get referrals is to ask for them. Some of your first clients will know that you are just getting started. If they like your service, they will be extremely eager to recommend you. If you get reliable and honest service from a repair shop, restaurant, or department store, you are probably only too happy to refer friends. The same is true of financial planners. The work sheet in **EXHIBIT 7.2** (see page 240) is an easy way to track referrals by source.

◆ **Niche positioning.** This chapter has described how to quantify your capture area, reach prospects, and convert interested consumers into loyal and productive clients. Although your prospects may be faceless, your clientele is full of character. Who are the people you want to call your own? Who is your niche customer? You simply cannot be all things to all people, so who are you going to cultivate? You must decide who you are comfortable working with, who will get your message, and go after that clientele.

A practical approach for the start-up planner is to use the marketing budget to reach and develop one market niche. A niche population consists of people with similar interests, language, cultural heritage, occupation, financial profile, or community. A niche might be high-net-worth families, unmarried high-income individuals, small business owners, or early retirees. Since a niche market is highly defined, you will need to become an expert on the sociology of the group. Understand the values, motivation, and cultural issues that may affect their accessibility and propensity to plan for financial security.

It is very common to target niches defined by occupations or demographic groupings. These may include professions (doctors, lawyers, architects, engineers), athletes and entertainers, couples with double incomes and no kids, military personnel, urbanites, farming communities, technologists, government employees, educators, and so on. You can also target your market by geographic location, as did FPC in the business plan presented at the end of Chapter 6. A geographic niche always has an economic, cultural, and educational profile. A local or regional niche improves accessibility and personalized service but is also cross-occupational and economically diverse. This may force you to use multiple marketing tactics and offer a broad product and service package. Once you select your niche market, define your practice image and product offering to reflect the needs and motivations of these individuals.

Developing Marketing Tactics: Understanding the Four Ps

PRODUCT, price, place, and promotion are the four Ps of marketing. Balancing these key tactics will help you to reach prospects and develop clients with a systematic and cost-effective approach.

PRODUCT

Product is what you offer the client: the services you provide and the products that make the services perform. Before you can choose the service and product portfolio to offer, you must form a clear idea of how service and product options satisfy client needs. Ask yourself the following questions:

◆ What is the purpose of the service or product?

◆ Is this service or product the newest, best possibility?

◆ If you are having trouble increasing your clientele, should you expand the types of services you provide or products you offer, such as income tax preparation, mortgage origination, and debt management? If you limit your services, you run the risk of a client moving to a competitor to receive one-stop financial shopping.

◆ What are the advantages of your services and products compared to those of your competitors?

◆ Are you offering the right mix of services and products?

PRICE

Price is the monetary return you expect for providing value to clients. Pricing is a dilemma. There is no de facto "right" price; it is only what the customer will pay. You must feel comfortable with what you charge as a representation of the fair market value of your services. Further, you must consider your target market. Do you want to be the Waldorf Astoria, charging a high price to a limited clientele for high service, or Wal-Mart, charging a low price to many clients for common products? Your pricing must take into account likely competitor action you identified as threats in your SWOT analysis. Challenge your thinking about pricing by asking yourself the following:

◆ **What are your pricing objectives?** Do you want to attract low-price clients and hope to build revenue on volume? Remember that a low-price client requires the same service as a high-price client. The more clients you have, the more service you must provide to retain your account base. Conversely, if you decide to be a high-price competitor, you will have to work harder for each new client, and the cost of losing high-price clients is steep.

◆ **Do you want to preserve pricing flexibility?** If so, you need price ranges to attract the different constituencies you serve. If you are targeting middle-income families, a fixed fee may be more appealing. Higher-net-worth clients may be willing to pay a commission as their asset base appreciates.

PLACE

Place is where and how you distribute your products. This is often the area most overlooked by planners. Matching the location where you provide service to different clients can affect the outcome of the transaction and its profitability. For instance, consider where you engage clients. A person-to-person meeting might be in a client's home or office. Indirect engagement may occur at seminars, through direct mail or cold-calling, or over the Internet. If you mostly meet in person, pick a location that fits your target market. If you deal with wealthy individuals, a downtown location is convenient. A traditional building, such as a Victorian or brownstone, fits a traditional, conservative approach to planning. Modern, all-glass offices suggest new thinking, breaking the mold, and risk taking. If your target market is commuters, an office in the suburbs might be appropriate.

Distribution strategies may also involve teaming up with specialists in insurance, investments, income tax, retirement planning, and estate planning. A firm can combine people in each specialty group, each with its own image.

PROMOTION

Promotion is how you get your message to your target market. It can involve advertising, public relations, or sales promotion. In advertising, you pay for media coverage, and you control the message. In public relations, you try to convince the media that they should write or talk about you as part of their editorial function. You may try to include the following types of media:

◆ Direct mail
◆ Outdoor advertising
◆ Local and regional magazines
◆ Newsletters from trade and membership associations
◆ Newspaper, radio, and cable television advertising

Choosing a media mix is complex. It depends on how accessible your target market is, the frequency of your promotion, and your budget. Direct mail, or shotgun marketing, is the least expensive medium per impression. At the other end of the marketing media continuum is a rifle-shot dinner meeting and seminar for six couples. Your annual marketing plan may include several types of marketing media aimed to generate awareness at one extreme and to focus on highly targeted prize clients at the other. Be careful not to diffuse the impact of your marketing program by trying too many ideas, or worse, none at all.

Developing a public image is very valuable. It could be self-directed, whereby you develop an image plan, or you could hire a public relations firm. A PR firm will place you in the news quickly but temporarily. Your own efforts could be more long lasting. Consider doing the following:

◆ writing a book

◆ writing a column for a community newspaper
◆ teaching a college course
◆ offering commentary and insight to local newspaper personal finance reporters
◆ establishing a seminar tour
◆ speaking at trade shows or industrywide conferences

In *The Guide to Financial Public Relations,* Larry Chambers urges planners to establish their own public relations program. The start-up entrepreneur should let his or her best instincts guide a public image campaign.

EXHIBIT 7.3 (see page 240) is a good tool to test the cohesiveness of your marketing thinking. Along the left side of the Marketing Planning Grid are the four Ps. Across the top is a place to write a brief description (one or two bullet points) of each P. Next, note the expected result—for example, of a direct mail project. Last, show the timing—when you want to implement each P. Once you complete the grid, look for overlap and redundancy of targets. Make sure your marketing tactics fit your targets. Do not crowd too much marketing into a short time span.

Creating Strategic Alliances

STRATEGIC ALLIANCES with allied professionals have multiple benefits. First, an alliance network is a barrier to entry. A network of alliances forces competitors to build their own relationships or remain narrow. Second, alliances maximize your productivity. You can continue to focus on your specialty and refer a client to a trusted colleague in another area of financial planning. Third, an alliance network is good marketing. Your A clients want one-stop shopping for broad financial services.

◆ **Partnering.** Partnering means pairing up with one or more professionals who have a similar business model but a different specialty. Your client bases remain separate, but you refer to each other to expand client revenues. Partnering is not always balanced. Often one party gains more than the other. Thus partnering can create healthy competition as well. The relationship is similar to that of running partners. You pace each other, strengthen each other, but neither of you wants to be last.

◆ **Networking.** Everyone talks about networking. The traditional approach is to ask a friend or a colleague if he or she knows someone with specific information. The best networking strategy is the simplest one: make good friends and colleagues, and give advice when asked. Oddly, the more you depend on a network for information, leads, and ideas, the further you stray from your business plan.

◆ **Brain trusts.** A corporate board of directors provides management with direction, depth of experience, and stability. Boards also hold management accountable for business ethics, performance, shareholder value, and employee satisfaction. For the same reasons, an entrepreneur needs a brain trust, a board of advisers. Your brain trust is a strategic alliance. You receive information and experience from your board, and they receive the intrinsic value of seeing you succeed. Your board should do the following:

—Help you think outside your business plan toward the future

—Be your eyes and ears to the outside world

—Provide sound guidance on business decisions

—Prod you to evaluate your progress against your business and marketing plans

—Bring the perspective of other businesses and professions to your firm

—Be a component of your referral network

The advisory board, partnering, and networking are ways to expand the competitive wall around your business and your clients and to deepen your wealth of knowledge and creativity.

The Marketing Budget

THE MARKETING budget amplifies the marketing line item in your business plan. It also serves the same purpose as the financial section of your business plan. The marketing budget is partner to your plan. While the plan explains what you intend to do and with what results, the budget explains how much it will cost. It should be easy for the reader or investor to grasp the logic and elements of your marketing plan in numbers. More so than your business plan financial data, the marketing budget is an ROI exercise. It shows what it will cost to get your message to a defined group of people who will buy a defined set of products in a defined period of time. How many dollars of gross margin (revenue less direct cost of services) will you generate with each marketing dollar? The greater the income, the greater the leverage. Marketing efficiency is measured in leverage. Reinvest cash from operations in marketing programs that create high leverage. Abandon those that do not. **EXHIBIT 7.4** (see page 241) presents a sample marketing budget.

The Action Plan

MARKETING PLANS are time- and resource-sensitive. The revenue stream you committed to in your business plan depends upon a sequence of events happening on time with the expected results and within budgeted cost. Thus you need to execute your marketing plan with confidence and thoroughness. Develop a game plan with very specific tasks, responsibilities, completion dates, and expected outcomes for each element in your marketing plan. Create an Action Blueprint as in **EXHIBIT 7.5** (see page 242).

Refer to your Action Blueprint weekly. As completion dates approach, check with the responsible person for an update, then look ahead to the next two or three tasks. Are you on target with the results you expect from each task? If so, are the subsequent marketing tasks still relevant, aggressive, opportunistic? If your action plan is not progressing as you intended, what adjustments should you make? Are you getting the overall benefit from your marketing spending, or are there better, more predictable ways to accelerate prospects into productive clients?

Auditing the Results

THE PRACTICAL marketer is constantly evaluating marketing-plan results in light of setbacks and new opportunities. Do not let pride of authorship color your willingness to kill a great idea that simply did not work. At the same time make sure your assessment is objective. You will want to audit the results of your marketing plan periodically using both *quantitative* and *qualitative* methods.

Qualitative information helps you fine-tune your message and marketing tactics, while quantitative information measures how effectively you are reaching your marketing goals.

◆ **Quantitative methods.** You made assumptions in your marketing plan about the size, accessibility, and value of your target market. Based upon these assumptions you set revenue goals for the first few years of your firm. Rather than waiting until the end of year one to confirm your assumptions and total your revenue, try to predict the impact of marketing as you move through your marketing plan. Prepare a simple, five-question survey like the one in **EXHIBIT 7.6** (see page 243) and mail it to one hundred people on your prospect list.

Notice the design of the questionnaire. It is very informal, friendly, personal, and easy to complete. The ratio of "yes" to "no" answers to question one will give a sense of your penetration. Any awareness over 5 percent from your prospect list is good. Question two measures which marketing tactic created awareness. This information helps you decide where to put additional marketing money. Question three tells whether your intended message was understood and remembered. Question four measures the respondents' readiness for planning help. If the respondents are familiar with FPC and understand how the company could help with money issues, how many of them are thinking about getting help? Question five queries the reasons why respondents have not acted to get help. These answers will help you to communicate more effectively with prospects in future marketing efforts. Finally, the questionnaire asks if the respondent would like to talk to FPC. The questionnaire itself is a marketing tool. Prepare statistics on each of the questions. The higher the frequency of response, the greater the predictive power of the information for future planning.

◆ **Qualitative methods.** Quantitative methods work best when enough time has passed after a marketing campaign to stimulate a significant group of prospects (or clients) to act. You are interested in the predictive power of the information. The limitation of quantitative methods is the survey itself. You get no more information than what you have asked for. There is no chance to explore questions in greater depth or study new areas. This is where qualitative methods are useful. Qualitative market research does not predict or add volume, it adds tone or richness to your knowledge base.

Peer review is one way to get feedback on your marketing program. Invite a potential partner to a seminar or workshop and ask him or her to evaluate your message, style, visual aids, and follow-through. Peer reviews can be mutually beneficial. Critique each other.

Never be afraid to talk to strangers. In the self-help or personal finance section of your local bookstore, look for the browsers. Do they seem upscale? What are they reading? What are they buying? Without appearing bold, ask a browser to recommend any of the books on the shelf. This is your entree to finding out what these people are thinking. You may use the same approach at your public library, a book fair, a continuing-education open house, or your local college.

Client-appreciation dinners demonstrate your appreciation but also let you find out what clients are thinking. Many planners have quarterly events, inviting three to six clients to each. Invite a partner or specialist to share the cost and the information. At the dinner, test some of your marketing and new-product ideas. Pass a draft brochure around the table and ask for feedback. Ask your clients why their friends do not use professional financial help. This information may add to what you learn from the prospect questionnaire suggested above.

Most clients will help you improve your practice. They too benefit from new ideas. Consider a questionnaire for clients. Unlike the prospect survey, you are not interested in how many clients think a certain way; you are interested in their ideas and their image of your practice. **EXHIBIT 7.7** (see page 244) is a sample client questionnaire.

Financial planning is an evolving business. Innovation in products, services, communication tools, and organization is occurring every day in your market. You need to stay ahead of the competition by understanding consumer needs before they do. No one told Apple Computer that a purple, see-through, all-in-one, plug-and-play desktop computer was what they wanted. Apple created the need *and* the market. You must do the same with your business. Continually ask yourself questions like the following:

◆ Why am I in business?

◆ What do I want from my business?

◆ Whom do I serve?

◆ What is my service? Is it valuable? How valuable?

◆ Are my business plan and marketing plan working? What can I do to make both work better?

The marketing plan is the blueprint that an enterprise pursues to accomplish its growth and image objectives. It is that path that leads and transforms a business from start-up to financial and personal success. The pathway includes market analysis, market targets and tactics, the four Ps, alliances, budget, action, and evaluation. Remember to plan the details very well. You need to understand more than the marketplace and where you fit in. You need to understand how to turn opportunity into reality.

EXHIBIT 7.1

Sample SWOT Analysis

Financial Planning Company:
Business Plan SWOT Analysis, July 2005

TOP STRENGTHS COMPARED TO COMPETITION

◆ Office manager skilled in direct marketing (in process of being hired away from a key competitor)

◆ Principal very comfortable making financial planning presentations to the public

◆ Location near downtown Denver, in modest office with easy access and parking

◆ Advisory board includes allied professionals serving middle-income families in target communities

◆ Strong program of follow-up communication with clients to encourage and reward referrals

TOP WEAKNESSES COMPARED TO COMPETITION

◆ No attorney on staff, so cannot integrate estate plans

◆ Key competitor has weekly column in Denver newspaper

◆ Competitors are highly computerized, especially in direct marketing

◆ Revenue estimate assumes premium fee driven by added value of education program

◆ Competitors are already established in two important suburban communities

TOP OPPORTUNITIES COMPARED TO COMPETITION

◆ Establish a strategic alliance with Alan Fields, estate-planning attorney

◆ Be the first to launch an interactive website, prepare press release, and seek interviews with community newspapers

◆ Hire freelance software developer to build a computerized database for prospecting and client management

TOP THREATS FROM COMPETITION

◆ Further price pressure from established competitors as more start-up planners enter the market
◆ Cash-rich competitors could leapfrog FPC Internet technology
◆ With repeal of Glass-Steagall Act, intensification of the trend for large investment service organizations to enter the general financial consulting business
◆ Commission-based sales representatives are becoming more common, increasing market penetration and noise factor

---

EXHIBIT 7.2

Sample Client Referral Work Sheet

Financial Planning Company: Client Referral Tracking, July 2005

REFERRAL	SOURCE	ACTION	RESULT
Williams, T.	Michael, A.	Phone, 3/19	Message
		Letter, 5/1	Call 5/20
		Meeting, 5/25	Proposal due 6/15

EXHIBIT 7.3

Marketing Planning Grid

Financial Planning Company

	DESCRIPTION	EXPECTED RESULT	TIMING
Product			
Place			
Price			
Promotion			

EXHIBIT 7.4

Sample Marketing Budget

Financial Planning Company:
Marketing Budget

PROGRAM	ANNUAL BUDGET	SPENDING: YTD Q3/05	ASSESSMENT
Advertising	$12,000	($6,000)	Stop
Direct mail	$9,000	$1,500	Continue Q4
Marketing audit	$4,000	0	Continue Q4
Market research	$7,000	$500	Stop
Prospecting: general	$15,000	($3,000)	Continue Q1
Public relations	$10,000	$2,000	Continue Q2
Seminars	$14,000	0	Continue Q4
Strategic alliances	$5,000	($1,000)	Continue Q4
TOTAL	**$76,000**	**$14,000**	

EXHIBIT 7.5

Sample Marketing Action Plan

Financial Planning Company:
Marketing Plan Action Blueprint

TASK	PERSON RESPONSIBLE	COMPLETION DATE
Prepare SWOT	Brian	July 7
Research target market	Sue (P/T planner)	August 1
Develop prospect list	Sue	August 30
Develop mailing for target market	Kathy (administrative (assistant)	September 1
Identify partnering candidates	Brian	August 1
Book Q4 speaking schedule	Kathy	August 30
Join local civic groups	Brian	August 1
Submit FPC launch article to newspaper	Sue	September 1
Book coffee break at Seniors Fest	Sue	October 18
Convene advisory board to brainstorm	Brian	August 30

EXHIBIT 7.6

Sample Market Survey

Financial Planning Company
Denver, Colorado

Dear Friend:

We would like to ask if you know about our company. Would you please take a moment to complete this short questionnaire, fold it, and return it as soon as you can? Thank you for your help.

1 Are you familiar with Financial Planning Company (FPC)?
Yes _____ No _____

2 If so, how did you hear about FPC?
Friend _____ Newspaper _____ Letter in the mail _____
Other (please describe) _____

3 If you have heard of us, what do you know about FPC?
FPC prepares income taxes _____
FPC specializes in helping families save money _____
FPC can help people prepare for retirement _____
FPC is a trusted source of help with money problems _____

4 Have you thought about getting professional help with financial planning? Yes _____ No _____

5 If no, is there a main reason?
It's too costly _____
I worry about losing the money I have _____
Financial planning is not important to me now _____
Other people have given me enough advice _____

Thank you for helping us.

Sincerely,

Brian Jones
President, Financial Planning Company

Would you like to be contacted by a professional planner from FPC to answer questions about money? There is no obligation.   Yes _____

EXHIBIT 7.7

Sample Client Feedback Questionnaire

Financial Planning Company: Client Questionnaire

Please tell us what you think about FPC.

1 What do you like best about our company?

_____

_____

_____

2 What do you like least about our company?

_____

_____

_____

3 What is your opinion about our office staff? Are they helpful? Are they pleasant? Do you get what you want when you call our office?

_____

_____

_____

4 Are you satisfied with the value you get from our company? Are our fees in line with the service you get? What other services would add value?

_____

_____

_____

5 Is there one message or phrase you think best describes FPC?

_____

_____

_____

Thank you for your interest in helping FPC serve you better.

Brian Jones
President, Financial Planning Company

CHAPTER 8

THE ART OF CLIENT COMMUNICATION

COMMUNICATION IS the intentional exchange of information among multiple parties. This working definition makes it easy to imagine how communication goes awry, missing its original intention. First, the number of parties affects communication. In financial planning it is more difficult to work with a husband and wife, father and son, or business partners than to plan with one person. Second, intention is very difficult to manage. You will encounter clients who are not ready to hear you. Your intention is supportive and positive, but it may be perceived as cold and blunt. Intention, then, is subject to interpretation, a force you cannot easily control. Exchange implies something happening in two directions. You, the planner, are exchanging information for money. Your client is exchanging information for financial security. Unless there is an overt balance in the exchange, one party may feel undercompensated. This issue, left unresolved, will ruin a relationship.

It is interesting to consider that on the surface the financial planner is simply providing a client with "numbers." However, in a far deeper sense the numbers are draped with meaning. Your financial analysis and planning proposal are very much like a report card on the life of your client. You may think that you are delivering good news: with proper planning your client can secure his or her future well-being. It is just as likely that you are the bearer of bad news: your client has failed to manage his or her financial security, and now the price must be paid—save or suffer. Money is mixed with emotion, and you need to be prepared to handle both.

Thus, communication is central to the professional relationship. It gives rise to a cycle of action and reaction. When one person communicates a message, the other will react. As a financial planner, you need to respect and understand the reaction you elicit from a client. The greater the sincerity of your understanding, the greater the trust and loyalty you will enjoy. Communication also involves motivating and influencing your clients to take action. Good financial planners know how to communicate, both by talking and by listening effectively to their clients.

Communication plays a significant part in the financial planning process described in Chapter 3. Communication begins even before a lead or prospect becomes a client. It begins by your understanding yourself. It continues through the first contact and preliminary interview, when both parties are deciding if they can work together. Communication continues through interviewing the client to determine goals and objectives, and reaches a maximum complexity when you give the client the "report card" and advise on alternative ways to achieve the client's objectives. At every point in the financial planning process, unburdened communication yields better information and therefore better planning. How you can communicate effectively in your new professional role is the subject of this chapter.

The Financial Planner Plays Many Roles

HIGHLY SUCCESSFUL financial planners are insightful. They know more than just the technical side of their business. They are skilled in helping the client handle the discomfort of money, past behavior, preparation for the unknown, and responsibility. Most financial planners may not think about the complexity of their relationship with a client. The issue of mutual dependency and the emotional energy involved are often not played out in communication. This can or cannot be a problem, but it should provoke awareness. Over time the adviser/client relationship will change. It may begin competitively. The client wants the planner to be impressed with his previous financial success: "I don't need you, but maybe you can help in some way." The planner wants the client to be impressed with his or her credentials, client base, or professional success: "This client doesn't realize how little he knows about investment strategy, but I'll teach him." This is not to suggest that client and adviser sit across from each other filled with devious thoughts. It does suggest that there are unnoticed issues going on in the background that both parties must try to tune in to and resolve. You are not a psychologist or therapist, but you are dealing with money and emotion, dangerous territory. Consider that a major reason for marital arguments and divorce is conflict over money.

What are the overt and hidden roles the financial planner will occupy in the course of a professional relationship? How do you know when these roles are likely to occur, and how do you manage them in a successful consultancy?

First, do you understand yourself? Why do you want to be a financial planner? If the answer revolves around working at home, keeping your own hours, being independent, making a lot of money, and dabbling in the stock market, think harder. These are not all the reasons. Is something else going on? What are your emotional attachments to the life of a financial planner? The need to help, the need to control, the need to parent, the need to be important? You must ask yourself honestly if any of these issues are involved. Your spouse or a close friend may help you see how your personality aligns with the roles of financial planner. Accept and manage whatever motivation you uncover. Awareness is the best way to keep background issues and energy in a positive direction for you and the client.

Why are leads, prospects, or clients seeking your help? Help them think through their dreams and worries, and you will help them understand what they will need to reach their expectations and prepare for financial independence. A good planner considers a client's entire situation by assessing the client's responses to the following questions:

◆ What is important to the client? Financial security, or feeling competent, or both?

◆ Why are these things important? To himself, to others, or both?

◆ How does the client feel about himself? Does he think of himself as a financial success or a failure?

◆ How does the client feel about money? Is money good or simply a necessity?

◆ Is the client willing and able to do what it takes to become financially secure? If not, why not?

◆ What issues could work against the client's achieving his or her goals? Do I have any control over these issues, or are they personal to the client? If I am unable to control these issues, can I be successful in helping the client? An organizational psychologist, Harry Levinson, uses a medical model to describe his work. Levinson says that sometimes a business consultant "opens up" an organization and finds that nothing can be done to solve its problems. If you "open up" a client and find that the client is not ready to be helped or cannot be helped, you are obligated to say so.

Most often, however, these questions help you get a picture of clients' intangible needs, which are as or more important than their tangible requirements. The questions help you learn very specifically what the clients' needs and goals are. The answers will point you toward some of the key issues in assembling an understanding of the client and in preparing a comprehensive financial plan.

The first question asks a client to describe what is important and allows the client to tell you about issues of concern. Do monetary or material things hold greater importance than intangible items? If so, then the focus should be on material accumulation to achieve wealth. It means helping the client organize goals to accumulate very specific tangibles, such as a second house, a fancier car, the latest technological equipment, a boat, and so on. If the client is interested in leaving a legacy to a child, school, or religious institution, ways to maximize these goals can be designed. Establishing a charitable lead or remainder trust can help pursue these dreams. These philanthropic goals may compete with or be complementary to the goals stated earlier. Indeed, there can be some combination of goals, which is fine. The point is to uncover the various motivations that precede strategies toward financial independence.

The second question asks "Why?" Clearly, there must be an underlying reason to explain why the client has these dreams. Finding out why delves deeper into a particular situation and ensures proper planning on your part. If clients come to you and say that their religious institution is struggling and they want to do good for the institution, you will feel a sense of joy in helping them achieve these objectives, possibly helping the clients establish a legacy in their own right. A client may feel a need for acquiring material objects because of childhood poverty or parental denial, and he and his spouse have made a pact that if they are fortunate enough to become wealthy, they will provide for their children. Again, the only way to find out is to ask.

The third question asks clients to evaluate their self-esteem. Their response reflects how they feel about themselves and others, such as friends and family. You will be able to tell whether they want to help themselves or their loved ones. It will also help them put in perspective just what are the critical factors in their life, which leads to the next question.

The fourth question asks clients why money is important to them. Ask your clients to relay their earliest experiences with money and the impact it has made on their lives. Ask these questions of each spouse in the presence of the other. Many times the responses will shed new light on an old subject about which the other spouse may have no clue. Lessons will be learned, and even more important, objectives will become clearer and the focus more obvious.

The fifth question asks whether the client is ready to do what it takes to create personal wealth; the answer is not quite as obvious as it would appear. There are many people who insist on living life to the fullest, doing things they can afford to do, such as traveling; attending the theater, concerts, and sporting events; dining out frequently; buying lavish items; and so on. Their objective can be to "zero out" at death, or, in other words, not to leave any money to their children, spending it all while they are healthy. These people are less intent on building assets on a balance sheet than on creating expenses on an income statement. There is no right or wrong response to this question. Clearly, though, you need to know which way the client is focused.

The last question asks why the clients believe that their long-term goals can be achieved. This reverts back to the basics, which are what is important to you, and how do you plan to achieve it? It involves ranking priorities from most important to least important and setting specific objectives for each (as described in Chapter 3). Do the clients have the fortitude to achieve goals over a long period of time? The objectives carry a time element, a monetary amount, and a person responsible for each accomplishment.

As a planner, you must learn to ask appropriate questions (as discussed in connection with the PIPRIM process in Chapter 3) and to listen closely to the answers as you record them. You will also need to communicate with clients in a way that ensures they expect services you can provide and they stay comfortable with the process. Once you begin asking these questions of enough clients, you will begin to feel a sense of direction as to what can or can't help a client's unique financial situation.

Information Processing

AS A FINANCIAL consultant, you must be aware of the different ways your clients process information. Experiences may be understood through one of the following lenses:

◆ **Visual.** Clients who communicate visually may do well by watching others, seeing a film, or studying diagrams.
◆ **Auditory.** This type of learning focuses on acquiring information through talking and listening.
◆ **Kinesthetic.** This type of learning focuses on active participation, trial and error, or physical activity.

Try to use some of each style in information collection from your client. Use graphs, for example, to explain difficult concepts as you talk about the issue. It is much easier to help clients understand issues in their preferred learning style than it is to use logical arguments to persuade them to change. Helping your clients to achieve their goals or to change their behavior is accomplished more easily if you help them process appropriate information in the mode best suited to their learning style.

How Do People Communicate?

COMMUNICATION is often thought of as verbal or nonverbal cues designed to provoke a response. In fact, everything we do communicates something. Even doing nothing is a statement of sorts. Effective communication takes place when the receiver interprets the sender's message in precisely the same fashion that it was sent. Difficulties arise when the receiver misunderstands the sender's message. Since an individual's intentions are private and rarely clearly stated, the receiver has the difficult job of decoding the message without knowing the sender's intentions.

You are the receiver trying to get the client to open up. Ask open-ended questions and pay attention to tone of voice, volume, and speed of expressions, as well as the words of the reply.

There are five "knowns" you need to remember to effectively communicate with your client.

1 Clients use words, space, tonality, rate, and volume of speech and other nonverbal actions to communicate facts and feelings.
2 Men and women, husbands and wives, young and older people communicate differently.
3 Initial impressions affect interaction for a long time.

4 Communication is constantly being influenced by multiple factors.

5 Personal life experiences leave a hidden mark on everyone.

Here is how to apply these five "knowns" to client communication.

◆ **Clients use words, space, tonality, rate, and volume of speech and other nonverbal actions to communicate.** Words themselves can mean different things to different clients. To one person, risk may mean going to Las Vegas with $100, while to another it may mean investing in futures.

Tonality, rate, and volume of speech are communication tools. Tone and pitch may indicate the speaker's feelings. For example, angry people often talk loudly, while sad people tend to talk in a flat tone. Furthermore, people sometimes mix signals, with the words communicating one thing and the tone and pitch transmitting just the opposite. Both messages may be important. Keep asking questions until the meaning becomes clearer.

The nonverbal channel is also used to communicate. A stare from a parent to a child often signifies that the child did something to merit disapproval. Eye contact, facial expressions, and gestures are other important nonverbal behaviors. Some clients look you square in the eye to ensure you are telling them the truth, or perhaps they sense anger or hostility. Clients who avoid looking at you may be fearful or uninterested. Facial expressions—smiles, frowns, bit lips, or nervous tics—can also demonstrate interest or a lack thereof. Try to notice these habits when the topic changes. See which topics are more sensitive. Gestures with the arm or hand can accentuate other statements. Tightly clasped hands can emphasize fear or anxiety, whereas free-flowing arm or hand gestures may display comfort. Frequent crossing or uncrossing of legs may indicate boredom or anxiety.

Look at overall body position. Clients who sit up straight are usually relaxed. If they lean slightly forward, it is usually a sign of interest and involvement in the planning session. If they slouch or seem to draw away from the planner, it may show that they have little interest in what the planner is saying. Good posture may signify high self-esteem or self-assurance, and poor posture the opposite. Body movements also send a signal. The client who frequently changes body position may be indicating physical or emotional discomfort or a lack of interest. People who bite their nails, pull at their hair, or fidget may be very nervous. People who greet friends and family with a kiss, hug, or warm handshake may be very open and warm.

Space between two people also conveys information. Americans normally stay at least thirty-six inches away from people they do not know. This is considered public space. The figure is thirty inches for those we know better, and twenty-four inches for those we know and trust. When two people are very comfortable together, they may stand closer than twenty-four inches apart. This is intimate space. Effective communicators are aware of how their use of space affects others, and consequently, they use it to make others feel comfortable.

◆ **Men and women communicate differently.** According to a study by Judy Cornelia Pearson, women tend to use formal words and phrases, whereas men often use more informal ones. Females appear to prefer the specificity that language can provide, whereas males appear to focus on the underlying issues. When working with a couple, you should provide language that allows everyone to understand the same message. Address both members of a couple together. If you talk with one spouse when the other is unavailable and one partner later communicates the message to the other, it may be interpreted differently than you intended.

◆ **Initial impressions affect communication long term.** In their book, *Contact: The First Four Minutes,* authors Leonard Zunin and Natalie Zunin conclude that the first four minutes of an interpersonal interaction are the key to establishing social relationships, family harmony, and business success. You can only make one first impression, so make it count. A firm handshake, a smile, or otherwise conveying warmth and sincerity can make a good impression.

◆ **Communication is constantly being influenced by multiple factors.** Communication is affected by motivation, credibility, organization, and style. It is crucial to help clients see the big picture and motivate them to take action. If the clients are not moving in this direction, you should be able to read the signs and adjust your presentation accordingly.

People act more readily if information comes from a credible source. Be extremely professional, sincere, up front, and direct about what needs to be done to improve the clients' financial situation. If they trust you, you can accomplish more. Organization is also critical. Information given at the beginning or end of a presentation is remembered more clearly than material in the middle. Make your most important points first or last.

Style describes your overall approach to a client. It can take several forms:

—Be an authoritative figure; when you speak, people listen.

—Emphasize the client's understanding of information to create self-confidence.

—Emphasize a low-key, low-pressure approach. You place the responsibility for action directly in the hands of the client.

In using any of these styles, remember that the planner controls the process. The client is responsible for content. We can only work with the information they give us.

◆ **Life experience leaves a hidden mark on everyone.** Experience has an effect on everyone. Perhaps clients went to a different financial planner before you. They began with $500,000 to invest, but after three years of working with that other planner, the nest egg dropped to $300,000. These clients will have great difficulty trusting another adviser as much as they trusted the first one. That is because their expectations were never managed. That makes your job more difficult. The key to building trust into the relationship is to be open, honest, and sincere. Mean what you say, and say what you mean. Tell them in advance whether you believe their objectives are realistic. Be frank. Tell them when it looks unlikely for them to achieve goals. Give difficult advice, such as their need to reduce current spending habits, when necessary. When you educate the client in all of these areas, it raises the trust and confidence level significantly. With clients on a higher plateau, questions become more focused on the key issues surrounding their surge into financial independence. This higher-level conversation between financial planners and clients enables their expectations to become managed. It also reduces the likelihood that they will sue you.

Structuring Communication

STRUCTURING a meeting determines the format and the subject matter of future communication. Make the purpose of the session clear to the client at the outset. Explain the process and forms involved, the amount of time required, and the confidential nature of the relationship, and give some prediction of what outcomes the client might reasonably expect. This structuring need not be long and cumbersome. Rather, it should be clear, concise, and straightforward. You might say, "Mr. and Mrs. Johnson, our relationship will consist of four in-person meetings plus unlimited phone support. Each in-person meeting will focus on a different part of the plan. In order to guide you throughout our relationship, any time something comes up or you need further clarification or you just want some quick advice, always call. We do not charge for phone time. Does this arrangement work for you?"

Attend to your clients' feelings immediately—do not put them off. Nip discrepancies or uncomfortable feelings in the bud, or they may come back to haunt you. For example, your client might say, "Mr. Smith, you never informed me that you were not going to notify me when certain asset classes went down by more than 15 percent." Or, "I don't believe you're listening to what I'm saying." In responding to this, you need to say to the client, "Are there other issues I have not addressed?" If the client seems agitated, you may explore the situation by asking, "Are other things happening that cause you concern, such as an impending divorce, forced layoff at work, or health condition?"

Structure allows you to help your clients manage their expectations. Clients may not even understand the nature of the planner-client relationship. Clients can misinterpret what they are expected to receive. For example, maybe you believed your relationship with a particular client was to involve only an up-front plan, whereas the client thought there would be numerous one-on-one sessions on an ongoing basis. Well, who is right? If you did not clearly state your understanding of the terms before, how do you determine when the relationship starts and when it ends? One way to alleviate this is through the use of an engagement letter (as explained in Chapter 3). You will need a few more rules to be a good communicator.

◆ **Be yourself.** Your clients must accept you for who you are and what you represent. Lay all your cards on the table at the first meeting. Be genuine—let the client see you as a real person. You do not have to wear a different hat for each client. Be yourself at all times.

◆ **Tune in to your client.** Listen to your clients. When the client says, "You're right on track," or "That's exactly right," you can feel confident that you have a good understanding. Learning to understand is not always easy. Your feelings and experiences must take a backseat to what is truly important to the clients. See the issues through their eyes, not yours. Listen carefully to both the subtle and the obvious content of what your clients say. Still, avoid getting too caught up in the clients' perspective. If you relate too closely to their situation, you cannot provide objective advice.

The most effective communication occurs when a message's receiver gives understanding responses, also called paraphrases. For example, if the client expresses doubt, such as "I don't believe that we can retire at age sixty-five. We may have to push it back," your response may be, "So you're not sure that you have the resources to retire at age sixty-five. My job is to see how we can either give you sufficient resources or make changes in your lifestyle that will enable you to achieve your dream of financial independence."

People rarely retract what they have stated to you. If they communicate financial planning facts to you, they believe it. To gain clarification, state in your own words the ideas they expressed to you. You will find that they will usually agree with your rephrasing.

In the end, the most important thing you can do for your clients is to make them feel important. Have them decide what works best, and concur with their decision.

◆ **Be positive.** Although there is no need to paint a rosy picture if it is not warranted, do put enthusiasm into the client's situation. Try to show the glass as half full rather than half empty. Avoid recommending ideas you do not believe in. Your sincerity and your positiveness must come from the heart. Remember, planners run into trouble when they do not adequately manage their clients' expectations. That means that whatever standards you set in the beginning for your clients and yourself should be understood, so that everyone knows what needs to be done to meet expectations.

◆ **Establish rapport.** To keep a friendly, open atmosphere between you and your clients, maintain a caring, interested concern. Proceed at an unhurried pace, and project an accepting, nonjudgmental attitude. Practice attentive, active listening. Put the client first in any discussions.

◆ **Let the client talk.** Ask open-ended questions. This lets clients give you complete and comprehensive information. Closed-ended questions, by contrast, typically generate only a one-word response. Both types of questioning are necessary to gain critical insight into a client's situation.

Open-ended questions might include the following:
—Tell me your first experiences involving money.
—What are you trying to accomplish by creating a financial plan?
—Why have you waited to begin saving for retirement?
—What are your thoughts about designing an asset allocation strategy?
—What do you hope your retirement will be like?

Closed-ended questions might include the following:
—Have you given any thought to retirement?
—Are you interested in developing a financial plan now?
—Are you worried about starting a retirement savings program now?
—Are you in favor of an asset allocation strategy?
—At what age do you plan to retire?

Of course, these questions should not feel like an interrogation, so try to mix questions and statements together. Remember, too much questioning may dilute its purpose, which is to find out as much as possible about your client's situation.

Be sure to stay away from leading questions. These questions usually begin with "Don't you think" or "Do you feel that." Leading questions can steer clients toward statements that may not reflect what they really think. Questions should help clients think through the situation and come up with their appropriate course of action.

TYPES OF CLIENT OBJECTIONS

Financial planners must learn to deal with client objections. Clients do not typically object to the services you provide or the products you recommend. They do object to planners they do not trust or expectations that are not met. Objectors come in the following types: a client whose needs are not understood; one whose plan has a risk/reward ratio that is too close; a client who fears making quick decisions; one who is not convinced your solution will work; and a client who was told to raise an objection.

◆ **Not understanding your client's needs.** Your clients come to you because of outstanding concerns that can hinder the prospect of their future financial independence. They want to address these concerns in a rational and systematic format. If you do not listen to what they say, your clients will become frustrated and seek advice elsewhere.

◆ **A risk/reward ratio that is too close.** Clients will be unwilling to implement new ideas and strategies if the risk for undertaking these developments is not significantly less than its reward. There must be some incentive for clients to act—to see the light at the end of the tunnel. Discuss with your clients the options available to help them achieve their goals while minimizing risk at the same time.

◆ **A client who fears making quick decisions.** Never put your clients on the spot to act immediately. That is a turnoff for the clients and a hindrance to your ability to get things done in the future. Present your plan to the clients in draft form and give them time to read it and digest its meaning. Then meet with them to address what the next step should be and what action would be appropriate to take.

◆ **A client who is not convinced your solution will work.** Your client should know that you do not have all the answers. You should not be expected to name the next great growth stocks or where interest rates are headed. That is not where your value is. It is in the education process you give clients so that they can dissect important information and learn how your solutions can help them achieve their ultimate goals. From your training, you are knowledgeable enough to guide them to the next level. They must be convinced of this fact and know that you are on their side. Your job is to help clients stay the course—and that can only be accomplished through a complete buy-in to the education process. It is only then, when the clients buy in to your approach to the financial planning process, that they will be willing to hear you out and adopt your recommendations.

◆ **A client who was told to raise an objection.** Many times your clients will raise objections or challenge you on issues whether they are valid or not. These clients were told, probably by others, to never accept recommendations from planners at face value and to be on guard against possible unnecessary sales.

OVERCOMING OBJECTIONS

Just because the client is not hearing you or responding to you does not mean all is lost. You can overcome objections by implementing these techniques:

◆ **Hear your client out.** Let your clients voice their concerns or frustration without interruption. Let them get off their chests issues that may cripple the planning process before it starts. What you can do to overcome these actions is to listen to these statements carefully and then educate them in these areas. Explain to them what is required and sincerely explain the pros and cons of both sides. There is never one way to do things, and perhaps their concerns are valid. But the only way to dig through uneducated objections or genuine concerns is to provide an understanding that brings out the other side of their objections.

◆ **Isolate the problem. Try to fix one thing at a time rather than everything at once.** It is nearly impossible to do everything for the client all at once. You must isolate the concerns of the client and be selective in your approach by addressing those issues of critical importance first, based on the client's life. Give them a way to save for their specific objectives in a piecemeal fashion so that some achievement is attainable.

◆ **Question the objection. Never accept or immediately answer an objection after it is given.** Ask the client to explain the objection in detail. This will allow you to determine what the underlying cause of the objection is and address solutions to overcome those stumbling blocks. You should never criticize the client or his or her objection. Rather, you should re-examine it in a positive light and help the client to see the benefit of turning it around.

◆ **Confirm criteria. This helps reestablish commitment.** Consistently during the process, reiterate to clients what their objectives are. Show them how they tie in to what they want to accomplish financially. Make sure they are clear about their objectives.

◆ **Answer creatively. Restate what clients tell you in their words to demonstrate that you understand exactly what they are saying. Then rephrase their comments while still trying to emphasize the main points.** Give the client something new. Avoid run-of-the-mill answers that clients can find using generic software programs or books. Restate your clients' concerns the first time you hear them and then rephrase their responses while still trying to emphasize the main points. Every time you provide solutions to address your clients' recommendations, repeat your main points in different ways. This approach helps educate the client and tells them many different ways how you will help them achieve their financial objectives.

◆ **Confirm your response. Make sure that you have answered the objection to the client's satisfaction.** Once you identify the client's concern and address that concern by educating the client, reconfirm your approach to ensure that your client understands how it ties together.

◆ **Understanding the client's value system.** Your clients have moral values that they live by. These moral values should tie in to the objectives they want to achieve. You should recognize their most important concerns and address your recommendations to each one.

Every client has a definite idea of what is acceptable and what is not. If your recommendations are to be successful, they must mesh with the client's value system. If socially conscious investing is important to a client, you probably should not recommend Philip Morris stock. Your job is to determine what it takes to make clients act within their value system in a way that will help them reach their goals. Develop a framework they are comfortable with. You must listen carefully to your clients as they sift through the various value choices, so that when they do finally make up their minds, they will do so with a high level of comfort. Clients must buy into the process and ultimately make choices that are consistent with their values.

Presenting Financial Plans and Reports to Your Clients

THE WAY you present a financial plan has a direct impact on what happens next. A bad presentation can turn clients away from your plan or even toward finding another planner to help implement your recommendations. A good presentation helps clients implement your findings. If your clients are a couple, explain the plan to both of them, or you risk the possibility of one partner explaining the plan to the other very differently than you intended.

Point out clients' positive actions. Show them the good things they have done so far and how they can add your recommendations. Show them that by positioning their existing assets in a certain manner, they can achieve more return with no additional risk (if true). Or show them how they can reconfigure their existing expenses to move them toward their goals a little faster. Show them where they are (point A) and where they want to be (point B). Then show them the road map that will get them from point A to point B. Communicate recommendations in a low-key, positive, definitive manner. Being too sales-oriented can work against you. You are not selling clients a product. Rather, you are devising a strategy to help clients reach the goal of financial independence.

Your plan should be simple—visually graphic and as clear as possible. There are many different software programs in the marketplace to help you prepare a dynamic presentation. What should the financial plan show?

◆ Multiple colors, not pastels
◆ Graphic design
◆ Simplicity
◆ Specifics
◆ Action items/recommendations

EXHIBIT 8.1 (see pages 263–266) illustrates pages extracted from the financial plan of Jeff and Sally Williams. The balance sheet measures assets owned, liabilities owed, and the ensuing net worth of the clients at a particular date. The cash flow statement summarizes the clients' inflow and outflow during the past year. Showing graphic charts like these to clients enables them to understand in clear and concise terms where they stand now and will help get them where they need to be in the future through the creation of a financial plan.

Look at the chart on page 264 entitled "Current Cash Flow Management." In the original, all the cash flow captions are in different colors. As explained before, many people are visual learners. They need to see ideas in front of them. The graph explains what they have currently. You can also include a graph on what they will eventually need to achieve in order to accomplish their objectives.

When explaining concepts to clients, always talk conversationally with them. Never make statements that clients cannot follow. Ask clients whether they understand. Ask, "Does this make sense?" "Do you have an idea of where you stand?" or "Are you comfortable with this?" Clients need to wholeheartedly support the plan and know what to do when they leave the office.

The Client Communication Checklist in **EXHIBIT 8.2** (see page 267) summarizes many of the points expressed in this chapter. To ensure that you have established effective communication with new clients or existing ones, complete the checklist for each client.

EXHIBIT 8.1

Financial Plan Sample Text and Supporting Charts

Personal Financial Plan Summary
Jeff Williams and Sally Williams
July 15, 2005

This is your personal financial plan, a profile and analysis of your current financial resources and your objectives. It is designed to be a starting point to help you develop plans and strategies to reach your financial goals. It covers many aspects of your financial situation.

YOUR CURRENT RESOURCES

◆ **Net worth.** You currently have a net worth of $1,274,992. You can increase your net worth by increasing savings or by reducing the amount of your debt.

◆ **Cash flow.** For 2005, we estimate that you will have $65,000 to fund your financial objectives. To fully fund these objectives will require 60 percent of your available cash in 2005, or $39,000. This will leave you with $26,000 cash to fund unforeseen spending. You may decide to increase this reserve by decreasing your variable expenses.

◆ **Income tax.** You are currently paying 39 percent of your income to various government entities in the form of taxes. This percentage does not include personal property, sales, or sundry taxes. See the Income Tax Planning section for ideas on steps you could take to reduce your tax burden.

FUNDING YOUR FINANCIAL OBJECTIVES

Jeff and Sally, this section shows your goals in the priority order that you indicated and summarizes what you will need to achieve these goals. Your total cash requirement to fund the areas below is $39,000.

◆ **Retirement.** When Jeff retires in 2019, you will need an additional $125,321 in today's dollars to fund your retirement. See the Retirement Planning section for details. Set aside $20,300 in 2005, or 6 percent of your gross income.

◆ **Education financing.** It will cost approximately $203,000 in today's dollars to fund education beginning in 2015. You have identified $0 of funds currently available, leaving you a shortfall of $203,000. See the Education Financing Summary for details. Set aside $12,000 in 2005.

◆ **Life insurance.** Jeff has $0 of life insurance in force and Sally has $0. Our review indicates that there may be an additional need of $500,000. See the Analysis of Life Insurance Requirements for more details. Set aside $3,800 in 2005.

◆ **Disability insurance.** Currently, Jeff does not have a disability insurance policy. The analysis shows that there may be a need for a monthly benefit of at least $16,000. Refer to the Disability Insurance Analysis for more details. Set aside $2,900 in 2005.

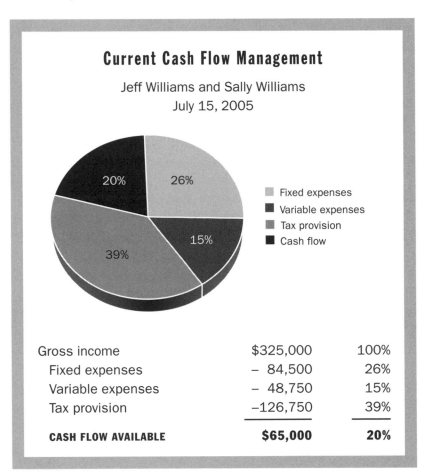

Current Cash Flow Management

Jeff Williams and Sally Williams
July 15, 2005

- Fixed expenses
- Variable expenses
- Tax provision
- Cash flow

Gross income	$325,000	100%
Fixed expenses	– 84,500	26%
Variable expenses	– 48,750	15%
Tax provision	–126,750	39%
CASH FLOW AVAILABLE	**$65,000**	**20%**

SOURCE: FINANCIAL PLANNING PROFESSIONAL LUMEN SOFTWARE (800-233-3461)

Net Worth

Jeff Williams and Sally Williams
July 15, 2005

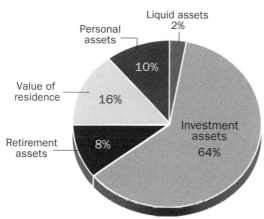

OVERVIEW

Your net worth is the best overall measure of your financial resources. It is the amount left after you subtract your liabilities (what you owe) from your assets (what you own).

YOUR CURRENT STATUS

Your net worth is currently $1,274,992.

	WHAT YOU OWN	WHAT YOU OWE	NET WORTH
Liquid assets	$30,000	$0	$30,000
Investment assets	814,992	0	814,992
Retirement assets	100,000	0	100,000
Business assets	0	0	0
Value of residence	2,200,000	2,000,000	200,000
Personal assets	130,000	0	130,000
TOTAL	**$3,274,992**	**$2,000,000**	**$1,274,992**

SOURCE: FINANCIAL PLANNING PROFESSIONAL LUMEN SOFTWARE (800-233-3461)

◆ **Asset management.** You currently have $914,992 in your investment portfolio. Review the Asset Class Mix for ideas that could enhance short-term cash (less tax obligation) to fund financial objectives in 2005 and beyond.

◆ **Estate planning.** Jeff and Sally have a combined estate of $3,274,992. Refer to the Estate Planning section for details on the composition of the gross estate and potential methods of saving estate taxes.

EXHIBIT 8.2

Sample Client Communication Checklist

Did you communicate your role to the client? ☐ Yes ☐ No

Does your client know what to expect from your relationship? ☐ Yes ☐ No

Did you come to an understanding of how your client will accomplish his or her goals? ☐ Yes ☐ No

Did you send the client a follow-up letter summarizing what was discussed in your office, and did your client sign off on it? ☐ Yes ☐ No

Did you use a combination of visual, auditory, and kinesthetic approaches to communicate with theclient? ☐ Yes ☐ No

Did you communicate how important it is for the client to take an active role in planning for financial independence? ☐ Yes ☐ No

Are you managing your client's expectations? ☐ Yes ☐ No

Did you consciously try to maintain the right tonality, pace, and volume as you spoke with the client? ☐ Yes ☐ No

Did you establish rapport during the initial four minutes of your meeting? ☐ Yes ☐ No

Did you allow the client to communicate needs and concerns? ☐ Yes ☐ No

Were you expressing yourself realistically to your client? ☐ Yes ☐ No

Were you positive in your approach? ☐ Yes ☐ No

Did you tune in to the client's discussions by displaying sincerity, openness, candor, and honesty? ☐ Yes ☐ No

Did you use open-ended questions? ☐ Yes ☐ No

Did you use closed-ended questions? ☐ Yes ☐ No

Was your communication approach creative? ☐ Yes ☐ No

Does your client understand your recommendations? ☐ Yes ☐ No

Does the client understand the risk of not implementing your recommendations? ☐ Yes ☐ No

RUNNING AN INTEGRATED PRACTICE

THE PRINCIPLES explained throughout this book are meant to help new advisers get started in developing, nurturing, and monitoring a financial planning practice. They can also help planners transform their practice's commission-based approach to a more process-oriented fee-based approach. Top-notch planners currently employing these principles in their practices have been asked to share some of their experiences.

Their responses have been incorporated into the following case studies. These case studies illustrate common situations that may be encountered while building a practice and show new advisers how to plan for their clients sensibly, efficiently, and effectively.

Case 1: Mary Leonard—Recently Widowed

MARY LEONARD is a seventy-two-year-old widow whose husband managed the family's financial affairs for fifty years. Her husband died one month ago. Another client referred Mary to Planner A.

How does Planner A begin? As was outlined in Chapter 3, the best place to start is with the PIPRIM system.

Preliminary meeting with a client
Integrated goal setting and data gathering
Putting it all together
Recommending solutions
Implementing the plan
Monitoring the plan

The PIPRIM system can be used for any case that presents itself. It is a process that will enable Planner A to make sure his clients are being handled properly. It also provides the framework for an orderly and organized approach to dealing with clients.

PRELIMINARY MEETING WITH A CLIENT

Planner A greets Mary in the waiting room, where his assistant has already offered her a beverage and made her feel welcome. He introduces himself and invites Mary into the conference room, where he begins the conversation by asking how she is doing. Mary begins by discussing her husband, what they did together, how he took care of all the financial issues, and how different it will be without him. Planner A informs her that he is here to help her get through this most difficult time and will work with her to create a financial plan that she is comfortable with.

Working with a client whose partner has died can be an emotion-filled and complex process. Mary must feel secure if she is to continue to open up to Planner A. With the appropriate amount of hand-holding, she will eventually trust him to invest and manage her money. Many planners are either not willing or not capable of providing such a time-consuming level of service. Therefore Planner A must be sure that it makes sense to add this type of client to his practice. The amount of client service this type of client requires may continue to increase substantially. As part of the practice's business plan, Planner A must determine whether he can make the sacrifices necessary to provide this type of client with the emotional support she will need.

When dealing with a client such as Mary, Planner A isn't looking for short-term solutions through inappropriate investments. Even though she is older, she is treated as a long-term client. That means Planner A won't suggest anything fancy or unsuitable. For example, he won't automatically put her in an annuity or another fixed type of investment program without first doing the appropriate analysis. She may be concerned about running out of money sooner rather than later, in which case an annuity could be a good choice for her. Unfortunately, approximately 93 percent of all annuities never pay out in full, an indication that they are sold for the wrong reasons.

Planner A summarizes the conclusions reached by and agreed upon by both parties in a formal engagement letter to ensure that the type of services he will provide meets Mary's expectations. A client may even want to meet with Planner A several times more before signing. She may be concerned about making a mistake or "signing her life away." Meeting with a client as often as necessary helps assuage any fears and solidify the relationship.

INTEGRATED GOAL SETTING AND DATA GATHERING

Now that Planner A is beyond the initial meeting, it is time to set Mary's goals. He begins by asking questions centered on her overall objectives. Does she plan to change anything about her current living situation? Has she considered moving to be closer to her children? Are her children committed to taking care of her should she become ill? Or would she downsize her house or move to an adult or assisted-living community? Does she have long-term-care insurance?

After Planner A identifies Mary's needs, funds must be allocated to her objectives. If funds aren't available to purchase long-term-care insurance, for example, alternative avenues must be pursued. Perhaps a relative is able to help fund Mary's long-term-care needs.

Planner A also reviews all of her estate planning documents, such as wills and trusts. Many times such documents were prepared years ago and are completely outdated, with deceased or divorced beneficiaries or incorrect addresses or other personal information, or they were drafted in a state other than where the client is now living (such as a community-property or common-law state).

Remember, goals and objectives are different; objectives quantify goals by setting definitive dollar amounts and time frames for each. Planner A needs to ensure that his client is as specific as possible in her descriptions and as direct as possible concerning her future plans. He makes sure Mary states what she wants to do, and he constantly summarizes and paraphrases what she is saying to ensure that they are both on the same page.

By this point, Planner A should have all the data he needs to incorporate into a financial plan for Mary that includes how much she can withdraw each month to live on; an appropriate investment policy; what, if anything, she plans to leave to her heirs; and all other issues that have been identified by the client during this process. The objective is for the client to address all of her immediate and future concerns so that she is financially prepared for every issue.

PUTTING IT ALL TOGETHER

At the conclusion of the interactive session, Planner A lets Mary know when she can expect to hear from him again. On her way out of the office, he suggests she meet with his assistant to set up a return visit, and gives her a one- to two-week range as to when he anticipates the plan will be ready for review.

Now that Planner A has all of his client's information, his assistant enters the raw data into the database. Based on the raw data, Planner A will be in a good position to make recommendations, pick investments, allocate funds, assess the objectives, and tie everything together to help create the opportunity for the client to achieve her goals.

The balance sheet and cash flow statements developed through this process provide Planner A with a good indication of what his client can and cannot do financially. In Mary's case, it can even tell him whether she qualifies for Medicaid or another type of subsidy. Planner A will see what assets there are to draw from and how much annual income can be expected.

RECOMMENDING SOLUTIONS

When Mary returns to the office for the follow-up meeting, Planner A is firm when explaining the likelihood of success based on the objectives Mary has stated and the resources she can depend on. He gives Mary a highlighter and makes the first mark on the financial plan to make the point that the plan should be used as a road map, not placed on a shelf somewhere and never referred to again. He tells Mary to highlight all the key information and mark up the plan so it will be easier for her to use in the future.

Planner A explains whether Mary's objectives are achievable based on the circumstances he has uncovered. It may be necessary to start over with some clients at this time, basically informing them that their existing or proposed scenario is not going to work. Sometimes the client is shocked; other times they are expecting it. But remember, Planner A is the realist. His job is to help the client attain her goals, and this type of feedback can be difficult for a client to accept. In Mary's case, there are only two choices: raise revenue or cut expenses. One way of increasing revenue might be to assume the risk of reallocating assets to a more aggressive portfolio. But that approach is inappropriate for a client who is not psychologically prepared to handle increased risk or radical changes. Such a client might react to a brief market downturn by insisting on selling those assets, defeating the plan's purpose. In Mary's case, a more aggressive investing approach probably would not work. With her shorter time horizon and an immediate need for cash, a conservative approach is the most logical answer.

The other option is to reduce Mary's expenses by creating a budget that will enable her to live a little less comfortably but with the security that she won't run out of assets. Planner A then looks at Mary's existing budget, determines which expenses are the first to go, tinkers with others, and develops a new lower budget that doesn't require as large a return on investments and can be stretched out over a longer period of time.

IMPLEMENTING THE PLAN

The plan won't be worth the paper it's printed on unless it is put into action. Therefore, Planner A provides a simple "to do" list for the client, as follows:

Sample Summary Action Plan

Action List for Mary Leonard
July 10, 2005

ACTION	PERSON RESPONSIBLE	DUE DATE	COMPLETED
Contact estate-planning attorneys	Mary	07/31/05	X
Begin reallocation of assets to ensure monthly income and a more overall conservative portfolio	Mary	08/15/05	
Update will	Mary	10/31/05	
Research long-term-care options	Mary	11/15/05	

This will serve as a starting point for items getting completed every time they meet. Planner A goes through the list with Mary to determine what has been done, and find out why things have not been done. He ensures that these basic points get covered so the client is protected and her situation is upgraded based on his recommendations. They decide to meet either by phone or in person every other month to ensure that things are getting done. This is also Planner A's chance to monitor progress and ask for referrals.

MONITORING THE PLAN

Because things can change, it is imperative that the client's situation is constantly reviewed. Mary is going to need attention to ensure that any adjustments she needs to make are implemented. After Planner A has met with her several times during the initial process, a semiannual or annual meeting is warranted and should be established in the engagement letter.

Planner A is now engaged in tweaking that plan to ensure that the client stays on course. Therefore, the fee should be either a percentage of what the client paid initially or a flat fee (perhaps 40 percent of what was initially charged). Most of the time-consuming things were done initially; at this stage, Planner A is refining the model already in place. And again, every time he meets with Mary, he asks for referrals.

Case 2: Ben and Kate Wilson— Professional Young Couple with Children

BEN, AGE THIRTY-FIVE, and Kate, age thirty-two, were a referral from a client who works with Ben. Ben is an engineer, and Kate is a homemaker, taking care of their three-year-old and one-year-old children. Ben earns $80,000 per year and has limited benefits— only health insurance and a 401(k) plan.

PRELIMINARY MEETING WITH A CLIENT

When Ben and Kate arrive at Planner B's office, her receptionist gives them a simple twelve-question questionnaire (see **EXHIBIT 3.2** on pages 76–77) to complete. The entire questionnaire takes about ten minutes yet prepares Ben and Kate for the issues the planner is about to raise. When Planner B greets Ben and Kate in the waiting room, they are visibly nervous, having never undergone this process before. The closest they have come to a financial planning discussion is when they spoke informally to Kate's brother about purchasing life insurance.

INTEGRATED GOAL SETTING AND DATA GATHERING

Once they are seated in the conference room, Planner B explains the purpose of financial planning. She tells the Wilsons it is a long-term process that essentially helps someone get from Point A to Point B. It is not a get-rich-quick scheme, nor is it about consistently selecting the best-performing investments. It's not a daily activity but one that is measured over the long term. Planner B tells them that the purpose of financial planning is to ensure that they will have funds available when they need them, depending on their particular objectives.

Planner B begins by asking a series of specific questions about money. Where do they intend to go in life? How much do they anticipate needing to accomplish all of their objectives? What's most important to them now? What are their priorities? It's very possible that Ben and Kate won't achieve all of these; yet, if they can attain several important ones, then Planner B's help will be worthwhile. That's the importance of prioritizing. Essentially, the plan is to make the objectives at the beginning of the list a reality, and then, depending on their other circumstances, work toward achieving the next set of objectives, and so forth. They seem overwhelmed by all of this questioning, so Planner B explains the importance of being very specific. Goals are open-ended broad statements that give generalities. It's more difficult to give specifics, which are objectives, but they are definite and measurable. This way accountability is established and specific needs can be provided for properly.

The Wilsons have never discussed life insurance in a serious way. Who will take care of their children if something unexpected happens? They never thought about these issues when their children were first born, because they were too busy taking care of more immediate concerns. Planner B proceeds with her line of questioning and determines all of their objectives, putting a price tag on each in today's dollars.

Planner B then tallies all of their objectives to quantify a grand number for life insurance needs. For Ben, a reasonable estimate of life insurance coverage is seven times his annual salary, or $560,000. Since Kate does not draw a salary, calculating her life insurance coverage requires a calculation of her "replacement cost." If Kate were to die, Ben would need to hire live-in help to care for the kids and handle all the housekeeping duties. Since Ben occasionally travels for business, overnight child care would be warranted. If the cost of bringing in a live-in nanny is $35,000 per year, and the youngest child will not be attending college for another seventeen years, and assuming the nanny gets a 5 percent raise every year, then Planner B enters the following into the financial calculator:

$35,000	PMT
17	N
5	1

The present value (PV) of that future payment stream equals $394,592. So Kate's life insurance requirement is roughly $400,000.

Planner B next works through the disability income numbers to ensure that they have coverage for 60 to 70 percent of their gross income. Since Ben's job doesn't provide for long-term disability, disability insurance is an important objective that goes to the top of the list. A ninety-day elimination period and benefits payable to age sixty-five would be warranted for a professional like Ben. He probably will be at or next to the highest classification for determining disability benefits and premiums. There is a greater concern about long-term disability since short-term disability needs would be met through the ninety-day emergency fund the Wilsons will create. Their health insurance coverage is provided by Ben's job. Because they are young, and because their resources are not yet adequate to address this need, long-term care should not be a concern for them at this time.

Their automobile insurance policy has a deductible of $250 and $500,000 liability coverage. Planner B tells them to raise the deductible, since the odds of submitting a claim for that little amount is far-fetched, considering that the raise in future premiums will cost them more than what they would receive from smaller claims. Planner B has them raise the deductible to $1,000 to save a few hundred dollars annually on the premium. Planner B also notices that the $500,000 liability limit does not coincide with their umbrella deductible of $1 million from another insurer. Therefore, she suggests that Ben and Kate raise this coverage amount to equal their underlying umbrella deductible. After all, in the event of significant liability claims, Planner B wants the payout to be seamless. That is, where the underlying automobile liability coverage stops, the umbrella policy kicks in. The umbrella policy will cover not only their liability needs beyond their underlying policy limits but also their defense costs associated with a lawsuit.

Their home owners coverage is also out of line. They just purchased their dream house last year for $600,000. Planner B notices that the home owners dwelling coverage (coverage A) is also for $600,000. She tells the Wilsons that they have too much coverage; based on the land-to-home value in their region, they should have approximately $480,000 of coverage. Planner B explains that even if the house burns down, the land will still be there; therefore, no insurance coverage for the land is necessary. Ben and Kate lower their dwelling amount to save money on the premium.

Many times planners see clients with *too little* home owners dwelling coverage. The rule of thumb is that insurance should cover 80 percent of the appraised value of the property. For example, if the clients' house would cost $500,000 to rebuild and the client currently has $300,000 of coverage A (dwelling coverage), they are roughly $100,000 low on total coverage. It should be suggested that the client bump up this coverage amount to $400,000 to ensure full coverage in the event of a loss. However, the land/ building ratio varies by region. Consult a real estate appraiser to determine the property's true value.

Planner B next has Ben and Kate create a budget, which is something they have never done before. After analyzing their entire situation, they are amazed at how much money they are

Objectives for Ben and Kate Wilson

Pay off all debt	$550,000
Establish a 90-day emergency fund	$25,000
Fund four years at a state college for two children	$120,000
Support children until youngest reaches age 18	$200,000
Provide pre-retirement support for spouse (until age 65)	$300,000
Provide post-retirement needs for spouse (ages 65 to 90)	$400,000
Purchase life insurance	$960,000 (Ben + Kate)
Make bequest to favorite charity	$50,000

wasting and how inefficient their whole household budget has become. They reallocate monies from discretionary expenditures and reroute those dollars into savings and investments to target the specific goals they have set out for themselves.

At this point, the infrastructure is in place and the investment planning process can begin with the development of an investment policy statement. Risk and insurance issues must always be covered first, without exception. The client must adequately plan for becoming ill, being unable to work, losing a house, or dying prematurely. Funds should always be set aside to cover these exposures. If these risks are not accounted for properly in advance, the client would have to raid any after-tax investments or retirement accounts to cover them.

The investment analysis covers after-tax investing, retirement (before-tax) investing, and saving for college. Planner B also coordinates cash surrender values of their newly purchased life insurance policies into the overall asset allocation.

Planner B then looks at their remaining documents to help put together their estate plan and determine a retirement needs analysis and any other analysis they may need. The estate-planning documents might include the clients' wills, trust documents, deeds, and pre- or postnuptial agreements. On the retirement-needs side, these documents would include an analysis of existing investments, a projection of potential revenue streams (such as Social Security and pensions), and an analysis of what future retirement expenses are likely to be incurred.

PUTTING IT ALL TOGETHER

These individual components are gathered to create a balance sheet and cash flow statement that spells out where Ben and Kate are and where they need to be. The results may be a little overwhelming for them, since they have never seen an analysis like this done for them before (see **EXHIBITS 9.1** and **9.2**).

Chances are Ben and Kate will be asset poor, in that their only major asset is their house. Their net worth will also be low, due to their huge mortgage balance. Drawing from other assets to earmark them for future goals is a little premature at this point. Their cash flow statement looks fine, since they have a sufficient amount of money coming in, more than enough to cover expenses and a surplus to invest. Planner B's job is to invest that money in a way that enables them to reach their known future goals.

RECOMMENDING SOLUTIONS

The recommendations Planner B has listed may have initially seemed far-fetched given Ben and Kate's immediate needs for raising their two young children. But after this careful and thorough analysis, Planner B helps the Wilsons put their options into perspective. Planner B has helped them identify the key issues and plan an appropriate course of action.

The following are some of the issues Planner B has identified during their analysis, and suggestions for ways to explain recommendations to clients:

◆ **Saving for the children's education should be a priority.** One way to do this is through the creation of a Section 529 educational savings account. With a 529 plan, monies grow tax-deferred and can be distributed income-tax-free if used for college. Significant amounts can be contributed to these accounts (approximately $270,000 as of this writing), and the client can take five annual gift tax exclusions up front ($55,000 on day one, which is the current annual exclusion of $11,000 per year for five years at the time of this writing). Different investment options and many state plans' state income tax deductions make this a worthwhile choice.

◆ **The Wilsons' current amount of life insurance and disability insurance stand out as insufficient.** Planner B's estimate should include all of the objectives the family will want to accomplish if Ben were to die today. The automobile and home owners insurance serve as the underlying deductible for the umbrella (or excess liability) policy, which is also a requirement. The umbrella policy can provide additional protection against both serious and frivolous lawsuits, since it covers the actual liability arising from the claim and the costs of a defense.

With young children and new expenses, the Wilsons have not saved as much as they need, nor have they paid attention to some of their longer-term objectives, such as college tuition and retirement. Their rationale has been that these other objectives are not a true immediate concern, since they are not in sight for them at this time. But nevertheless, Planner B needs to reiterate that the only true path for achieving them is through a disciplined approach beginning now.

IMPLEMENTING THE PLAN

Planner B drafts a "to-do" sheet the Wilsons can follow to ensure that all the items she has identified get done. This is their scorecard for getting things done in a timely manner. Any deviations from this game plan will need to be addressed in future revisions of the plan.

MONITORING THE PLAN

Ben and Kate will be undergoing much change over the next few years as the children grow and additional funds will be needed on their behalf. They will go into their peak earnings years, and

ACTION ITEM	PERSON RESPONSIBLE	DUE DATE
1 Decrease home owners insurance (coverage A)	Ben	04/05/05
2 Purchase umbrella insurance policy	Ben	04/05/05
3 Examine investments in retirement plan	Kate	04/12/05
4 Create a revocable living trust	Kate	05/01/05
5 Set up 529 plan	Kate	05/05/05
6 Buy life insurance	Ben	05/15/05
7 Buy disability insurance	Ben	05/15/05

those newfound monies will need to be rerouted to ensure that their infrastructure remains strong. Parents this age will probably have an active social life, with mom-and-tot classes, sports leagues, and the like. The Wilsons' social contacts can lead to numerous referrals, which Planner B requests.

Case 3: Ed and Tami Johnson— Wealthy Married Couple Nearing Retirement

ED AND TAMI, both age fifty-eight, have had Planner C's name for years. They've long meant to call her but have only now gotten around to it. They have seen their children graduate from college, settle down, and begin families of their own. Ed is an attorney who is a partner with a large national law firm and earns $400,000 per year. He's been with the firm for twenty-five years. Tami works as a teacher's aide, has been with the school system for seventeen years, and earns $30,000 per year. This highly active couple has a sizable nest egg, and they want to begin enjoying their resources and possibly assist their children down the road. But, as they will tell Planner C, "Let's not plan on those large inheritances for the kids just yet. There is still a lot of living for us to do."

PRELIMINARY MEETING WITH A CLIENT

Planner C's assistant gives them the twelve-question questionnaire to complete. Planner C meets them in the waiting area and invites them back to the conference room. After small talk about what they have accomplished, the Johnsons begin telling Planner C about their objectives. Retirement is their big issue; they want to retire in two years, at age sixty, while they are in good health. Ed is concerned about giving up his big salary and making sure they have things to occupy their time. Planner C informs them that they have to plan for a retirement period equaling about one-third of their lifetimes, or about thirty years. That's a long time to be withdrawing the funds they will have contributed primarily during the previous thirty years, between the ages of thirty and sixty.

Another concern is taking care of Ed's mother, whose care during her remaining years they are partially responsible for funding. Also, now that their kids are on their own, Tami and Ed want to travel. They hope to vacation outside their metropolitan area frequently throughout their retirement.

INTEGRATED GOAL SETTING AND DATA GATHERING

Now the key is to find sufficient funds to accomplish Ed and Tami's objectives. They tell Planner C that every objective is a priority, and since retirement is only two years away, they want to know what they can do now to achieve their objectives. When Planner C asks if they have ever had a financial plan done for them, they answer no. "Just never got around to it," they further reply. Planner C asks them about their house and their future plans for residing there, downsizing, or possibly moving away, perhaps to be closer to their kids. Two of their three children live nearby, and the third lives a few hours away by car. They also don't want to leave their friends and Ed's mom, so they plan to use their house as home base for their adventures.

Planner C asks them about their wills and any other trust documents. Their wills were set up thirty years ago, when guardianship of their children was their key issue. A lot has changed since then, considering they moved from a common-law state to a community-property state. Planner C informs the

Johnsons that their wills need to be updated every three to five years to ensure that their wishes are communicated exactly as they want them to be.

Since at a glance it looks like their estate is over the "magic threshold" where estate taxes will be due at death, Planner C begins to discuss retitling certain assets and making use of irrevocable trusts, including moving some insurance policies into irrevocable life insurance trusts (ILITs). The Johnsons also have a concern about paying estate taxes. They would like to leave money to their children, if possible, but they won't sacrifice the way they live during retirement to do so. Since both of them are in good health, Planner C tells them that she will investigate the feasibility of life insurance on both to accomplish this goal. Some planners may also show their clients a matrix of the recommended policy types and companies, explaining the pros and cons of each, and letting them make the ultimate choice. Premiums are compared, cash values are looked at, expense ratios are analyzed, company ratings are reviewed, and anything else that may concern them is addressed.

Ed's mother is an ongoing concern, since she needs hands-on care. So Planner C begins looking into an assisted-living facility for her. She is too old for a long-term-care policy and not in the best of health. Planner C tells them that she'll investigate various options for Ed's mother. Finding the funds should not be an issue, since Ed's brother and sister have agreed to help with the expense. Ed will do all the legwork and come out with a viable recommendation for the entire family.

PUTTING IT ALL TOGETHER

Planner C determines which retirement benefit works best given their situation, since both have defined benefit plans. A matrix will be drawn explaining the benefits under various scenarios. Since Tami's benefits would not be sufficient if Ed were to die first, a joint-and-survivor benefit should be present. Planner C works out several alternatives here to make sure she is in line with the expenses they plan on incurring.

Planner C then consolidates their information into a balance sheet and cash flow statement. She sees a net worth of about

$1.6 million, yet their current expenses total $15,000 per month ($180,000 per year). Based on Planner C's analysis of what their income will be during retirement and the amount they can begin liquidating, she tells them their assets won't be sufficient. Cutbacks are needed. They have two choices: reduce expenses or raise revenue through the reallocation of their current investments. The Johnsons choose to lower their expenses. Planner C analyzes the cash flow statement's discretionary expenses and find several categories to remove and reduce.

RECOMMENDING SOLUTIONS

Planner C recommends that the Johnsons' discretionary expenses be reallocated into their investment portfolio. By reviewing their objectives again, she helps the Johnsons reduce their monthly expenditures to a more manageable $9,000 ($108,000 per year). The key here is that this can be done with minimal interruptions and little hassle. In essence, they won't miss these expenses. Work-related expenses, high-end vacations, and impulse buying are some of the things to be done away with. These reductions will enable them to retire at age sixty as planned.

Planner C provides a grid of assisted-living facilities for Ed's mom for several states based on cost, benefits, and transferability. Planner C proceeds to go over them with the client, but the client makes the final decision.

Planner C also provides the clients with a list of three attorneys who specialize in estate planning so they can interview them all. When they choose an attorney, Planner C seeks permission to release a copy of the financial plan to the attorney so the attorney can understand their background and the important issues surrounding their decisions.

Based on their health and the newly found money from rearranging their expenses, life insurance policies are needed to handle any estate taxes that may arise. Planner C recommends the policies be placed into an established irrevocable life insurance trust (ILIT) to ensure that these policies' death benefits will not be part of any gross estate.

ACTION ITEM	PERSON RESPONSIBLE	DUE DATE
1 Increase disability coverage through work	Ed	09/10/05
2 Increase life insurance coverage through work	Ed	09/10/05
3 Provide planner with list of 401(k) plan options	Tami	09/12/05
4 Change beneficiary on personal life insurance policy	Tami	09/15/05

IMPLEMENTING THE PLAN

Since the clients' time horizon is relatively short (two years till retirement), actions need to be taken quickly. Monthly follow-ups to ensure that tasks are met are a necessity. Planner C has the Johnsons begin to allocate the time regularly into their schedules to ensure that these items get done.

The assisted living for Ed's mother is also key because there could be a waiting period for entrance. If the period is too long, alternative suggestions need to be developed, including contacting Ed's brother and sister for the possibility of all of them assuming some responsibility until Ed's mom is provided for. Ideally, Ed and Tami want to ensure that this issue is taken care of before their retirement; otherwise further reliance on Ed's brother and sister may be warranted.

MONITORING THE PLAN

Although Planner C has set up a plan for the Johnsons' retirement, that doesn't mean it's going to be carried out automatically. The Johnsons are to cut their expenses drastically, and they need to learn to live under these newly defined parameters, so constant monitoring is essential.

Planner C meets with them quarterly in the beginning, then semiannually. She reviews investment performance, annual dividends, and interest payments to ensure that cash flow remains strong. Any discrepancies are immediately investigated and corrected.

FINANCIAL PLANNERS shoulder a huge responsibility. Clients come to them for advice, guidance, and help with everything they refuse to deal with themselves, don't want to get involved with, or simply don't understand. A planner can be their guiding light. A planner doesn't dictate to them what to do, but rather suggests ways they can accomplish their objectives, given their particular circumstances. Planners should not make the final decisions; rather, they should act as a sounding board and point out to clients what steps they can take now to achieve long-term success. When a planner works with sincerity, understanding, and real-life compassion to help people maximize their current situation and be the best they can be, the rewards of the profession are boundless.

Ben and Kate Wilson
Statement of Financial Position
as of December 31, 2004

ASSETS[1]		LIABILITIES AND NET WORTH	
Cash/cash equivalents		Liabilities[2]	
Checking	$_____	Consumer loan	
CU savings/		balance	$_____
passbook	$_____	Mortgage	
Money market		balance	$_____
accounts	$_____	**Total liabilities**	**$_____**
Life insurance			
cash value	$_____		
Total cash/			
cash equivalents	**$_____**		
Invested Assets			
Stocks/bonds/funds	$_____		
IRAs	$_____		
Vested retirement			
accounts	$_____	**Net worth**	**$_____**
Total invested assets	**$_____**		
Use Assets			
Residence	$_____		
Vacation homes	$_____		
Personal property	$_____		
Total use assets	**$_____**		
TOTAL ASSETS	**$_____**	**TOTAL LIABILITIES**	
		NET WORTH	**$_____**

Explanations for the planner:

[1] All assets are listed at fair market value.

[2] All liabilities are listed with the outstanding principle balance accrued interest, if applicable.

EXHIBIT 9.2

Ben and Kate Wilson

Cash Flow Statement for the Year Ending December 31, 2004

INFLOWS[1]

Gross salaries	$ 80,000	$ 0
Dividends/Interest	$ 3,000	$ 2,500
Other	$ 0	$ 0
Total inflows	$ 86,000	

OUTFLOWS

Savings and investments[2]	$ 8,600	0
Fixed outflows[3]		
Mortgage payments	$ 34,871	$ 0
Auto payments	$ 0	$ 0
Insurance premiums	$ 4,000	$ 0
FICA taxes	$ 6,120	$ 0
Other	$ 2,500	$ 0
Total fixed outflows	$ 47,491	
Variable Outflows		
Federal and state taxes	$ 9,609	$ 0
Debt reduction	$ 0	$ 0
Food	$ 6,000	$ 0
Transportation	$ 3,000	$ 0
Entertainment	$ 1,800	$ 0
Vacations	$ 4,000	$ 0
Charitable contributions	$ 1,500	$ 0
Clothing	$ 3,000	$ 0
Gifts	$ 1,000	$ 0
Total variable outflows	$ 29,909	
TOTAL OUTFLOWS	**$ 86,000**	

Explanations for the planner:

(1) Gross inflows
(2) Including reinvested dividends and interest
(3) Relatively predictable, recurring and little control

CHAPTER 10

RESOURCES AND TRAINING

CHAPTERS 1 THROUGH 9 provide a strong base on which

to build a financial planning practice. This chapter gives

you outside resources that will help make your practice

more efficient.

Joining a Professional Group

JOINING A group of your peers is one way to improve your

practice. Professional groups have various resources,

including software, journals, and newsletters. Many

also have support or specialty groups that discuss technical and/or practice management issues. Members of these groups are typically sincere, helpful, smart, and willing to share information.

Many organizations represent the interests of financial planners. The following six are among the more popular ones.

1 American Institute of Certified Public Accountants (AICPA) Personal Financial Planning (PFP) Division. This organization represents 4,000-plus certified public accountant (CPA) financial planners in the United States. Membership requirements include having a valid CPA license and being a member in good standing of the AICPA. As discussed in Chapter 2, the AICPA offers a professional designation: Personal Financial Specialist (PFS). Member benefits include a bimonthly division newsletter called *The Planner,* an annual PFP practice handbook called *Responsibilities in PFP Practice,* discounts to the AICPA-PFP Technical Conference, and the opportunity to buy consumer brochures.

The division's goal is to enhance public awareness of CPAs and the CPA/PFS designation and to become known as the premier providers of PFP services. It also plans to launch an Investment Advisory Service Center, expand educational materials, and work closely with the state CPA societies. For more information, call 888-777-7077 or visit the institute's website at www.aicpa.org.

2 Chartered Financial Analyst (CFA) Institute. This association of 70,000-plus members represents investment analysts in the United States, Canada, and abroad. Membership requirements include having a bachelor's degree from an accredited institution or relevant work experience, and passing the Chartered Financial Analyst (CFA) examination. Member benefits include access to the CFA Institute JobLine, local programs provided by CFA Institute societies, discounts to CFA Institute seminars and conferences, website programs, and videoconferences. Its publications include *CFA Digest, Financial Analysts Journal, CFA Magazine,* and *CFA Institute Conference Proceedings.* For more information, call 800-247-8132 or visit the CFA Institute website at www.cfainstitute.org.

3 Financial Planning Association (FPA). This association of 28,000-plus planners, which began in January 2000 and represents a broad spectrum of financial planners, includes licensed planners as well as CFP licensees. It represents a merger of the former Institute of Certified Financial Planners (ICFP) with the former International Association for Financial Planning (IAFP). It offers a variety of conferences, publications, and other member benefits. For more information, call 800-322-4237 or visit FPA's website at www.fpanet.org.

4 Investment Management Consultants Association (IMCA). This association represents investment consultants in the United States, Canada, United Kingdom, and Australia. Member benefits include a legislative network, discounts on publications, various conferences, and the Certified Investment Management Analysts Course. Its publications include *Facts About Investing, Using ERISA to Develop New Business, Maximizing Your Investment Results, Consultant's Math Primer, Marketing Kit,* and *Professional Module Series.* For more information, call 303-770-3377 or visit its website at www.imca.org.

5 National Association of Personal Financial Advisors (NAPFA). This 750-member U.S.-based organization represents fee-only financial advisers. Members must agree to a code of ethics and a fiduciary oath; have a bachelor's degree, specialized education, or training; adhere to continuing education requirements; have three years of experience; offer comprehensive financial planing services; and submit a comprehensive financial plan. Members receive the *NAPFA Advisor* and *Newslink.* NAPFA holds an annual conference. For more information, call 800-366-2732 or visit its website at www.napfa.org.

6 Society of Financial Service Professionals. This organization of more than 22,000 members represents financial service professionals from all segments of the financial services industry. Membership requirements include holding any of the following designations: Chartered Life Underwriter (CLU), Chartered Financial Consultant (ChFC), Registered Health Underwriter (RHU), Registered Employee Benefits Consultant (REBC), Certified Financial Planner (CFP), Certified Public Accountant

(CPA), Juris Doctor (J.D., licensed), Chartered Leadership Fellow (CLF), or Master of Science in Management (MSM) and Master of Science in Financial Services (MSFS) degrees granted by the American College. Member publications include the *Journal of Financial Service Professionals, Keeping Current,* four client newsletters, and nine special-interest newsletters. In addition, a member can belong to any of the nine professional interest sections and sign up for advanced continuing education programs or courses. Importantly, members have access to industry products, Internet-based research capabilities, industry news, national advertising and public relations campaigns, networking, chapter meetings, promotional publications, and a national consumer referral service. The society also has an annual conference. For more information, call 610-526-2500 or visit its website at www.financialpro.org.

Tools for Your Practice

FULL-TIME planners benefit tremendously from automated tools in the form of advanced financial planning software programs. It may take you a while to learn the ins and outs of these tools, but once you become familiar with some of them, you will have the knowledge to go out and test others in order to locate the product that best suits your practice. As with all computer technology, this field is changing very rapidly. This section gives you a starting point for evaluating these tools and choosing the ones that make the most sense for you without sacrificing much time. It does not represent an endorsement of any product or service.

Turnkey Programs

IF YOU WANT to work within an established system that defines every step of the financial planning, investment planning, and management programs, you may want to consider a turnkey program. In theory, just like with a car, you turn the key and it goes.

A turnkey program for an asset management system is called a TAMP (turnkey asset management program). You contract with a back-office operation to provide all the compliance, research, and hand-holding you need. This type of program is good for the novice planner, but it does have drawbacks. You split part of your fee with this back office every time you do business. Still, TAMPs can get you up and running in a much shorter time than you can probably do it on your own.

A turnkey program for personal financial planning services can operate in a variety of ways. With one type you contract with a company that makes all the financial plans after you complete a data-gathering form and submit it, either electronically or on paper, to your turnkey provider. The company then enters the data, goes over the numbers with you, and sends back a completed plan within seventy-two hours. You present the plan to the clients. This is a good approach for planners who want to be in front of clients most of the time and have someone else be responsible for the back-office work.

A second program takes over and provides plans for the clients you refer. If you are licensed, you receive a part of the commission if your referral results in product sales. The benefit of this approach is that you do not have to learn the business. The downside is that you will never make as much money as you likely will if you do learn the business.

Still another approach is to form your own turnkey program. Join forces with other planners, each with a particular specialty—investment, retirement, insurance, estate planning—and a CPA for income tax issues. Clients see the combination of professionals they need to address their needs. Most planners these days are specialists, so this arrangement often works well.

Selecting a Software Program

BUYING A software program is not easy. It is a big investment and requires a great deal of research before you write a check. Worse, few or no programs will do exactly what you want, and you will not know precisely how a program works until you use it for many clients, even though you try out a demo.

To aid in the evaluation process, take a moment to consider the following twenty questions before you buy a computer program.

1 What are the pros and cons of buying one integrated system versus several programs separately to accomplish particular tasks?

2 Will you have to pay an annual support fee for this financial planning software? What does that charge include?

3 What is involved when this software interfaces with another program?

4 Does the software require third-party programs for operation? If so, does this pose special issues to look out for?

5 What skills should you have to operate this financial planning software program?

6 How much time should you expect to spend evaluating a financial planning software program?

7 What trial period is available on this program?

8 How long does it take to get up to speed on this financial planning program?

9 What type of training is available and where?

10 What user groups exist for this software vendor? How much weight should you give input from existing users?

11 Will this software vendor download data from the companies you do business with on a client-by-client basis?

12 Will this vendor do a sample plan with you for one of your clients?

13 Is this software bug free?

14 How often is the software updated?

15 How often should you expect to have to upgrade the hardware?

16 Is a fact finder included? Can you modify it?

17 Can you copy the software and use it on different computers?

18 If you switch from Software X to Software Y, can you expect to get your data from X to Y?

19 Is this software company likely to go out of business?

20 Will this software vendor be able to answer questions about computer operation, aside from questions about its software programs?

Contacting the Vendors

ONCE YOU DECIDE what type of software you want, the next step is to contact vendors for a request for proposal (RFP). The RFP lets you compare the programs. Send this or a similar form to the vendors, or visit the exhibit area at one of the many industrywide conferences. Many of the software vendors listed in this chapter will be there, and you will be able to get a personal demonstration of their programs.

The following questions are general—you may want to modify them to reflect your needs.

◆ Software product _____

◆ Company _____

◆ Address _____

◆ Telephone number _____

◆ Fax number _____

◆ E-mail address _____

◆ Website _____

◆ Sales representative _____

SERVICE AND TRAINING

1 Do you provide training tapes?

2 Do you provide initial training? If so, when and where are classes held?

3 Do you provide advanced training for enhancements?

4 Based on my experience level, how many hours will it take me to adjust to your system?

5 Do you provide different levels of training for different functions?

6 How much is the annual maintenance fee? What does it include?

7 What future enhancements are included in this fee?

8 What enhancements do you plan to introduce over the next two years?

9 Do you provide technical support?

TECHNOLOGY

1 What hardware (including disk space) do I need to run your program?

2 What other software do I need to run your program?

3 Can I run the software on a network? Does the software come with multiuser access?

4 What software is included in your program?

5 What additional features cost extra?

6 Can I change the program's default assumptions to fit the needs of my individual clients?

7 Does the software offer an audit trail of calculations for reports?

8 Does the system have decision-making features?

9 If yes, then on what are the decision-making assumptions based?

10 What attitudes or goals does the system take into account when making decisions?

11 Does the software offer online capabilities?

12 Can the system support multiple simultaneous users?

13 What kind of support package is included?

14 What kind of training package is included?

15 Are there any discounts (i.e., broker-dealer, membership, etc.) offered?

OUTPUT

1 How many pages is the longest plan? The shortest?

2 Can the program generate a summary plan?

3 Can the program generate a single-use or modular plan for retirement, education, or investment planning?

4 How many years in the future will the reports project? Can a planner change the number of years?

5 Are the federal and state taxes exact or estimated?

6 How many schedules are included in each section?

7 Can all the schedules be graphed?

8 Does the text integrate with a word processing program such as Microsoft Word?

9 Is there a text library?

10 What auxiliary reports are available?

11 Can outprint be printed to a disk file?

12 How does the system handle what-if scenarios?

13 Does the system produce client review reports for ongoing client communication?

INPUT

1 For whom is your questionnaire designed?

2 Is required information highlighted in the questionnaire?

3 Can someone without financial planning knowledge input the data?

4 Do the data entry screens look like the fact finder?

5 Are fields numbered or coded?

6 What error trapping is built into data entry?

7 Are there help screens for data entry? Are help screens field specific or generalized?

CORPORATE BACKGROUND

1 Who founded your company and why?

2 When did your company start selling software?

3 How many employees does your company have?

4 How many software products do you sell? Are they all related to financial planning?

5 Can you provide financial information about your company?

6 Is your company a subsidiary or affiliated with another company?

7 Who is your main software competitor?

8 Why is your product better than those of your competitors?

THE BASICS

1 How much does the software cost?

2 Is there a full-refund period?

3 Do you offer a network version of the software?

4 Do you also sell hardware? If yes, what types and for how much?

5 How much is the annual maintenance?

6 Do you expect the software or maintenance costs to change in the next year?

7 Can you provide the names of three planners who would be willing to talk about your software?

8 I need to review the following software items before I make a decision:

    (a) a completed fact finder or questionnaire

    (b) a sample plan based on the completed fact finder

    (c) all schedules

(d) all auxiliary reports

(e) all graphs

(f) text library (if non-decision-making)

(g) information about your company

(h) sales literature

(i) technical explanations

(j) sample software license agreement

9 Does your system do any of the following in addition to planning?

(a) portfolio management

(b) asset tracking

(c) practice management

(d) order entry

(e) batch processing

(f) client management

(g) interface to outside data services

Technology Central

THE FOLLOWING companies make financial planning software programs. If you want further information, call the vendor and ask for a demo disk and sales brochure.

Financial Planning Software Programs

PROGRAM	DEVELOPER	PHONE NUMBER
Enteract	CCH	800-224-7477 x4622
Estate Planning Tools	Brentmark	800-879-6665
ExecPlan v5.03	Sawhney Systems	800-850-8444
Financial Analyzer II	Leimberg Associates	610-924-0515
Financial Planning Professional	Lumen Systems	800-233-3461
Financial Planning Suite	Cheshire Software	800-734-6734
FPlan Professional Advisor	First Financial Software	800-354-4929
Golden Years	Money Tree Software	877-421-9815

Harvest-Time.net Retirement Planning Software	The Advisors Edge	704-549-1100
MasterPlan Financial Software	MasterPlan Financial Software	800-229-5080
NaviPlan	EISI	888-694-3474 x2135
PFP Notebook	Brentmark	800-879-6665
Profiles+ Professional	Financial Profiles	760-431-9400
Viewplan Advanced Estate Planning Software	CCH	800-224-7477 x4622
WealthMaster	WealthTec	443-535-8675

Mutual Fund Information Programs

PROGRAM	DEVELOPER	PHONE NUMBER
CDA Weisenberger-HY Sales	CDA Weisenberger	800-232-2285
FundScope	The Planner's Edge	800-859-8039
Investor Square	Manhattan Analytics	800-251-3863
Monocle II	Manhattan Analytics	800-251-3863
Mutual Fund Expert 5.8	Steele Systems	310-478-4213
Mutual Fund Explorer	InvestorSquare	800-251-3863
Net Funds Navigator	No-Load Fund Shareholders	800-966-5623
Principia for Closed-End Funds	Morningstar	800-735-0700
Principia for Mutual Funds	Morningstar	800-735-0700
Principia Plus for Mutual Funds	Morningstar	800-735-0700
Standard & Poor's Fund Service	Standard & Poor's	800-596-5323
Value Line Fund Analyzer	Value Line Publications	800-654-0508

Portfolio Reporting Software Programs

PROGRAM	DEVELOPER	PHONE NUMBER
Advent Office Essentials	Advent Software	800-685-7688
Captools Professional Investor	Captools Co.	800-826-8082
Centerpiece	Schwab Performance Technologies	800-528-9595
dbCAMS+	FCSI	877-432-2267
Unified Managed Account Platform	Advisorport	610-834-8910

Contact Management

PROGRAM	DEVELOPER	PHONE NUMBER
ACT! 4Advisors	ACT4Advisors	800-831-7636
Advisors Assistant	Client Marketing Systems	800-799-4267
Broker's Ally	Scherrer Resources	800-950-0190
Ed Morrow's Text Library System	Financial Planning Consultants	800-666-1656
Junxure-I	CRM Software	866-276-8665
ProTracker Systems	ProTracker Software	603-926-8085

Investment Planning

PROGRAM	DEVELOPER	PHONE NUMBER
Advisor Insight	Standard & Poor's	800-221-5277
Advisor Workstation	Morningstar	800-735-0700
Crystal Ball Professional Edition	Decisioneering	800-289-2550
Decipher	Financial Numerics	410-992-0623
Integrated Capital Engine	Advisory World	800-480-3888
Portfolio Strategist	Ibbotson Associates	800-758-3557
Principia	Morningstar	800-735-0700
Steele Mutual Fund Expert	Steele Systems	800-315-9002

Compliance Software

PROGRAM	DEVELOPER	PHONE NUMBER
AdvisorMail	LiveOffice Corp	800-251-3863
Advisory Agreement	The Consortium	805-987-6115
Investment Policy Statement	The Consortium	805-987-6115
RIA Solicitors Agreement	The Consortium	805-987-6115
RIA Written Policies	National Compliance Services	800-800-3204
RIA Written Supervisory Procedures Comp Manual	The Consortium	805-987-6115
Sample Investment Advisory Contracts	National Compliance Services	800-800-3204
Form ADV Software	National Compliance Services	800-800-3204

Client Education Programs

PROGRAM	DEVELOPER	PHONE NUMBER
Back Room Technician	Kettley Publishing	800-777-3162
Financial Planning Omniscience	FP Publications	505-269-2955

Financial Planning Books

THE FOLLOWING books cover many of the technical and/or practice management aspects of personal financial planning. Certainly, you can never have too much knowledge of a particular subject. You may want to develop a work habit of focusing on a different part of your practice each month and looking for a specific book in that area that can help take you to the next level. The books listed below are groundbreakers in their respective fields.

Bachrach, Bill. *Values-Based Selling* (Aim High Publishing, 1998).

Beam, Burton Jr. *Fundamentals of Insurance for Financial Planning* (The American College, 2000).

Bowen, John Jr., and Daniel C. Goldie. *Creating Equity: Building a Hugely Successful Asset Management Business* (SDC Publishing, 1997).

————. *The Prudent Investor's Guide to Beating Wall Street at Its Own Game,* reprint ed. (McGraw-Hill, 1998).

Burg, Bob. *Endless Referrals Updated Edition* (McGraw-Hill, 1998).

Chambers, Larry. *The First-Time Investor* (McGraw-Hill, 1998).

————. *The Guide to Financial Public Relations* (CRC Press–St. Lucie Press, 1999).

Crowe, Robert M., and Charles E. Hughes. *Fundamentals of Financial Planning* (The American College, 1993).

Donahue, Robert J. *An Introduction to Cash Flow Analysis* (The Regent School Press, 1998).

Drucker, David J., and Joel P. Bruckenstein, *Virtual-Office Tools for a High-Margin Practice: How Client-Centered Financial Advisers Can Cut Paperwork, Overhead, and Wasted Hours* (Bloomberg Press, 2002).

Duff, Richard W. *Preserving Family Wealth Using Tax Magic* (Berkley Publishing Group, 1995).

Durrie, Douglas H. *The Financial Planner's Guide to Moving Your Practice Online: Creating Your Internet Presence and Growing Your Business* (Bloomberg Press, 2001).

Ehrlich, Evelyn, and Duke Fanelli. *The Financial Services Marketing Handbook: Tactics and Techniques That Produce Results* (Bloomberg Press, 2004).

Ellis, Charles. *Investment Policy: How to Win the Loser's Game* (Business One/Irwin, 1993).

Evensky, Harold R. *Wealth Management: The Financial Advisor's Guide to Investing and Managing Your Clients' Assets* (Irwin, 1997).

Evensky, Harold, and Deena B. Katz, ed. *The Investment Think Tank: Theory, Strategy, and Practice for Advisers* (Bloomberg Press, 2004).

Fontaine, Constance J. *Fundamentals of Estate Planning* (The American College, 1999).

Fowler, D. Larry, William Mears, and Jeffrey H. Rattiner. *Personal Financial Planning Portfolio Library* (Harcourt Professional Publishing, 2000).

Garrett, Sheryl. *Just Give Me the Answers* (Dearborn, 2004).

Gerber, Michael E. *The E-Myth Revisited* (Harper Business, 1995).

Gibson, Roger. *Asset Allocation: Balancing Financial Risk* (Irwin, 1996).

Ibbotson Associates. *Stocks, Bonds, Bills, and Inflation* (Ibbotson Associates, 2004).

Jones, Charles Parker. *Investments: Analysis and Management,* 8th ed. (John Wiley & Sons, 2003).

Katz, Deena B. *Deena Katz on Practice Management for Financial Advisers, Planners, and Wealth Managers* (Bloomberg Press, 1999).

————. *Deena Katz's Tools and Templates for Your Practice for Financial Advisers, Planners, and Wealth Managers* (Bloomberg Press, 2001).

Kirsch, Clifford E., ed. *The Financial Services Revolution* (Irwin, 1996).

Krass, Stephen J. *Pension Answer Book: The 2004 Edition* (Aspen Publishing, Panel Publishers, 2003).

Landis, Andy. *Social Security: The Inside Story,* 2nd ed. (Crisp Publications, 1997).

Lehmann, Michael B. *The Irwin Guide to Using the Wall Street Journal* (McGraw-Hill, 1997).

Leimberg, Stephan R. *The Tools and Techniques of Financial Planning,* 6th ed. (National Underwriter Company, 2002).

Leimberg, Stephan R., and John J. McFadden. *The Tools and Techniques of Charitable Planning,* 1st ed. (National Underwriter Company, 2001).

Leimberg, Stephan R. et al. *The Tools and Techniques of Employee Benefit and Retirement Planning,* 8th ed. (National Underwriter Company, 2004).

————. *The Tools and Techniques of Estate Planning,* 13th ed. (National Underwriter Company, 2004).

————. *The Tools and Techniques of Income Tax Planning,* 1st ed. (National Underwriter Company, 2004).

————. *The Tools and Techniques of Life Insurance Planning,* 3rd ed. (National Underwriter Company, 2004).

Levin, Ross. *The Wealth Management Index* (Irwin, 1997).

Levy, Donald R. *Individual Retirement Accounts Answer Book: Special Supplement—Quick Reference to IRAs* (Aspen Publishing, Panel Publishers, 2003).

Littell, David A., and Kenn B. Tacchino. *Planning for Retirement Needs* (The American College, 2004).

Loewe, Raymond D. *A Professional's Guide to College Planning* (National Underwriter Company, 1998).

Lucal, Jane B. *Plan Now or Pay Later: Judge Jane's No-Nonsense Guide to Estate Planning* (Bloomberg Press, 2001).

Matson, Mark E. *Flashpoint: Mastering the Art of Economic Abundance* (McGriff Publishing, 2000).

Mayo, Herbert. *Investments,* 7th ed. (Dryden, 2003).

McCarthy, Ed. *The Financial Advisor's Analytical Toolbox* (McGraw-Hill, 1997).

Mitchell, William D. *Estate and Retirement Answer Book,* 2nd ed. (Aspen Publishing, Panel Publishers, 1999).

Mittra, Sid, and Jeffrey H. Rattiner. *Practicing Financial Planning: A Complete Guide for Professionals* (Mittra & Associates Publishing, 2000).

Moeller, Steven. *Effort-Less Marketing for Financial Advisors* (American Business Visions, 1999).

Morrow, Edwin P. *Personal Coaching for Financial Advisors* (Financial Planning Consultants, Inc., 1999).

National Underwriter Company. *Social Security Manual, 2004* (National Underwriter Company, 2004).

Rattiner, Jeff. *Rattiner's Financial Planning Bible: The Advisor's Advisor* (John Wiley & Sons, 2002).

————. *Rattiner's Review for the CFP® Certification Examination Fast Track Study Guide* (John Wiley & Sons, 2003).

Research Institute of America. *Federal Tax Handbook* (Research Institute of America, 2004).

Rowland, Mary. *Best Practices for Financial Advisors* (Bloomberg Press, 1997).

———. *The New Commonsense Guide to Mutual Funds* (Bloomberg Press, 1998).

———. *In Search of the Perfect Model: The Distinctive Business Strategies of Leading Financial Planners* (Bloomberg Press, 2003).

Siegel, Jeremy J., and Peter L. Bernstein. *Stocks for the Long Run: The Definitive Guide to Financial Market Returns and Long-Term Investment Strategies,* revised ed. (McGraw-Hill, 1998).

Stein, Michael K. *The Prosperous Retirement: Guide to the New Reality* (Emstco Press, 1998).

Trone, Donald B., William R. Allbright, and Philip R. Taylor. *The Management of Investment Decisions* (McGraw-Hill, 1996).

Vaughan, Emmett, and Therese M. Vaughan. *Fundamentals of Risk and Insurance,* 8th ed. (John Wiley & Sons, 1999).

Vessenes, Katherine. *The Compliance Liability Handbook* (IAFP Press, 1992).

———. *Protecting Your Practice* (Bloomberg Press, 1997).

Wilson, Carol Ann. *The Financial Advisor's Guide to Divorce Settlement* (Irwin, 1996).

Personal Financial Planning Periodicals

American Association of Individual Investors' *AAII Journal* (312-280-0170)

American College's *Journal of Financial Service Professionals* (800-392-6900)

Bloomberg Wealth Manager (800-681-7727)

Crain's *Investment News* (313-446-0450)

Financial Planning Association's *Journal of Financial Planning* (800-322-4237)

Institutional Investor's *Journal of Investing* (212-224-3185)

Financial Planning (212-803-8200)

CODE OF ETHICS AND PROFESSIONAL RESPONSIBILITY: SECTION I

Certified Financial Planner Board of Standards Code of Ethics and Professional Responsibility

◆ **Preamble and Applicability.** The *Code of Ethics and Professional Responsibility (Code of Ethics)* has been adopted by Certified Financial Planner Board of Standards Inc. (CFP Board) to provide principles and rules to all persons whom it has recognized and certified to use the CFP®, Certified Financial Planner™, and certification marks (collectively "the marks"). CFP Board determines who is certified and thus authorized to use the marks. Implicit in the acceptance of this authorization is an obligation not only to comply with the mandates and requirements of all applicable laws and regulations but also to take responsibility to act in an ethical and professionally responsible manner in all professional services and activities.

For purposes of this *Code of Ethics,* a person recognized and certified by CFP Board to use the marks is called a CFP Board designee. This *Code of Ethics* applies to CFP Board designees actively involved in the practice of personal financial planning, in other areas of financial services, in industry, in related professions, in government, in education, or in any other professional activity in which the marks are used in the performance of professional responsibilities. This *Code of Ethics* also applies to candidates for the CFP® certification who are registered as such with CFP Board. For purposes of this *Code of Ethics,* the term *CFP Board designee* shall be deemed to include current certificants, candidates, and individuals who have been certified in the past and retain the right to reinstate their CFP certification without passing the current CFP® Certification Examination.

◆ **Composition and Scope.** The *Code of Ethics* consists of two parts: Part I—Principles and Part II—Rules. The Principles are statements expressing in general terms the ethical and professional ideals that CFP Board designees are expected to display in their professional activities. As such, the Principles are aspirational in character but are intended to provide a source of guidance for CFP Board designees. The comments following each Principle further explain the meaning of the Principle. The Rules in Part II provide practical guidelines derived from the tenets embodied in the Principles. As such, the Rules describe the standards of ethical and professionally responsible conduct expected of CFP Board designees in particular situations. This *Code of Ethics* does not undertake to define standards of professional conduct of CFP Board designees for purposes of civil liability.

Due to the nature of a CFP Board designee's particular field of endeavor, certain Rules may not be applicable to that CFP Board designee's activities. For example, a CFP Board designee who is engaged solely in the sale of securities as a registered representative is not subject to the written disclosure requirements of Rule 402 (applicable to CFP Board designees engaged in personal financial planning) although he or she may have disclosure responsibilities under Rule 401. A CFP Board designee is obligated to determine what responsibilities he or she has in each professional relationship including, for example, duties that arise in particular circumstances from a position of trust or confidence that a CFP Board designee may have. The CFP Board designee is obligated to meet those responsibilities.

The *Code of Ethics* is structured so that the presentation of the Rules parallels the presentation of the Principles. For example, the Rules which relate to Principle 1—Integrity are numbered in the 100 to 199 series, while those Rules relating to Principle 2—Objectivity are numbered in the 200 to 299 series.

◆ **Compliance.** CFP Board requires adherence to this *Code of Ethics* by all CFP Board designees. Compliance with the *Code of Ethics*, individually and by the profession as a whole, depends on each CFP Board designee's knowledge of and voluntary compliance with the Principles and applicable Rules, on the influence of fellow professionals and public opinion, and on disciplinary proceedings, when necessary, involving CFP Board designees who fail to comply with the applicable provisions of the *Code of Ethics*.

Part I—Principles

THESE *Code of Ethics* Principles express the profession's recognition of its responsibilities to the public, to clients, to colleagues, and to employers. They apply to all CFP Board designees and provide guidance to them in the performance of their professional services.

◆ **Principle 1—Integrity.** *A CFP Board designee shall offer and provide professional services with integrity.* As discussed in "Composition and Scope," CFP Board designees may be placed by clients in positions of trust and confidence. The ultimate source of such public trust is the CFP Board designee's personal integrity. In deciding what is right and just, a CFP Board designee should rely on his or her integrity as the appropriate touchstone. Integrity demands honesty and candor which must not be subordinated to personal gain and advantage. Within the characteristic of integrity, allowance can be made for innocent error and legitimate difference of opinion; but integrity cannot co-exist with deceit or subordination of one's principles. Integrity requires a CFP Board designee to observe not only the letter but also the spirit of this *Code of Ethics*.

◆ **Principle 2—Objectivity.** *A CFP Board designee shall be objective in providing professional services to clients.* Objectivity requires intellectual honesty and impartiality. It is an essential quality for any professional. Regardless of the particular service rendered or the capacity in which a CFP Board designee functions, a CFP Board designee should protect the integrity of his or her work, maintain objectivity, and avoid subordination of his or her judgment that would be in violation of this *Code of Ethics.*

◆ **Principle 3—Competence.** *A CFP Board designee shall provide services to clients competently and maintain the necessary knowledge and skill to continue to do so in those areas in which the CFP Board designee is engaged.* One is competent only when he or she has attained and maintained an adequate level of knowledge and skill, and applies that knowledge effectively in providing services to clients. Competence also includes the wisdom to recognize the limitations of that knowledge and when consultation or client referral is appropriate. A CFP Board designee, by virtue of having earned the CFP® certification, is deemed to be qualified to practice financial planning. However, in addition to assimilating the common body of knowledge required and acquiring the necessary experience for certification, a CFP Board designee shall make a continuing commitment to learning and professional improvement.

◆ **Principle 4—Fairness.** *A CFP Board designee shall perform professional services in a manner that is fair and reasonable to clients, principals, partners, and employers, and shall disclose conflict(s) of interest in providing such services.* Fairness requires impartiality, intellectual honesty, and disclosure of conflict(s) of interest. It involves a subordination of one's own feelings, prejudices, and desires so as to achieve a proper balance of conflicting interests. Fairness is treating others in the same fashion that you would want to be treated and is an essential trait of any professional.

◆ **Principle 5—Confidentiality.** *A CFP Board designee shall not disclose any confidential client information without the specific consent of the client unless in response to proper legal process, to defend against charges of wrongdoing by the CFP Board designee, or in connection with a civil dispute between the CFP Board designee and client.* A client, by seeking the services of a CFP Board designee, may be interested in creating a relationship of personal trust and confidence with the CFP Board designee. This type of relationship can only be built upon the understanding that information supplied to the CFP Board designee will be confidential. In order to provide the contemplated services effectively and to protect the client's privacy, the CFP Board designee shall safeguard the confidentiality of such information.

◆ **Principle 6—Professionalism.** *A CFP Board designee's conduct in all matters shall reflect credit upon the profession.* Because of the importance of the professional services rendered by CFP Board designees, there are attendant responsibilities to behave with dignity and courtesy to all those who use those services, fellow professionals, and those in related professions. A CFP Board designee also has an obligation to cooperate with fellow CFP Board designees to enhance and maintain the profession's public image and to work jointly with other CFP Board designees to improve the quality of services. It is only through the combined efforts of all CFP Board designees, in cooperation with other professionals, that this vision can be realized.

◆ **Principle 7—Diligence.** *A CFP Board designee shall act diligently in providing professional services.* Diligence is the provision of services in a reasonably prompt and thorough manner. Diligence also includes proper planning for, and supervision of, the rendering of professional services.

Part II—Rules

AS STATED IN Part I—Principles, the Principles apply to all CFP Board designees. However, due to the nature of a CFP Board designee's particular field of endeavor, certain Rules may not be applicable to that CFP Board designee's activities. The universe of activities engaged in by a CFP Board designee is indeed diverse, and a particular CFP Board designee may be performing all, some, or none of the typical services provided by financial planning professionals. As a result, in considering the following Rules, a CFP Board designee must first recognize what specific services he or she is rendering and then determine whether or not a specific Rule is applicable to those services. To assist the CFP Board designee in making these determinations, the *Standards of Professional Conduct* includes a series of definitions of terminology (see page 2) used throughout the *Code of Ethics*. Based upon these definitions, a CFP Board designee should be able to determine which services he or she provides and, therefore, which Rules are applicable to those services.

RULES THAT RELATE TO THE PRINCIPLE OF INTEGRITY

◆ **Rule 101.** A CFP Board designee shall not solicit clients through false or misleading communications or advertisements:

(a) *Misleading Advertising:* A CFP Board designee shall not make a false or misleading communication about the size, scope, or areas of competence of the CFP Board designee's practice or of any organization with which the CFP Board designee is associated; and

(b) *Promotional Activities:* In promotional activities, a CFP Board designee shall not make materially false or misleading communications to the public or create unjustified expectations regarding matters relating to financial planning or the professional activities and competence of the CFP Board designee. The term "promotional activities" includes, but is not limited to, speeches, interviews, books and/or printed publications, seminars, radio and television shows, and videocassettes; and

(c) *Representation of Authority:* A CFP Board designee shall not give the impression that a CFP Board designee is representing the views of CFP Board or any other group unless the CFP Board designee has been authorized to do so. Personal opinions shall be clearly identified as such.

◆ **Rule 102.** In the course of professional activities, a CFP Board designee shall not engage in conduct involving dishonesty, fraud, deceit, or misrepresentation, or knowingly make a false or misleading statement to a client, employer, employee, professional colleague, governmental or other regulatory body or official, or any other person or entity.

◆ **Rule 103.** A CFP Board designee has the following responsibilities regarding funds and/or other property of clients:

(a) In exercising custody of, or discretionary authority over, client funds or other property, a CFP Board designee shall act only in accordance with the authority set forth in the governing legal instrument (e.g., special power of attorney, trust, letters testamentary, etc.); and

(b) A CFP Board designee shall identify and keep complete records of all funds or other property of a client in the custody, or under the discretionary authority, of the CFP Board designee; and

(c) Upon receiving funds or other property of a client, a CFP Board designee shall promptly or as otherwise permitted by law or provided by agreement with the client, deliver to the client or third party any funds or other property which the client or third party is entitled to receive and, upon request by the client, render a full accounting regarding such funds or other property; and

(d) A CFP Board designee shall not commingle client funds or other property with a CFP Board designee's personal funds and/ or other property or the funds and/or other property of a CFP Board designee's firm. Commingling one or more clients' funds or other property together is permitted, subject to compliance with applicable legal requirements and provided accurate records are maintained for each client's funds or other property; and

(e) A CFP Board designee who takes custody of all or any part of a client's assets for investment purposes, shall do so with the care required of a fiduciary.

RULES THAT RELATE TO THE PRINCIPLE OF OBJECTIVITY

◆ **Rule 201.** A CFP Board designee shall exercise reasonable and prudent professional judgment in providing professional services.

◆ **Rule 202.** A financial planning practitioner shall act in the interest of the client.

RULES THAT RELATE TO THE PRINCIPLE OF COMPETENCE

◆ **Rule 301.** A CFP Board designee shall keep informed of developments in the field of financial planning and participate in continuing education throughout the CFP Board designee's professional career in order to improve professional competence in all areas in which the CFP Board designee is engaged. As a distinct part of this requirement, a CFP Board designee shall satisfy all minimum continuing education requirements established for CFP Board designees by CFP Board.

◆ **Rule 302.** A CFP Board designee shall offer advice only in those areas in which the CFP Board designee has competence. In areas where the CFP Board designee is not professionally competent, the CFP Board designee shall seek the counsel of qualified individuals and/or refer clients to such parties.

RULES THAT RELATE TO THE PRINCIPLE OF FAIRNESS

◆ **Rule 401.** In rendering professional services, a CFP Board designee shall disclose to the client:

(a) Material information relevant to the professional relationship, including conflict(s) of interest; the CFP Board designee's business affiliation, address, telephone number, credentials, qualifications, licenses, compensation structure, and any agency relationships; and the scope of the CFP Board designee's authority in that capacity; and

(b) The information required by all laws applicable to the relationship in a manner complying with such laws.

◆ **Rule 402.** A CFP Board designee in a financial planning engagement shall make timely written disclosure of all material information relative to the professional relationship. In all circumstances and prior to the engagement, a CFP Board designee shall, in writing:

(a) Disclose conflict(s) of interest and sources of compensation; and

(b) Inform the client or prospective client of his/her right to ask at any time for information about the compensation of the CFP Board designee.

As a guideline, a CFP Board designee who provides a client or prospective client with the following written disclosures, using Form ADV, a CFP Board Disclosure Form, or an equivalent document, will be considered to be in compliance with this Rule:

—The basic philosophy of the CFP Board designee (or firm) in working with clients. This includes the philosophy, theory, and/or principles of financial planning which will be utilized by the CFP Board designee; and

—Résumés of principals and employees of a firm who are expected to provide financial planning services to the client and a description of those services. Such disclosures shall include educational background, professional/employment history, professional designations and licenses held; and

—A statement that in reasonable detail discloses (as applicable) conflict(s) of interest and source(s) of, and any contingencies or other aspects material to, the CFP Board designee's compensation; and

—A statement describing material agency or employment relationships a CFP Board designee (or firm) has with third parties and the nature of compensation resulting from such relationships; and

—A statement informing the client or prospective client of his or her right to ask at any time for information about the compensation of the CFP Board designee.

◆ **Rule 403.** Upon request by a client or prospective client, the CFP Board designee in a financial planning engagement shall communicate in reasonable detail the requested compensation information related to the financial planning engagement, including compensation derived from implementation. The disclosure may express compensation as an approximate dollar amount or percentage or as a range of dollar amounts or percentages. The disclosure shall be made at a time and to the extent that the requested compensation information can be reasonably ascertained. Any estimates shall be clearly identified as such and based on reasonable assumptions. If a CFP Board designee becomes aware that a compensation disclosure provided pursuant to this rule has become significantly inaccurate, he or she shall provide the client with corrected information in a timely manner.

◆ **Rule 404.** The disclosures required of a CFP Board designee in a financial planning engagement described under Rule 402 shall be offered at least annually for current clients, and provided if requested.

◆ **Rule 405.** A CFP Board designee's compensation shall be fair and reasonable.

◆ **Rule 406.** A CFP Board designee who is an employee shall perform professional services with dedication to the lawful objectives of the employer and in accordance with this *Code of Ethics.*

◆ **Rule 407.** A CFP Board designee shall:

(a) Advise his/her employer of outside affiliations which reasonably may compromise service to an employer;

(b) Provide timely notice to his or her employer and clients about change of CFP® certification status; and

(c) Provide timely notice to clients, unless precluded by contractual obligations, about change of employment.

◆ **Rule 408.** A CFP Board designee shall inform his or her employer, partners, or co-owners of compensation or other benefit arrangements in connection with his or her services to clients, which are in addition to compensation from the employer, partners, or co-owners for such services.

◆ **Rule 409.** If a CFP Board designee enters into a personal business transaction with a client, separate from regular professional services provided to that client, the transaction shall be on terms which are fair and reasonable to the client and the CFP Board designee shall disclose, in writing, the risks of the transaction, conflict(s) of interest of the CFP Board designee, and other relevant information, if any, necessary to make the transaction fair to the client.

RULES THAT RELATE TO THE PRINCIPLE OF CONFIDENTIALITY

◆ **Rule 501.** A CFP Board designee shall not reveal—or use for his or her own benefit—without the client's consent, any personally identifiable information relating to the client relationship or the affairs of the client, except and to the extent disclosure or use is reasonably necessary:

(a) To establish an advisory or brokerage account, to effect a transaction for the client, or as otherwise impliedly authorized in order to carry out the client engagement; or

(b) To comply with legal requirements or legal process; or

(c) To defend the CFP Board designee against charges of wrongdoing; or

(d) In connection with a civil dispute between the CFP Board designee and the client.

For purposes of this rule, the proscribed use of client information is improper whether or not it actually causes harm to the client.

◆ **Rule 502.** A CFP Board designee shall maintain the same standards of confidentiality to employers as to clients.

◆ **Rule 503.** A CFP Board designee doing business as a partner or principal of a financial services firm owes the CFP Board designee's partners or co-owners a responsibility to act in good faith.

This includes, but is not limited to, adherence to reasonable expectations of confidentiality both while in business together and thereafter.

RULES THAT RELATE TO THE PRINCIPLE OF PROFESSIONALISM

◆ **Rule 601.** A CFP Board designee shall use the marks in compliance with the rules and regulations of CFP Board, as established and amended from time to time.

◆ **Rule 602.** A CFP Board designee shall show respect for other financial planning professionals, and related occupational groups, by engaging in fair and honorable competitive practices. Collegiality among CFP Board designees shall not, however, impede enforcement of this *Code of Ethics*.

◆ **Rule 603.** A CFP Board designee who has knowledge, which is not required to be kept confidential under this *Code of Ethics,* that another CFP Board designee has committed a violation of this *Code of Ethics* which raises substantial questions as to the designee's honesty, trustworthiness, or fitness as a CFP Board designee in other respects, shall promptly inform CFP Board. This rule does not require disclosure of information or reporting based on knowledge gained as a consultant or expert witness in anticipation of, or related to, litigation or other dispute resolution mechanisms. For purposes of this rule, knowledge means no substantial doubt.

◆ **Rule 604.** A CFP Board designee who has knowledge, which is not required under this *Code of Ethics* to be kept confidential, and which raises a substantial question of unprofessional, fraudulent, or illegal conduct by a CFP Board designee or other financial professional, shall promptly inform the appropriate regulatory and/or professional disciplinary body. This rule does not require disclosure or reporting of information gained as a consultant or expert witness in anticipation of, or related to, litigation or other dispute resolution mechanisms. For purposes of this Rule, knowledge means no substantial doubt.

◆ **Rule 605.** A CFP Board designee who has reason to suspect illegal conduct within the CFP Board designee's organization shall make timely disclosure of the available evidence to the CFP Board designee's immediate supervisor and/or partners or co-owners. If the CFP Board designee is convinced that illegal conduct exists within the CFP Board designee's organization, and that appropriate measures are not taken to remedy the situation, the CFP Board designee shall, where appropriate, alert the appropriate regulatory authorities, including CFP Board, in a timely manner.

◆ **Rule 606.** In all professional activities a CFP Board designee shall perform services in accordance with:

(a) Applicable laws, rules, and regulations of governmental agencies and other applicable authorities; and

(b) Applicable rules, regulations, and other established policies of CFP Board.

◆ **Rule 607.** A CFP Board designee shall not engage in any conduct which reflects adversely on his or her integrity or fitness as a CFP Board designee, upon the marks, or upon the profession.

◆ **Rule 608.** The Investment Advisers Act of 1940 requires registration of investment advisers with the U.S. Securities and Exchange Commission, and similar state statutes may require registration with state securities agencies. CFP Board designees shall disclose to clients their firms' status as registered investment advisers. Under present standards of acceptable business conduct, it is proper to use registered investment adviser if the CFP Board designee is registered individually. If the CFP Board designee is registered through his or her firm, then the CFP Board designee is not a registered investment adviser but a person associated with an investment adviser. The firm is the registered investment adviser. Moreover, RIA or R.I.A. following a CFP Board designee's name in advertising, letterhead stationery, and business cards may be misleading and is not permitted either by this *Code of Ethics* or by SEC regulations.

◆ **Rule 609.** A CFP Board designee shall not practice any other profession or offer to provide such services unless the CFP Board designee is qualified to practice in those fields and is licensed as required by state law.

◆ **Rule 610.** A CFP Board designee shall return the client's original records in a timely manner after their return has been requested by a client.

◆ **Rule 611.** A CFP Board designee shall not bring or threaten to bring a disciplinary proceeding under this *Code of Ethics,* or report or threaten to report information to CFP Board pursuant to Rules 603 and/or 604, or make or threaten to make use of this *Code of Ethics* for no substantial purpose other than to harass, maliciously injure, embarrass, and/or unfairly burden another CFP Board designee.

◆ **Rule 612.** A CFP Board designee shall comply with all applicable renewal requirements established by CFP Board including, but not limited to, payment of the biennial CFP Board designee fee as well as signing and returning the Terms and Conditions of Certification in connection with the certification renewal process.

RULES THAT RELATE TO THE PRINCIPLE OF DILIGENCE

◆ **Rule 701.** A CFP Board designee shall provide services diligently.

◆ **Rule 702.** A financial planning practitioner shall enter into an engagement only after securing sufficient information to satisfy the CFP Board designee that:

(a) The relationship is warranted by the individual's needs and objectives; and

(b) The CFP Board designee has the ability to either provide requisite competent services or to involve other professionals who can provide such services.

◆ **Rule 703.** A financial planning practitioner shall make and/or implement only recommendations which are suitable for the client.

◆ **Rule 704.** Consistent with the nature and scope of the engagement, a CFP Board designee shall make a reasonable investigation regarding the financial products recommended to clients. Such an investigation may be made by the CFP Board designee or by others provided the CFP Board designee acts reasonably in relying upon such investigation.

◆ **Rule 705.** A CFP Board designee shall properly supervise subordinates with regard to their delivery of financial planning services, and shall not accept or condone conduct in violation of this *Code of Ethics.*

TRENDS IN STAFFING AND COMPENSATION

THE FOLLOWING STATISTICS are from the *2003 FPA Compensation and Staffing Survey*. The survey was done by The Financial Planning Association in cooperation with Moss Adams, LLP, the tenth largest CPA firm in the nation. The overall conclusion of the study is that the financial advisory community is becoming more sophisticated in the development of its human capital plan. For more information about the FPA, membership opportunities, or to purchase the entire study, visit their website at www.fpanet.org or contact them at 800-322-4237.

Recruiting and Retention

◆ During the past two years, advisory practices increased full-time staffing by 15 percent.

◆ Firms are becoming more sophisticated and careful in their recruiting. More than half (51.9 percent) of the multiprofessional (ensemble) firms use tests to screen their prospective employees.

◆ More than three-quarters (78.4 percent) of all firms conduct employee evaluations, 14.9 percent use upstream evaluations, and 12.6 percent use peer evaluations.

◆ Firms continue to invest heavily in their employees; 86.2 percent reimburse some education expenses.

Staffing Models: Smaller Firms

◆ Advisory firms are typically solo practices with a median of one administrative staff member and one support person.

◆ The principals/owners of advisory practices typically hold a CFP Certificate (43.9 percent). Other common designations held by principals include ChFC (18.2 percent) and CLU (18.2 percent).

◆ CFP certificate holders who practice as planners and paraplanners earn more than their noncertificate counterparts.

◆ The typical adviser works with 75 to 190 clients and generates a median of $2,500 in revenue per client relationship.

◆ 90.9 percent offer investment policy decisions and perform buying and selling of securities on behalf of their clients.

◆ 59.1 percent offer securities trading, such as brokerage accounts.

◆ 74.2 percent offer portfolio administration.

◆ 69.7 percent offer investment research.

Staffing Models: Larger Firms

THE LARGEST FIRMS achieve their size by:

◆ Merging practices together to reach critical mass and create overhead efficiency

◆ Standardizing client delivery processes and including support staff to achieve leverage

◆ Employing non-owner professionals to further increase the capabilities of the practice and to further leverage the reputation of the firm

◆ Institutionalizing their brand, systems, and human resource practices

Elite Firms and Virtuoso Practices

THE TOP 25 PERCENT of ensemble firms (as measured by pretax income per owner) are termed "elite." The top 25 percent of solo practices (as measured by pretax income per owner) are termed "virtuoso." Both elite and virtuoso firms exhibit clear characteristics that have contributed to their success:

◆ The median operating profit per client of an elite firm is ten times that of other firms, at $1,440. The median assets per client for an elite firm approaches $850,000, compared to $350,000 for other firms.

◆ Virtuoso practices generate $1,050 of operating profit per client versus $194 for their peers, with $290,000 of assets per client contrasting with $125,000 for their peers.

◆ Elite firms have roughly three times the assets under management than that of other firms, and virtuoso firms have approximately two times the assets under management than that of other firms.

◆ Elite firms have more than 2.5 times the revenue of other ensembles at $1.3 million.

◆ Elite firm owners generate 3.5 times the pretax income of other ensemble firms.

◆ Elite firms in particular have captured a much wealthier client base.

◆ Both elite and virtuoso firms have several more years of experience in the advisory business than their peers.

Continuing-Education Exam

for CFP Continuing-Education Credit
and PACE Recertification Credit

EARN TEN HOURS of credit toward your CFP Board CE requirement as well as PACE Recertification credit by passing the following exam online at www.bloomberg.com/ce.

All the material has been previewed by the CFP Board of Standards. If you wish to find out if this book and exam can be used to fulfill the CE requirement for a different organization, please contact its governing board directly.

CHAPTER 2

1. Which is not a reason to use a sole proprietorship?
   a. The owner is not concerned about transferring interests.
   b. The business is in its early stages.
   c. Adequate liability insurance is available.
   d. Two or more owners want to form a joint venture for profit.

2. Which is not a reason to use a general partnership?
   a. The new business generates significant start-up costs that can be passed through to the partners.
   b. Tax benefits can be passed through to each partner's contributions to the business.
   c. The business performs financial services with the inherent risk of errors-and-omissions claims.
   d. Cash distributions can be taken from the business in order to reduce the partner's basis.

3. Which is not a reason to use an S corporation?
   a. Owners want limited liability.
   b. Owners want to draw high fringe benefits.
   c. Owners want a pass-through entity.
   d. Current owners can meet the strict eligibility rules.

4. Which is not a reason to use a C corporation?

   a. Owners' personal assets will be protected from creditors.

   b. Owners want the benefits of pass-through taxation.

   c. Owners see the need to borrow from qualified plans.

   d. Owners want to maximize retained earnings within the business.

5. Which is not a reason to use an LLC?

   a. Members want to continuously issue new shares of stock.

   b. Members want to pass ownership to heirs and retain management control.

   c. The start-up expects to have pass-through losses.

   d. The business plan has venture capital investments that permit pass-through investments.

6. Which is not a reason to use an LLP?

   a. Owners want pass-through taxation.

   b. Owners want to avoid double taxation.

   c. Qualifying as an S corporation is more convenient.

   d. Owners want to make tax-free distributions of appreciated property.

7. The exam required by a planner who desires to become a Registered Investment Advisor is the:

   a. Series 24

   b. Series 6

   c. Series 65

   d. Series 7

CHAPTER 3

8. Which is not an example of quantitative data?

   a. names, addresses, and phone numbers of family advisers

   b. risk tolerance level

   c. pension plan information

   d. copies of wills

9. Which is not an insurance recommendation as discussed in the text?

   a. strength of the issuing company

   b. contingent beneficiary named

   c. HO 15 endorsement

   d. $100,000 minimum automobile liability coverage

10. When purchasing insurance, planners should stress:

   a. the availability of client resources

   b. the number of agents working for the company

   c. evaluation of the client's current economic situation where assets and not liabilities are taken into consideration

   d. none of the above

11. Which are the financial statements necessary during the PIPRIM process?

—I Statement of financial position

—II Cash flow statement

—III Statement of current analysis

—IV Statement of uses of funds

   a. I and II only

   b. I, II, and III only

   c. II and IV only

   d. I, II, III, and IV

12. The monitoring stage includes:

   a. starting with the assumptions

   b. considering personal and economic changes

   c. re-evaluating goals when necessary

   d. all of the above

13. Which is not a stage in the PIPRIM process?

   a. monitoring the plan

   b. referral process

   c. preliminary meeting with client

   d. implementing the plan

14. The most common reason a client seeks legal restitution from a planner is:
- **a.** loss on investments
- **b.** mismanaged client expectations
- **c.** poor tax advice
- **d.** failure to adjust the client's account quickly enough

15. Which is not an immediate issue when recommending disability insurance for a client?
- **a.** obtaining 60 to 70 percent of gross monthly earnings
- **b.** obtaining an occupation definition
- **c.** obtaining a residual disability rider
- **d.** obtaining a noncancelable rider

16. Which is not part of a client's financial plan as discussed in the text?
- **a.** overview of short-term goals
- **b.** mutually selected recommendations
- **c.** step-by-step implementation
- **d.** detailed analysis of all financial conditions of the client

CHAPTER 4

17. Which of the following is not one of the reasons clients fail to plan for their financial future?
- **a.** They already have sufficient assets.
- **b.** They think they have insufficient assets to warrant planning.
- **c.** They are putting off the complex.
- **d.** Their gift taxation is higher than necessary.

18. What are the three steps to cash-flow planning?
- **a.** establishing reasonable goals and objectives, successfully implementing the recommendations, and determining the client's current financial situation
- **b.** establishing reasonable goals and objectives, determining the client's current financial situation, and monitoring the probable outcome

c. successfully implementing the recommendations, monitoring the probable outcome, and forecasting future expenses

19. Which is not a cash-flow planning strategy to increase disposable income?
   a. initial asset allocation
   b. debt restructuring
   c. establishing qualified plans
   d. separate treatment of children's assets

20. Which type of life insurance requires level annual premiums for the entire lifetime of the insured?
   a. term life
   b. whole life
   c. universal life
   d. variable universal life

21. Which type of life insurance has two different death benefit options?
   a. term life
   b. whole life
   c. universal life
   d. variable life

22. Which is not one of the investment parameters defined in the text?
   a. time horizon
   b. estate-tax considerations
   c. liquidity
   d. marketability

23. Which is not a type of systematic risk?
   a. business risk
   b. market risk
   c. purchasing-power risk
   d. interest rate risk

24. In the text, midcapitalization is defined as companies with assets of:
   a. $10 million to $300 million
   b. $500 million to $1 billion
   c. $1 billion to $5 billion
   d. more than $5 billion

25. According to the text, which is not a category of equity investments?
   a. blue-chip stocks
   b. growth stocks
   c. value stocks
   d. defensive stocks

26. Which of the following is not part of the nine-step college-education planning process?
   a. compare and evaluate every financial aid award
   b. teach your clients and their children how to select the appropriate colleges
   c. integrate any college–borrowing plan into a retirement plan
   d. negotiate financial aid packages with the appropriate school

27. Which is not an appropriate technique for accelerating expenses at year-end?
   a. charge deductible expenses on your credit card
   b. defer bonuses until after year-end
   c. increase withholding of state and local taxes
   d. bunch miscellaneous expenses together

28. Which of the following is a valid technique for deferring income until subsequent years?
   a. installment sale
   b. capital gain deferral
   c. ordinary income acceleration
   d. delay capital losses until the subsequent year

29. Which of the following is not a tax-planning move described in the text?
- **a.** increase level of participation in business activity
- **b.** increase or decrease vacation home use
- **c.** consume expiring loss carryovers
- **d.** establish traditional IRA accounts for those taxpayers who earn more than $100,000 and are covered under a qualified retirement plan through their employers

30. Which of the following is not a vesting schedule as defined in the text?
- **a.** five-year cliff
- **b.** three-to-seven-year graded
- **c.** three-to-ten-year graded
- **d.** none of the above

31. Which does not fall under a defined contribution plan?
- **a.** money-purchase plan
- **b.** target-benefit plan
- **c.** profit-sharing plan
- **d.** tandem plan

32. Which retirement plan provides company stock to employees?
- **a.** ESOP
- **b.** 401(k)
- **c.** savings or thrift plan
- **d.** defined benefit plan

33. Which is not an exception to the 10 percent penalty regarding individual retirement account distributions?
- **a.** series of substantially equal payments
- **b.** disability
- **c.** separation from service by an employee after age 55
- **d.** dividend paid on stock held by an ESOP

34. When the decedent dies without a will, he is said to have died:
   a. testate
   b. intestate
   c. codicil
   d. QTIP

35. All of the following are will substitutes except:
   a. operation of law
   b. contract
   c. trust
   d. intestate

36. The type of property and casualty policy that protects renters is an:
   a. HO2
   b. HO4
   c. HO8
   d. HO15

CHAPTER 5

37. The regulatory act that deals primarily with new-issue securities and provides for full disclosure is:
   a. The Securities Act of 1933
   b. The Securities Exchange Act of 1934
   c. The Investment Company Act of 1940
   d. The Investment Advisors Act of 1940

38. Under the Securities Investor Protection Act of 1970, the total amount of cash and securities covered per customer is:
   a. $0
   b. $100,000
   c. $400,000
   d. $500,000

39. All of the following are exceptions to the definition of investment adviser except:
- **a.** bankers
- **b.** lawyers
- **c.** accountants
- **d.** architects

40. In order to register as an investment adviser, the planner must meet the definition of an investment adviser. Which of the following is not part of that definition?
- **a.** analysis
- **b.** advice
- **c.** business
- **d.** compensation

INDEX

About Bloomberg

Bloomberg L.P., founded in 1981, is a global information services, news, and media company. Headquartered in New York, the company has sales and news operations worldwide.

Serving customers on six continents, Bloomberg, through its wholly-owned subsidiary Bloomberg Finance L.P., holds a unique position within the financial services industry by providing an unparalleled range of features in a single package known as the Bloomberg Professional® service. By addressing the demand for investment performance and efficiency through an exceptional combination of information, analytic, electronic trading, and straight-through-processing tools, Bloomberg has built a worldwide customer base of corporations, issuers, financial intermediaries, and institutional investors.

Bloomberg News, founded in 1990, provides stories and columns on business, general news, politics, and sports to leading newspapers and magazines throughout the world. Bloomberg Television, a 24-hour business and financial news network, is produced and distributed globally in seven languages. Bloomberg Radio is an international radio network anchored by flagship station Bloomberg 1130 (WBBR-AM) in New York.

In addition to the Bloomberg Press line of books, Bloomberg publishes *Bloomberg Markets* magazine.

To learn more about Bloomberg, call a sales representative at:

London: +44-20-7330-7500
New York: +1-212-318-2000
Tokyo: +81-3-3201-8900

About the Author

Jeffrey H. Rattiner, CPA, CFP, MBA, is president and chief executive officer of the JR Financial Group, Inc., a financial planning, money management, and tax information firm with offices in Centennial, Colorado, and Scottsdale, Arizona. He is also the founder of the nationwide Rattiner's Financial Planning Fast Track educational program that trains advisers to become certified financial planner (CFP) licensees in an accelerated alternative format.

A popular speaker and frequently quoted practitioner, Rattiner has authored several books, including *Rattiner's Review for the CFP Certification Examination Fast Track Study Guide* (Wiley, 2003), *Rattiner's Financial Planner's Bible* (Wiley, 2002), *Financial Planning Answer Book* (CCH, Inc., 2009), and *Financial Planning for Divorce* (Wiley, 2009). He has served in director capacities in several industry organizations, including the Institute of Certified Financial Planners, the Certified Financial Planner Board of Standards, and the Personal Financial Planning Division of the American Institute of Certified Public Accountants. Rattiner received a BBA from Bernard M. Baruch College and an MBA from Hofstra University.

He can be reached at jeff@jrfinancialgroup.com, 720-529-1888, or www.jrfinancialgroup.com.